OP
995

D0845781

Over My Shoulder

Over My Shoulder

An autobiography
Jessie Matthews
as told to
Muriel Burgess

ARLINGTON HOUSE·PUBLISHERS
NEW ROCHELLE, N. Y.

© JESSIE MATTHEWS AND MURIEL BURGESS, 1974

THIS BOOK OR PARTS THEREOF MAY NOT BE REPRODUCED
IN ANY FORM WHATSOEVER WITHOUT PERMISSION IN WRITING

PRINTED AND BOUND IN GREAT BRITAIN BY BUTLER & TANNER LTD
LIBRARY OF CONGRESS CATALOG CARD NUMBER 75-1453
ISBN 0-87000-311-9

For my sister Rose with love
and in memory of Dr Henry Rowan.

Acknowledgements

My grateful thanks to everyone who has helped with this book, especially Archie Currie and sisters Rose and Lena. Thanks also to Victor Saville, Lord Elwyn Jones, and Sir Carol Reed.

Extracts from songs are here reproduced by kind permission of:

Ascherberg, Hopwood and Crew (*Limehouse Blues*).

Chappell and Co. Ltd. (*My Heart Stood Still, Dancing on the Ceiling, A Room with a View*).

The Estate of Noël Coward (*A Room with a View*).

Title *Over My Shoulder* and extract from the song come by kind permission of Cinephonic Music Co. Ltd.

The extract from the screenplay of J. B. Priestley's *The Good Companions* is reprinted by permission of A. D. Peters & Co. and by courtesy of The Rank Organisation Ltd.

'Over my shoulder goes one care,
Over my shoulder goes two cares,
Why should I cry, it's blue above . . .'

Chapter One

A gentle voice said in my ear, 'Wake up, Jessie, wake up.' Through layers of sleep I tried to resist. I did not want to wake up. In this oblivion I had found safety. I pressed my eyelids closer together.

The voice was insistent, 'Please open your eyes, Jessie. Don't be frightened.'

Frightened! All my life I had been frightened! From the first time I stared down into that black menacing pit: from the first time Rosie had shouted, 'My sister can do it better.' I'd been frightened in New York, frightened in London, and yesterday . . . what had they done to me yesterday?

A hand touched my shoulder, someone bent near me and I heard the rustle of a uniform and caught the whiff of clean antiseptic. Sudden knowledge jerked me back to consciousness. Oh God, was it happening all over again? How many times had I opened my eyes to this?

'It's all right, Jessie. Please wake up.'

She had an Irish accent the owner of this gentle voice. She sounded kind. Obedient, as from past experience I knew I must be, I opened my eyes and looked up at the fresh young face of a nurse. Slowly my surroundings filtered in: a row of beds, people. . . . I was in a long hospital ward, and the first thing that came into my mind was: 'This time I'm having it on National Health. Thank God, I won't have those awful bills to pay.'

The nurse could not know why I smiled, but she seemed satisfied. 'Would you like a cup of tea?' she asked gently, then added reassuringly, 'My name is Norah.'

I

Almost happy, I closed my eyes again and relaxed for a moment. Whatever had happened—and I wouldn't think about it now—had saved me. I need not go back. It was only when I reached out for the cup of tea and saw the identification tape around my wrist that I was shocked into awareness. Saved me from what? What had I done that I should be labelled like a dead body?

Memories jostled their way into my mind. I could see again the lights of Waterloo Bridge on that wet evening, hear the surge of the traffic; there was the Festival Hall lit up like a gigantic glass box . . .

Norah steadied the cup in my hand. 'Don't think about it, you are safe here.'

Yes, I was safe in this bed. I need not go back, need not hold another bouquet of carnations, smile radiantly and go through that terrible torture again. The National Film Theatre could open its doors without me.

And yet it had all started so well.

I'd gone to tea that afternoon with Victor and Phoebe Saville in their flat in Curzon Street. It was years since I'd had a real meeting with Victor, the last time must have been in Hollywood in 1941 when he'd left Gaumont-British to take up a contract with Metro-Goldwyn-Mayer. As soon as we saw each other the years fell away. The friendship that had its roots in the early thirties was as strong as ever and I felt the same bond between us.

We talked about the old days when he'd been our leading British film director and he'd just met the girl he was to lead to stardom. 'Remember how frightened you used to be of the camera?' he laughed. When we made our first film together I used to shrink every time a camera came near me. The film camera, I felt, was like a creeping serpent ready to pick up all my nerves and exaggerate every defect.

Victor recognised that in the past another director with his highly critical remarks had given me an inferiority complex. He took me aside. 'Listen, Jessie,' he told me. 'Every time that camera creeps up, stare it in the face and say, "I am beautiful. I am beautiful!" And, by God, you *will* be beautiful.'

I followed his advice and to my amazement when I saw the rushes next day, the whole expression of my face was completely different. The cowed look had gone. There was a new

2

tilt to my head and a different personality was coming over, one full of confidence.

Victor Saville did that for me. He was a tower of strength, someone to lean on and be guided by. 'Victor's in charge,' I used to think. 'He'll look after me.'

Phoebe, Victor's wife, was an old friend too. We'd been at Madame Terry's Dancing School together when we were girls. The afternoon passed full of warmth and reminiscence that lasted until we left for the theatre.

As we took our seats I was surprised at the youth of the audience that filled the cinema to capacity. Immediately I felt apprehensive. Would these young things be interested in a film that had been made before some of them were born?

Back in 1936, *It's Love Again* had been a great hit, breaking all records at the Roxy in New York, but how would it stand up now, watched by critical young eyes? Was it going to be just another old film with old-time stars viewed with indifference and settled with a patronising smile? As the lights dimmed I felt tense and nervous. I was going to be judged by these young people. If only they knew what these old films had done to us who made them, but they must be oblivious to the flesh and blood eroded in these celluloid reels. And then I told myself that I was a fool to worry. What did it matter what they thought. It was all over and done with years ago, along with yesterday's worn-out emotions.

Soon my anxieties evaporated. I forgot everything but what was happening on the screen in front of me. The film seemed alive, pulsating with vitality. *It's Love Again* was a crazy story about a girl who impersonates a society beauty aided and abetted by two newspaper reporters. Robert Young, over from Hollywood, was one of the journalists, and Sonnie Hale the other.

I remembered how Sonnie, my husband, had had the time of his life making this film. He loved dressing up, he was a real ham, and in his make-up as an Indian Rajah, he had fooled everyone. He had gone round the studio pretending to be a visitor, asking the way in a sing-song accent and the results had been hilarious. Robert Hale, Sonnie's father, was in the film too. Seeing them now on the screen together, they looked almost like brothers. What a darling Robert had been, always

3

so kind to me, although he knew perfectly well that the rest of his family loathed me.

And then, there was the girl!

She was lovely, a beautiful stranger who sang and laughed and danced. How she danced! Even Madame Clare would have applauded. 'You have good fortune, my child.' I'd stood in front of this strange little figure when I was ten years old: Madame in her fur tippet, her grey spats over black buttoned boots, and in her hand that dreaded long stick that could hurt so much. 'Balance, posture, a supple back, you have all those, but to be a great dancer,' her stick tapped my shoulder, 'discipline! You need discipline!'

This girl on the screen with the round dark eyes, so young and gay, had learned all about discipline. Rosie had bored a hole through the bedroom wall so that unobserved, she could make sure I was practising. But it had been worth it, the dancing was good, very good. The audience, too, seemed caught up in the magic of the film. In the scene where the girl pretends to be a crack shot they laughed aloud. I remembered that we had an expert marksman on the set who did the real shooting, but as chandeliers crashed to the ground and bullets whizzed overhead, the effect was extremely funny, and the audience began to applaud. I glowed with pleasure, it's not often that a comedy scene gets applause. The joy of living fairly bounced off the screen at us. The young audience loved the film, there was so much happiness oozing from it.

Things had been so right for Sonnie and me then. We were young and happy, our hopes were bright, our futures assured. We were going to live for ever and be happy ever after. It had been a good marriage. Even when we quarrelled it often ended in laughter.

'Tell that red-nosed comic of a father of yours to shut up,' I'd shout to Katie, our daughter.

'Tell that stuck-up leading lady of a mother of yours to go to blazes,' Sonnie would yell back.

Little Katie would run back and forth delivering our highly coloured comments until the three of us were helpless with laughter.

We were both on top of the world. 'Mouse,' he'd told me when the last take of *It's Love Again* was printed and the film was in the can, 'start packing. We're off on holiday.'

Mouse was his pet name for me. He said I never opened my mouth when we went to high-class dinner parties. He was right of course. I was petrified of making mistakes. I used to sit and listen, making mental notes, learning all the time. Learning how to pronounce words, how to use the English language properly. God, I had so much to learn, and I was so frightened of making a fool of myself. Not that I should have worried overmuch, I didn't ever get a chance to talk; when Sonnie was around he always hogged the conversation. Those theatrical stories he told, how they went on and on.

We went on holiday, the two of us. We swam and sunbathed in the little Spanish fishing village called Cadaqués that no one knew about then. Of course halfway through our holiday the telegrams arrived ordering us back to London to get ready for our next film. We ignored them for another week because we were at the top of our profession and the film moguls didn't frighten us—much.

We came back to London and then it all began. . . . That girl dancing up there on the screen, had anyone told her this film was the end of her happiness, would she have believed them? Would she have believed that soon her life was going to disintegrate around her? Poor little creature, why did it have to happen to her? What had she done to deserve it?

Imperceptibly I felt my mood change. Bitter memories edged out the happy ones, bringing an arid yearning for what might have been. A shudder ran through me. I'd buried this part of my life too deeply to have it resurrected in front of me scene by scene. Why had I let myself in for this? I was watching a parade of phantoms. Sonnie . . . Robert . . . they were both dead. I couldn't bear to watch them. Sonnie, dying as he did at the wrong time, and in the wrong way. . . . My hands began to tremble, I felt perspiration gather on my forehead. I clutched my hands desperately together. Hold on, I prayed, hold on! For God's sake don't make a scene. Hold on, it will be over soon.

By the time the film ended, the shaking had subsided and I was in control of myself. But it was a control balanced on a knife-edge. I decided that as soon as I could I'd thank Victor and get out. My hand was on Victor's arm ready for my whispered goodbye when the lights came up. To my utter confusion and surprise the whole audience began to rise. They

5

stood up, turned and faced us where we sat. I watched them uneasily. And then the clapping broke out, a crescendo of noise. We were getting a standing ovation.

Victor whispered, 'Stand up, Jessie. It's for you.'

An immense wave of gratitude swept over me. So it hadn't all been in vain. I'd left something behind that people still applauded.

Standing on the stage, a bouquet of pink carnations and maidenhair fern was placed in my damp hands. I gazed out at the sea of faces hoping the right words would come.

'Thank you,' I murmured unsteadily. 'Thank you, you've been so kind.'

They had been kinder than they knew, giving me an assurance that my career hadn't been wasted. But what could I tell them? That I was shaking like a leaf? That it had taken all my will-power to sit and watch my past unfold before my eyes? And then I remembered, they'd liked my dancing. 'Sir Michael Balcon,' I began, 'the producer of this film, once said that I had no talent, he didn't want to use me, but I thought the dancing tonight came over superbly. Whatever he thought of the girl in this film, even he must admit—*she could dance!*'

At the back of the theatre Victor was surrounded by well-wishers. He came forward and took my arm. 'They want you to come back and be present at another film next week, Jessie. They're arranging for one of the new young stars to make a presentation to you.'

'I'm not sure,' I said uncertainly.

He brushed my words aside, 'Of course you are. It's *Evergreen.*'

I stared at him, unwilling to accept what he said.

He misunderstood my blank look and laughed. 'You can't have forgotten *Evergreen*?'

Forgotten! Does one forget a recurring nightmare? I'd managed to sit through *It's Love Again*, and that had been a happy film. How could I come back and watch *Evergreen*, the film that had given me some of the deepest misery of my life. *Evergreen*, that was when it all began. No! No! Never!

I did my best. I talked and laughed with the kind people around me. The platitudes of the theatre came easily and my smile seemed stuck on with Sellotape. But in the car that drove me to Baker Street Underground station, Victor's words, 'Come back and watch *Evergreen*', echoed again and again in my mind, until they were like a vice tightening around my head. He might just as well have said, 'Come back and watch your crucifixion.'

The train ground along the Metropolitan Line . . . Wembley Park . . . Harrow. . . . A few more stations before I reached my sanctuary at journey's end. A nice motherly woman got up to leave from the seat opposite. 'What lovely flowers,' she said. 'Have you been to a celebration?' She beamed at me expecting a cheerful answer. I tried to smile. *Had* I been to a celebration? Dear God, I'd been to a burial. I'd looked at people I loved, dead and gone. I'd sifted the ashes of a career that had once pierced the skies like a shooting star. To my horror a tear rolled down my cheek, then another, and another. I lowered my head and wept.

By the time I got home I was ashamed of my breakdown on the train and ready to act the part of the successful actress coming home from a triumphant performance. Rosie, my sister, always wanted to hear exactly what had happened, learn every minute detail. I arranged the flowers and told Rosie and George, her husband, about meeting Victor and Phoebe again. But when I came to the showing of the film I hesitated. I couldn't bear the thought of breaking down in front of them. If I could keep busy I might ward off difficult questions until I went to bed. Tomorrow was another day—I'd tell them then.

Eventually I had to sit down and drink the tea Rosie brewed. The silence grew between us. I knew they were waiting for me to begin. Rosie took my hesitation to mean something else.

'Didn't they like the film?' she asked carefully.

'They loved it.'

Like the devoted sister she was, Rosie's face lit up, and the questions poured out. I had to tell her.

'The whole audience turned and faced us. They gave us a standing ovation. Oh, Rosie, they liked the film so much. And it was such a happy film.' It seemed easy to talk, about the laughter, the applause, even about Sonnie and his father. But when we came to the part where Victor said I must go back and see *Evergreen*, my voice tightened. 'I can't go back.'

Rosie looked puzzled. 'But you must, Jessie. It's in your honour.'

7

I stood up. In spite of myself, my voice rose. 'I can't. I can't go back and watch all that unhappiness.'

Rosie didn't seem to understand. 'Don't be childish, Jessie. You'll sail through. There's nothing to it.'

Against my will the trembling began again, tension knotted my insides. 'They're all dead, Rosie,' I cried. 'Dead and gone. Only that poor kid is left. I can't watch her again. She didn't know what was coming to her.'

Rosie stared at me, 'What poor kid?'

'Me!' I shouted. 'Me!' And then I was weeping. Terrified at the thought of having to go back and watch *Evergreen*. Distraught that even my sister could not understand my unreasoning panic.

In the bathroom I jerked open the door of the medicine cabinet. I fumbled for my bottle of sleeping pills. I must block out my misery. I must forget. I must sleep. The panic grew until it devoured me, until the only thought in my mind was to find a way out. *I could not go back!* And as I was putting one pill after the other into my mouth, I cried for a little girl called Jessie Matthews who might have been happier if she'd stayed where she was born in Berwick Market, Soho, and never, never tried to climb up there to the stars.

Chapter Two

High in the sky a carnival of lights exploded, blue and yellow chased red and green; a circle of red electric lights flashed into blue. Then a split second blackout and a man's head made up of lights switched on. He was smoking a cigarette with a red burning tip and his hand moved. Magic!

'Coo! Rosie! Look!' I'd never seen anything like it in my life.

Rosie tugged my hand impatiently. 'It's only Piccadilly Circus. Come on.' She pulled me energetically through the traffic to the other side of the wide street.

Piccadilly! What a lovely name. And I'd never been here before. Swarms of people, flashing lights, big red buses swooping by, their open decks crammed with passengers. It was like fairyland. 'Look! Rosie! Look!' Flower girls wearing wide-brimmed straw hats and shawls sat on the steps around a little statue: roses and carnations filled the baskets at their feet. One of them held out bunches of violets, 'Violets! Who'll buy my violets?'

My seven-year-old eyes were wide with wonder as Rosie turned out of the broad highway and marched me into a narrow street, and then an even more exciting world burst upon us. A barrel organ. Gay music made to dance to. While a man with a red bandana round his neck turned the handle a little monkey in a green jacket pranced on his shoulder.

'Stop gawping,' ordered Rosie as she dragged me past.

Lace curtains thinly veiled plate-glass windows and I could see people inside sitting at tables. A waiter in a long white apron opened a door and spicy smells gushed out. He shouted in a foreign language to the man with the barrel organ. Imagine, just half an hour ago we'd been in the quiet streets of Camden Town, and now a bus ride had brought us to this exotic city.

'Is this it?' I cried excitedly, 'Is this where we're going to live?'

'No,' said Rosie sharply. 'It's round the back, behind the market.' I sensed that Rosie's patience was drying up fast, another question and I might get a cuff round my ear. Rosie, my eldest sister, was seventeen. That spring she'd put up her long black hair and skewered her straw hat on with a fancy hat-pin. Although she wasn't very tall and didn't look very old, Rosie had now joined the grown-ups. Rosie had always frightened me, and today there was a special reason for her displeasure. That morning the Matthews family had moved from Camden Town to Soho and Rosie had to stay behind to bring me home from my school concert.

We left the barrel organ, the gaiety and the bright lights behind and turned a corner. The gutters were piled with rotting vegetables. I stepped carefully, avoiding the squashed tomatoes, the blackened banana skins and the empty boxes. 'Coo! I don't like it here,' I muttered.

'You'd better not let our Dad hear you,' snapped Rosie, 'he works here. This is Berwick Market.'

The streets were empty now and the fading light made them look sad and grey. We passed a dirty looking public house, the yellow paint peeling from its walls, and through the open door I smelled the sour odour of beer. Rosie crossed the road and halted outside high iron gates. I could just make out 'King William and Mary Yard' in worn gold letters across the top of them. Rosie let go of my hand and rattled urgently at the locked gates. Beyond them I saw a cobbled stone yard backed by wooden sheds and stables and over them a soot-stained ramshackle building.

I grabbed Rosie's sleeve, 'It's not here, is it?'

'Oh be quiet. I've wasted enough time on you. I should have been here helping Mum hours ago.'

This couldn't be our new home. We'd left our lovely garden in Camden Town for this? A drab yard, a dingy building that looked like a slum? In Camden Town we'd had a shed in the garden where we played sweet shops and there was a pond with goldfish.

A window was pushed up in the building over the sheds, a woman's voice shouted, 'We're locked up for the night.'

'I'm Rosie Matthews. I've come to live here.'

The window slammed down and a few minutes later a woman walked across the yard and opened the gate with a large iron key. 'Hallo, Rosie.' She had a warm sibilant voice. 'Remember me? I'm Mrs Phillips. The caretaker's away so I'm here to let you in. Now, who's this one?' She bent down to inspect me.

'She's the one in the middle. Our Jessie.'

'So this is Jessie.' I caught a glimpse of black hair and olive skin as she patted my cheek. 'I remember you being born, my darling. Just round the corner, it was, over a shop in Berwick Market.'

My head jerked up. 'No, I never,' I said indignantly. 'I'm from Camden Town.' How dare this woman say I was born in such a dirty place.

Mrs Phillips laughed and Rosie joined in. They were still laughing and chatting as I followed them sulkily across the cobbles to a flight of wooden steps at the far end. On the bottom step a boy sat strumming a banjo. 'One of the Dawsons from the middle,' said the woman as she pushed past him. 'Place is full of kids. Your Mum's got nine, hasn't she?'

I was snivelling as I climbed the stairs after Rosie. I hated this place called 'William and Mary Yard'. I wouldn't stay. I'd go back to Camden Town. And then the door at the top of the stairs opened and there she stood, the centre of my world. Long pearl earrings swinging, her dark hair coiled in a great mass at the nape of her neck, a blue overall tied round her middle and her smile as loving as when I'd left her this morning.

I threw my arms around her ample waist and sobbed, 'Mum, Mum! It isn't true? I wasn't born in this horrible place, was I?'

She took off my straw hat and straightened the ribbon bow on my hair. 'Berwick Market a horrible place, is it?' She laughed, 'Don't let your Dad hear you. Look,' she turned me round, 'we're all here waiting for you, and there's Dolly the parrot in her cage and Tiger the cat . . .'

It wasn't often that I saw all my brothers and sisters sitting together round the long kitchen table. It was usually first come, first served when there was any food around. And there were sausages tonight, I could smell them cooking.

Georgie, fifteen, sat at the top, head in a comic as usual, ignoring what the rest of the family did. Then came Billy, thin and wiry, a year younger. Jenny and Carrie, my older sisters, sat close together whispering; then there was Lena who came after me; Eve the toddler, and Eddie the baby sitting in his high chair banging his dish with a spoon.

'Come on Mum. When we going to have our supper?' Billy shouted, he was always after food.

'All right, all right.' My mother gave me one of her rare kisses and then picked up the big cottage loaf. She always carved bread with the loaf perched on top of her pregnant stomach. Mum had to hold things where she could see them. She was always pregnant with another baby and she said she hadn't seen her toes since Jenny was born.

Without removing her hat, Rosie slapped the marge on the bread, dished out the sausages and poured the tea from the big brown teapot.

'How'd it go, Rose?' Mum asked. 'What was the concert like?'

I stopped chewing bread and marge and listened attentively. I didn't expect Rose would give me a very good report.

'Mum, she was really lovely.'

I stared at Rose in astonishment. She was smiling.

'The headmistress was ever so pleased with her. D'you know what she said?' Was this *me* Rosie was talking about? 'The headmistress said Jessie ought to go on the stage. She's got more talent than she's ever seen in a child. She ought to be trained, that's what she said.'

'No!' Mum's voice was full of awe. 'Did she really?' They both turned and looked at me. I grew red at being caught out listening and I gave Lena a shove to hide my embarrassment. But before Lena started yelling I saw Rosie's face. She was looking at me in a strange way, her face shone with pride as if I'd done something extraordinary, as if she loved me very much.

I was sorry I'd pushed Lena. She was only five and having trouble with her eyes. Mum took her regularly to hospital and now she had to wear a pair of glasses with a black patch over one lense. I gave her half my sausage to shut her up.

Why was Rosie so pleased that I'd done well at the concert?
I always did well when I sang and danced. Teacher made a
fuss of me every time we had a concert and this year she'd
made me a special flowered kimono and given me a little paper
fan so that I could pretend to be a Japanese girl. But Rosie
was more important than my teacher now. I'd left Camden
Town and Rosie was the power in the home when Mum was
out working. Maybe I'd have a better time if I played up to
Rosie.

'I did ever so well at the concert,' I shouted, excitement
going to my head. 'I sang a song.'

·'You push Lena again and I'll give you something to sing
about,' declared Rosie.

'Show off,' whispered Carrie, and pushed me off the bench.

A quick wipe with a wet flannel round the face and hands
and we younger children were sent to bed. There were three
rooms upstairs, and on the day we moved into William and
Mary Yard they all looked equally forlorn. Bare boards on the
floor, sagging beds, and nails on the wall where we hung our
clothes. One room was for the girls, one for the boys and the
other for Mum and Dad and the two babies. We five girls had
to share two beds, and Carrie, Lena and I were the fighting
threesome. Lena, being the youngest, slept in the middle, and
keeping her toes out of my face was a constant battle.

I was still awake when the older girls came to bed. Through
the grimy window I could see flashes of green and gold, and
crimson rays lit up the sky as the advertisements snapped on
and off over Piccadilly Circus. Perhaps it wasn't going to be so
bad after all with Piccadilly just around the corner. And tomorrow I'd go down and see the stables. Jenny the carthorse
(she was named after my mother) who pulled Dad's van was
asleep down there. In a way it might be better than Camden
Town for Mum would be working just round the corner at
Dad's stall in Berwick Market and I could always find her, and
Georgie, who'd left school last year, would be there too.

I yawned, everything was going to be all right. Then I
heard the noise of people coming out of the pub across the
street and immediately I was wide awake again. The one
person who could spoil everything would be coming home
soon. He'd been in that pub with his mates all evening, and
now he'd come home drunk and there'd be trouble.

Shortly after, I heard him come in, loud and argumentative as always. Ever since I could remember I had been frightened when I heard him come home late at night. So often when he shouted I heard my mother pleading with him. If he hit my mother again . . . I sat up in bed. I pulled back the covers.

'Jessie,' Rose whispered to me from the other bed. 'Stay where you are. Mum can manage our Dad.'

It was quite true I had been born over a butcher's shop in Berwick Market. We didn't stay there long. Some weeks before I was born the butcher told my parents that he wanted their flat for his son who was getting married but they could stay on until the new baby was six weeks old.

My mother took this new move philosophically. Ever since she married my father at the age of eighteen her life had been precarious, moving from one drab flat to another. The rooms were always around Covent Garden where my father worked at first and afterwards Berwick Market where he had his stall. After my birth their next move was to Livonia Street in Soho, but after Lena was born someone he met in a pub offered my father a house in Camden Town. We had a garden and an almost suburban life until 1914 when money was short and my mother had to help my father on his stall, so we moved back to Soho and into William and Mary Yard. We were poor, there was never enough money, but we always managed somehow. Working in the markets as my father did, meant that at least we should never starve.

Jenny Townsend, my mother, had been born in Islington, North London, and for reasons none of us ever discovered, Jenny and her sisters were brought up by their grandparents. I remember being taken to see them once. Great-grandfather was ninety and he was dying. The house was terraced and in the small bedroom where he lay everything looked spotless. There were white sheets and a snowy counterpane on the bed, and the frail old man was propped up with white pillows, his thin face looking as yellow as old ivory against the whiteness. I remember a little old lady full of energy, bustling around finding me a book to look at and lemonade to drink, and yet on the day her husband died my great-grandmother took to her bed and three days later she died too.

Not much is known about my mother's family. There was

supposed to be some Irish blood and my mother certainly had the look of a Celt; her long black hair was her pride and joy. She told us stories of how she used to sit on it, and there was a tale we loved to hear, how she'd nearly been killed because of her hair. It happened when she worked at the Peerless Silk Factory when she was a girl. In those days there were no regulations about guards on machines, and as she worked winding silk thread onto reels, her long black hair caught in her machine. Only the prompt action of a quick-witted friend saved my mother from being scalped.

My mother had a wonderful walk. In spite of her broad hips, for constant childbearing had made her stout, her step was light and her well-shaped head was carried high. I can see her now, sitting in her favourite ladder-backed chair in our kitchen/living room, her face so pretty and round, her glossy hair parted in the middle looking like some dark beauty from an Italian painting. And there was always a baby in her lap. Her heart was big enough for all her children, and before she'd finished she had sixteen, although only eleven of us survived.

We were so lucky to have such a mother. It may have been three or even four in a bed, bread and scrape for supper some nights, and a swipe from Dad if we got in his way, but we had the kindest, most lovable mother in the world. She only let me down once and that was my own fault.

It happened at my new school, the Pulteney L.C.C. School in Peter Street, Soho, where all the Matthews children under the age of fourteen were enrolled. At my old school in Camden Town I had always been allowed to use my left hand when I wrote. But Miss Steel, my new teacher, was going to make me use my right hand if it killed me. She was a very large woman, man-sized, and she wore mannish clothes, high collars with a tie and thick skirts over her solid hips.

A large boney hand would grasp my left wrist, shake the pen from my hand, and then I'd get a blow on the back of my head. 'Use your right hand,' she'd command. Any chance that I might become a scholar was killed stone dead by Miss Steel. She gave me an inferiority complex about my lack of education that lasted all my life. My school days became ink-stained, futile and miserable.

'Mummy,' I complained one evening, 'Miss Steel's ever so

15

nasty. I heard her say that my knickers were a disgrace. "Fancy sending a child to school like that," I heard her say it.'

I was delighted at my mother's instant, hurt reaction. I neglected to tell her that my knickers had become black after an hour on the slide in the playground. 'Did you hear that, Rose?' she said over my head. 'Well, I don't know.' There were many things the Market might say about sketchy house-keeping, but to call one's children dirty!

Next morning I didn't protest when I was scrubbed under the kitchen tap and ceremoniously dressed by Rose. We were right in the middle of sums when someone tapped on the class-room door and my mother walked in. She looked pale and agitated, and she was wearing her Sunday hat, a black straw with a bluebird's wing across the brim.

Welcoming any interruption, we laid down our pens and sat back. 'It's about Jessie,' my mother announced. Miss Steel looked thunderous. 'Come here, Jessie,' my mother called.

I hadn't expected this. What misfortune had brought my mild-mannered parent to school? Uncertainly I crossed to her side. My mother laid her worn leather reticule on Miss Steel's desk. Then, with infinite care she began to unbutton the back of my gingham dress. She lifted it up and slipped it over my head. Shame and horror overtook me. 'Is this dirty, Miss?' my mother demanded. She held the dress out for Miss Steel's in-spection. Next over my head came my cotton petticoat. 'And how about this, Miss?'

The class watched in enthralled silence. I wanted to die very quickly. My liberty bodice was unbuttoned next. A tear ran down my cheek and I hugged my bony chest. Not my knickers, I prayed, please Mum, not my knickers.

'Turn round, Jessie,' said my mother, 'now bend over. Quite clean, Miss, aren't they?'

Miss Steel cleared her throat ready for the attack. But my mother was silent, never one to argue in public. She had made her point, saved the honour of the Matthews family and now she dressed me quickly, led me back to my desk, gave my head a pat, and left the classroom.

I sat at my desk weeping bitterly. It was the first time in my life that my mother had let me down and I knew it was all my own fault. Why hadn't I kept my mouth shut? As I rubbed the tears from my cheeks I wished desperately that I

16

was miles away from Soho. That I lived somewhere where little girls wore white buttoned shoes and spotless white dresses and no one would dare to mention the state of their knickers.

Three families lived in the buildings over the stables at William and Mary Yard: the Phillips at one end, the Dawsons in the middle, and the Matthews on the other side.

The Phillips family were Jewish. Mrs Phillips, a warm-hearted inquisitive woman, had seven children, and her husband also sold fruit and vegetables in Berwick Market. The Dawsons in the middle had three children and Mr Dawson was stage manager at the London Palladium at Oxford Circus. I think my father's friendship with Mr Dawson was the reason we moved to William and Mary, for if there was an animal act on at the Palladium, they would be housed in the stables and my father would look after them. Dad loved animals, sometimes I thought he preferred them to human beings.

The Yard was a wonderful playground for the twenty children who lived there. In the sheds and stables most of the paraphernalia of Berwick Market was kept every night—the stalls, the vans, the horses that pulled the carts from Covent Garden with meat for the butchers and fruit and vegetables for the stalls. Ladders were left leaning against all the walls to climb up, there were empty packing cases to hide in and there was always a stable boy or two around to join in a game of cricket or a fight between cowboys and Indians. And there were the animals my father looked after to play with, the dogs, the cats, a goat, two rabbits and the chickens.

George Matthews, my father, could put his hand to anything, earn a shilling anywhere. From the age of nine he had been on his own and fought for his existence; toughness had grown on him like an outer skin. My mother, who found fault with no one, called him a hard man but she alone understood why he had become what he was. Throughout my childhood I was frightened of my father. As I grew up I thought my mother was too weak with him, but later, when I knew the story of his life, I could understand him better, although I did not always forget—or forgive.

Chapter Three

Grandma Matthews came to tea every Sunday afternoon and one afternoon she told us that she was making a fur coat for Queen Mary. When Grandma was young she used to work for Revillon, the high-class furriers in Regent Street. Now that she was too old to go out to work they sent the fur pieces round to her little cottage in Poplar.

Whenever Grandma came my father would say he'd got things to do down in the Yard. There was always a certain amount of coolness between him and Grandma, for Grandma was the mother who had deserted him when he was a baby.

My father was born in an East End slum near Poplar with back-to-back houses and an outside lavatory that served a row of houses. He came into a home filled with brutality, poverty and misery. When his mother could stand no more she left her husband, taking the four elder children with her. The baby, George, was left behind. I always remember my mother shaking her head when she told me, 'Fancy leaving a baby behind. What a terrible thing to do.'

From babyhood George was beaten and half starved. When he was nine he ran away, sleeping in cellars, stables and doorways, running errands, selling newspapers and scrounging for food. He learned to use his fists to protect himself. Perhaps his violent temper stemmed from his early fight for survival, but when Dad was in a temper you kept well away from him.

When he was about twenty and working in Covent Garden, a friend told him there was a girl called Matthews working in Hatton Garden who looked dark and Welsh, just like George.

That was how my father found his sister and she took him out to Poplar to meet her mother. My father looked at the small, trim woman with the large dark eyes, and said coldly, 'How do I know you're my mother?'

'How do you know, George?' said the small woman in the same cool tones. 'Come over to the looking-glass.' Mirrored before him were their two faces, both olive skinned, with slim pointed noses, flashing brown eyes; two identical faces from the same mould.

There was never any show of affection between Dad and Grandma. I don't think he ever forgave her for leaving him behind. But they were very much alike: tough, with a flintlike quality that was hard to pierce. Grandma, however, was devoted to my mother, and she often stood up to my father on her behalf. Like the time when Rosie decided that I must have dancing lessons and my mother tried to get the money out of him.

In the free and easy way of Soho and especially William and Mary Yard, we children were always in and out of each other's homes with or without an invitation. I always liked going to the Phillips' flat. There'd be a pot bubbling on the stove and Mrs Phillips would see me sniffing the air and say, 'Want a bowl of chicken soup and noodles, Jessie?' Fay Phillips was about my age and I envied her tremendously. There was an air of comfort amounting almost to luxury in contrast to our bare boards and curtainless windows.

One evening when Rosie and I were round at the Phillips' flat, Fay's elder sister and her boyfriend came in. The boy-friend worked at Gamba, the theatrical shoe shop in Old Compton Street, and he'd brought Fay a present, a pair of pink satin ba llet slippers. Fay put them on and tried a few steps, not very successfully. Devoured with envy I watched her; those pink satin slippers seemed the most desirable things in the world.

'Let me try them on, Fay,' I wheedled. 'Go on.'

The young man fitted the slippers onto my feet. They were a size too big but he tied the tapes tightly round my ankles, and then held out his hand. I took it and then sprang straight onto my toes. It was a lovely feeling. I was tall and straight. I could do anything. I ran across the room on my points.

Mrs Phillips and her daughters laughed and applauded and

I noticed that Rosie joined in. The boyfriend untied the tapes. He held my foot in his hand. 'Look at this,' he said in an interested voice. 'Just look at that arch. What a strong foot she's got. A real dancer's foot.'

We had a good supper that evening. Dad had brought home a sack of live eels and emptied them writhing and wriggling on the wooden table. He chopped off their heads and cleaned them and Rosie stewed them in water. They still wriggled when they were on the table but who cared. There was plenty to eat that night and we all loved eels for supper.

When we'd finished, Mum lay back in her chair with baby Eddie asleep in her lap and little Eve curled up at her feet. Jenny and Carrie squabbled over a hair slide Carrie had pinched from Jenny. Georgie and Billy were practising sparring in a corner and Dad was resting in his chair prior to going out to the pub. His top trouser buttons were undone and his collarless shirt was open at the throat. Dad never wore a collar or tie if he could help it.

The kitchen where we gathered was the only living room in the house. It was clean. We all had to help. One of us scrubbed the bare wooden floor every day and sanded the long deal table. The big iron cooking range had to be black-leaded, and the sink with the cooking pots underneath cleaned out. The mangle stood next to the sink to be used on washday, and over in one corner was a broken-down divan where Dad took his naps. The rest of the furnishings were spartan, but somewhere in the room there was usually one article of value. My father was always picking up something in a junk yard or a sale that might fetch a good price in the right quarter. He knew something about furniture, and he'd bring home a little table that might be Chippendale, or a chair with a tattered silk cover that might be Hepplewhite. He could always tell a gilt picture frame from one that contained gold leaf, so there was often a picture frame or two standing against the wall.

Rosie was at the sink doing the washing up. She accepted her position as chief cook and bottle washer without complaint. Her mother had to work at the stall and in our society once a girl was fourteen her place was to help at home. When Jenny was fourteen it would be her turn.

She wiped her hands on her apron and turned round. 'Dad,' she called. Rosie was the one child who didn't flinch away when her father walked by. She resembled Dad to a certain extent, she had the same flashing dark eyes and black hair, but that was as far as it went. I always watched my step with Rosie, but there was never any real fear in our relationship. I recognised that there was no cruelty in her character. 'Dad,' she said, 'I want to tell you something.'

Dad belched and said, 'Tell your mother.'

Rosie left the sink and walked over to where I sat on the floor playing with Tiger the cat. 'Jessie's going to be a dancer,' she announced.

Dad turned his head. 'That skinny little 'aporth! Get 'orf!'

Rosie stood her ground. Small as she was, under five foot, she had an indomitable look. 'That's how dancers have to be, thin like our Jessie. Her headmistress at her school in Camden Town said she'd go far.'

'Garn!' said Dad.

'She's got to have lessons and some special shoes.'

'Some 'opes,' sneered Dad.

'If you won't give me the money,' I could hear Rosie getting nervous, no one ever disagreed with Dad, 'I'll get it myself. There's a job going in Brewer Street.'

My father swung round in his chair. 'What did you say, my girl?'

The atmosphere in the kitchen changed abruptly. Jenny and Carrie stopped quarrelling, Georgie moved nearer the door to the stairs, and I let Tiger go and got ready to move rapidly.

'George,' my mother's gentle voice broke the tension. 'I can manage. Let Rosie go out to work if she wants. Jenny's a good help now, and we can always ask Carrie to give a hand.'

Dad glowered at Rosie for a moment, then he jerked his head towards me. 'Here,' he said, 'you! Come here!'

Nothing on earth would make me go to my father. If I was going to be beaten I'd take it here. Rosie leant down and jerked me to my feet. There were twin spots of crimson in Rosie's cheeks. She was just as frightened as I was, but that didn't matter, not to Rosie. She pulled me over to Dad's chair.

'Show him your foot,' she hissed.

I held out my bare and dirty foot.

'Look,' Rosie said shrilly, 'that arch. It's a dancer's foot . . .' She grabbed at an illustration that might help. 'It's just like Pavlova's.'

'Get 'orf,' rumbled Dad. But she'd got him on a raw spot. He didn't know what a dancer's foot looked like. Neither did I, and until this evening in the Phillips' flat, I'm sure that Rosie didn't either. 'All that foot needs is a wash.'

Dad turned away, reached over and pulled one of Georgie's comics from the table. He studied it with apparent great interest. As we all knew that Dad couldn't read or write properly, this show of indifference meant that the battle was over—for the moment. Ten minutes later he went off to the pub, where he knew he'd get a welcome. Dad was a popular man in the market and in the pub; he always bought his round and more. That was where the money went, Mum said, playing Mr Big in the pub.

Much later that night I heard Dad come home from the pub. His voice came straight up to the bedroom where I lay with Lena and Carrie. I tensed for the drunken argument that might follow. But he was in a good temper. 'Here, Jenny, my love,' I heard him say. 'Something I got for you.'

When I heard him come up to bed, I tiptoed down the stairs and peeped round the door. On the table was a large basket of eggs. But even more interesting was the little scene being enacted by my mother and Rosie. Mum had Dad's trousers in her hands and she was going through the pockets. 'Here you are, love,' she said to Rosie. 'Two bob, for a start. Put that in your purse. That'll help towards those lessons.'

Rosie went out to work. She found a job making buttons and buttonholes at a shop in Brewer Street, and her first week's wages went towards buying me a pair of black practice shoes. I know Grandma had a 'go' at Dad and made him pay for some of the lessons, and my mother also contributed, but the idea was Rosie's, and it was Rosie who marched me off to my first lesson.

One Saturday morning Rosie took ten minutes off from her job and met me on the corner of Brewer Street. The dancing class was held in a large bare room on the first floor of a house in Carnaby Street. She tied on my shoes, straightened my cotton frock, warned me to do everything teacher said, then hurried back to her buttons and buttonholes. I was left to face the blank stares of an assorted group of small girls. My heart was pounding with anxiety by the time the door opened and a seeming goddess walked in. Miss Shortiss was young and slender, her dark hair was pulled back into a classic chignon and she wore black practice clothes. I loved her from the moment I saw her. Miss Shortiss, I never found out her first name, was a professional ballet dancer and she had all the grace and poise of her profession.

A middle-aged lady sitting at a piano in the corner began to play. The girls lined up by a horizontal bar fixed along one wall. Miss Shortiss looked at me in an absent-minded way. 'You, too, little girl.'

I don't know what the music was, it might have been a Chopin waltz, but for me it was a melody straight from heaven. I remember the joy that flooded through me, the sheer happiness that now I was going to learn to dance and look like the beautiful Miss Shortiss.

I copied what the other girls did, not knowing that they were the routine exercises that all ballet dancers begin with: *Turn-out First position, Second Position.* I wondered when the lesson would really start and we would float round the room like thistledown. Eventually we left the bar, ran into the centre of the room, and although we didn't float, I found the effect in the mirror very pleasing.

Rosie came back and waited hesitantly until Miss Shortiss took a towel from a chair and mopped herself, and the other girls put on their coats. Miss Shortiss walked over to us. 'She's very good,' she said. 'Who taught her?'

Rosie looked desperate. 'She's never had a lesson in her life. I thought I told you.'

'Oh!' Miss Shortiss exclaimed. 'What have I done? But she followed everything so naturally. And that beautiful line she has, it's perfect.'

'What did she mean, Rosie?' I asked, as I skipped down Carnaby Street. 'Where's the line she says I've got?'

'How do I know?' snapped Rosie. 'Why didn't you listen, like I told you to?'

Much later I discovered that 'line' is the ability of a dancer to move and stand in such a way that the whole body, head, arms and legs always form a harmonious and attractive pattern. My training helped, but instinctively the quality of line came to me easily. It wasn't a hard won accomplishment, it was a natural gift.

*   *   *

Lena and I sat on the narrow wooden staircase outside the kitchen, hugging each other for comfort, and trying not to cry. The ambulance men gently eased the stretcher down the steps. My mother's face was wan and yellow and her hair was damp and bedraggled. 'Be good girls,' she whispered, as they carried her down to the ambulance and off to the Middlesex Hospital.

That evening we were overjoyed to learn that our mother wasn't dead after all, but following a difficult labour, had given birth to her fourteenth child, our new sister, Rachel. When she came back from hospital Mrs Smith from Brewer Street was employed for a small wage to come in to mind the babies and do the chores while Mum went back to work on the stall.

All us girls had to help but we didn't mind, anything rather than have Auntie Nellie from Islington come to live with us again.

Aunt Nellie was my mother's youngest sister. Like her, Nellie was small and dark-haired with a lovely English skin, but there the family likeness ended. Instead of the sweetness and goodness that glowed from my mother's face, Auntie Nellie wore a permanently spiteful expression. In the old days when we lived in Camden Town she often came to stay while Mum went off to work. We grew to dread her visits for not only did we have to keep out of Dad's way, but Auntie Nellie dealt out blows even faster and with less reason. We were completely at her mercy, for our mother was far away working in Berwick Market and could not see what was happening.

I don't know what made her so mean to us; Carrie said it was because no one wanted to marry her. She did have boy-friends, but none of them could stand her for long. One of them fell for Rosie and there was a lively row, witnessed by Carrie and me, when Rosie put her in her place.

'If you don't leave me alone,' cried Rosie, 'I'll tell my Dad about your carryings-on.'

Rosie declared that one of Auntie Nellie's followers had climbed a ladder and got in through Auntie's bedroom window while the rest of the family slept. Morals were very strict in the Matthews' home. Dad was the Victorian head of his household and very prudish about our upbringing. If he found out that 'carrying-on' was taking place under his roof, Auntie Nellie would be out on her ear.

Auntie Nellie did get the boot in the end. Carrie caught her finger in the mangle and when my mother came home from the stall she found her weeping in the garden. She inspected the injured finger. 'You know you shouldn't play with the mangle, my darling.'

'I wasn't playing,' wailed Carrie. 'Auntie Nellie makes me do the mangling. And she locked me in the coal shed yesterday.'

All our childish complaints poured out. 'And she makes me black the range every day,' I shouted.

'And we don't get enough to eat,' cried Jenny.

This really upset my mother. She was giving her sister all the money she could spare to buy the food. 'But she says you get a good dinner every day.'

'Chips,' I cried, 'that's all we get.'

'Chips! Chips! Chips!' shouted Carrie and Jenny.

Auntie Nellie was banished to Islington next day, and if we children had anything to do with it, that is where she would stay.

Dad was now a special constable, and although he was a provider of the nation's food and thus had a reserved occupation, his police duties, real or imagined, kept him away from the stall in the daytime. My mother and Georgie had to run it on their own. And Georgie, although he was only sixteen, kept talking about joining up. Twice Dad had hauled him back from the Recruiting Office in Trafalgar Square.

We all loved it when my mother could be at home with us. Her presence in the kitchen was such a comfort. Sometimes she'd sing as she peeled the potatoes for dinner. She had a lovely voice but her favourite songs were all very sad. Lena always wept when she sang:

> Only a penny and then I can buy,
> A small loaf of bread for my baby and I,
> Only a penny, sir, don't turn away,
> Her tiny face is so cold and so grey.

Chapter Four

'You watch that Alice Marks,' said Rosie belligerently. 'She's had money spent on her. But you can do it better.'

You can do it better! That was the phrase that echoed throughout my childhood. I had to dance better than anyone else or Rosie would want the reason why. 'You haven't watched. You haven't listened,' she'd cry or, 'You haven't tried hard enough.'

Little Alice Marks, aged ten, who wore white gloves and white kid shoes, arrived at the theatre in a chauffeur-driven car with a Nanny in attendance and watched over by a posh mother who lived in St John's Wood. But I'm sure that when Alice became Alicia Markova, prima ballerina, and danced before the crowned heads of Europe, Rosie would still have it: 'You can do it better.'

It was a wonderful spur having someone like Rosie with supreme confidence in my ability, but there were times when I wished that Rosie had stuck to making buttons and left me alone. At the age of nine when Rosie decided to make me a professional dancer, my only reaction was to hope that I could stay away from school.

The beautiful Miss Shortiss had re-joined the corps de ballet at Covent Garden and closed down her Carnaby Street studio at about the time when Rosie saw an advertisement in the *Evening News* for children to be auditioned for a Christmas Show.

The auditions were held at the Charlotte Street school of Madame Elise Clare. Rosie and I, together with about one hundred other hopefuls and their proud mothers, presented ourselves. Madame Clare had once been understudy to the famous Dame Adeline Genée who danced at the Empire Theatre. I was fascinated when I first saw Madame, for never before had I seen a lady wearing spats. She sat in a high-backed chair, a tiny figure dressed in black: a little toque with an eye-veil perched on her head, a black fur tippet round her shoulders, little black mittens, and over her black buttoned boots she wore the extraordinary dove-grey spats. She was well over seventy when I first saw her, as frail as a humming bird, but she had enough presence to terrorise small girls, and in her hand she held a long stout stick.

Dressed in our practice clothes of woollen leotards and tights we had been waiting for a long time before Madame appeared and even then, before the audition began, we were asked to watch a performance by Madame's star pupil, a girl called Audrey Betts.

Audrey finished her dance with a series of superb spins, and the mothers applauded enthusiastically.

'See that,' whispered Rosie. 'You do one of those at the end of your dance.'

Madame spoke for the first time in her high precise voice. 'My standards are high. I do not expect any child here to dance like that, however.'

Rosie's grip on my hand suddenly tightened. 'My sister can,' she called out in a shrill voice. 'My sister can do it better.'

In the hush that followed I wanted to die with shame. Everyone turned to stare at us and Madame visibly froze in her seat. 'Indeed!' she sounded very displeased. 'I am surprised you think so.'

The mothers who were darting poisonous glances our way now laughed happily.

'I don't *think* so,' cried Rosie, crimson with anger at being kept waiting, losing a morning's work at her button shop, and now being laughed at. 'I *know* she can.'

'Indeed!' Madame composed herself and sat back in her chair. 'Then I will see her dance. Bring over your music.'

If I could have escaped from that long high-raftered room I would have, but when I saw the fierce expression on Rosie's face as she came back to me, I knew there was only one way I could get home to my mother and that was to dance. 'That spin,' hissed Rosie. 'Don't forget.'

I knew every step of the dance I had often performed at

Miss Shortiss's little charity concerts, but I had never danced for an audience of hostile women and a terrifying old lady before. This was my first audition and I was very nearly paralysed with fright. The pianist played the opening bars of 'Valse des Fleurs' and I found myself running into the centre of the room. I counted the steps to myself desperately . . . one . . . two . . . three . . . If I kept counting I might get through, but Rosie wanted that awful spin at the end. I'd never done it, I'd never even seen it before.

The last chord and the pianist stopped playing. Now I had to do it. I started the spin on the point of one foot just as I had seen Audrey do, then I whipped the other foot round at knee level . . . it was working . . . I was doing it . . . I'd done it! I'd executed a fouetté for the first time in my life.

I stood uncertainly in the centre of the room, not knowing what to do next. Someone started clapping, then someone else, soon they were all clapping. Rosie *would* be pleased.

'Come here, child,' Madame called.

She reached out and took my chin in her hand, her black mitten scratched my skin. 'Why do you look so unhappy when you dance?' she asked. 'Are you in pain?'

I stared at her, too frightened to answer.

She drew me towards her; she spoke quietly as if we were alone in the room. 'No matter how frightened you are, you must never let the audience know. You must float through the air as if you really enjoy your dancing.'

'How old is this child?' she demanded imperiously of the room at large.

'Nine,' I heard Rosie's husky voice.

'She is too young. She cannot perform on the professional stage until the age of ten. Next child, please.'

I have never forgotten the first time I saw Rosie go into action on my behalf. It was to happen often again, usually when I auditioned for a job. Something in her chemistry seemed to ignite when she wanted me to succeed; it was like having a small dynamo propelling me forward. Rosie wasn't a typical theatrical mum, at all. She never demanded special favours from a management, she just wanted everyone to know that her sister could do it better than anyone else.

I think Rosie's outburst appealed to Madame Clare. Before we left the school word came that Madame was prepared to take me in as a pupil, and I was a lucky child to have been chosen. Rosie didn't need any urging; she had seen the difference between Miss Shortiss's class and the professionalism of Madame Clare's ballet. There was one enormous problem, however, the lessons would be quite expensive, and as Rosie sighed all the way home, 'Would Dad pay for them?'

Rosie made us a stew for supper that night. There wasn't much meat in it but there were lots of onions and carrots and dumplings. Rosie did most of the cooking, my mother wasn't very good at it. As the iron pot bubbled on the hob I heard Rosie and my mother working out how to bait a trap for my father to make him fork up for the lessons. We all knew that the exact timing was important. He must have eaten and be relaxed, but not too long after or he'd be off to the pub, and not too soon, or he might lash out at someone.

My mother with baby Ray in her lap was looking tired tonight. She was pregnant again and uncomfortable and weary most of the time. Ironically, after fourteen children, she was about to give birth to twins. Knowing about the argument that was to take place there was a general air of anxiety amongst us children. Only Billy, practising shadow boxing in a corner, seemed unaffected.

'Dad,' Rosie began uncertainly, 'Jessie's going to dance in a Christmas Show at the Metropolitan Theatre, Edgeware Road.' She paused to let the importance of the theatre sink in. 'She'll earn money.'

Dad looked interested, 'How much?'

Rosie chose her words carefully. 'She's under age, so it won't be till next year.'

'And what bloody good's that, eh?'

Rosie rushed headlong into the heart of the matter. 'She's got to have lessons first to bring her up to standard.'

Crouched behind my mother's chair, I held my breath. What was he going to say?

The floor beneath us suddenly seemed to shake, the whole ramshackle William and Mary building moved on its uneasy foundations. A terrible noise erupted in the street outside as if every big gun in Great Britain was blasting straight at us.

The door burst open. Georgie rushed in. 'Zeppelins!' he cried. 'They're coming over! Hear the guns! There's a full moon! They've got the searchlights up.'

'Christ,' shouted my father. He was out of his chair pulling on his big market coat and off down the stairs, blowing his special constable's whistle as he went, ready to marshal the inhabitants of Soho towards shelter.

'Come on,' shouted Georgie. 'Come on down to the tube, quick!'

Pandemonium broke out. 'Billy,' yelled Georgie, 'you get hold of Eddie. I'll take Eve. Rose, you carry the baby.'

'The babies,' cried my poor mother, 'they've got to have their milk.'

Rose took charge. 'Jenny, fill the milk bottles! Carrie, cut the bread! Jessie, put some jam on it. Lena, get the condensed milk and the babies' dummies.' At least we weren't going to starve down in the bowels of the earth. Blankets were grabbed, pillows gathered. I raced upstairs and found my dancing shoes. Lena took her injured sparrow in a box. Then off, loaded like refugees, we went down Brewer Street. Whistles blew, and out of every doorway hurried people on their way to Piccadilly Underground. Eve and Eddie started to whimper with fright and then, catastrophically, I had hysterics. Tears poured down my cheeks, wails rent the air. It was all too much: that terrifying audition this morning, then no money from Dad for the lessons, and now we were all going to be blown up.

We came up again at six next morning completely unscathed. It had been quite a jolly night underground. Everybody danced and sang and shared their food. It wasn't the last night we should spend in the tube; in 1917 when the raids grew heavier, the Germans even dropped a bomb on Piccadilly Circus. Billy swore he saw the Zeppelin caught in the searchlights looking like a long silver cigar.

I always loved the winter in Berwick Market when the stalls were lit by yellow paraffin flares and there was a smell of roasting chestnuts in the air. Dad's fruit stall outside the Blue Posts Pub would look a picture with the oranges, apples and pears arranged in pyramids. At Christmas he always had a toy stall. He sold wooden soldiers, spinning tops, skipping ropes and dolls: baby dolls, dolls with long flaxen hair and white kid shoes, dolls with black curly hair and bright blue eyes. How I yearned for a doll, any of them would do, even a celluloid baby doll. I never got one. The toys were for sale, not for our

Christmas stockings. I remember that Rosie's present that year was a little fur tam o' shanter, sewn together with scraps my father had salvaged from a fur shop fire. When Grandma Matthews came to tea she picked it up and said to Rose. 'You know what you've got there, my girl, sable! You've sewn up bits of sable, just like the coat I made for the Queen.'

On Saturday mornings Dad would sometimes take one of the children with him to market. Jenny never went with him. She was the one who was always in trouble, she would answer him back. Jenny got more hidings from Dad than any of us. She was growing up to look just like Grandma Matthews and, like Dad and his mother, Jenny had a violent temper.

I came downstairs one Saturday morning about six o'clock and helped Dad harness Jenny the horse in the Yard, and then we drove off to Smithfield Market to fetch the meat and poultry for the Jewish butchers of Soho. Saturday, being the Jewish Sabbath, meant that we children often picked up a copper or two lighting fires or running errands for the orthodox. One old Jewish lady who wore a black wig gave me a regular Saturday penny for running her errands.

Jenny jogged along the empty roads that had been hosed down during the night and smelled fresh and clean. The rhythmic jingle of the harness, the smell from the black tarpaulin wrapped round my legs made me feel very important. Jenny halted to have a drink of water at the horse trough outside the Bank of England and Dad and I went over to the vanman's stall for a cup of coffee and a currant bun.

'My kid, Jessie,' Dad introduced me. 'She's going to be a dancer, aren't ya gel?' He wagged a finger at me. 'Fight, that's what you gotta do. Fight your way to the top, 'cos you're a Matthews and you gotta be good.'

What with Rosie on one side urging me on, and now my father telling me to fight my way up, I wondered why they talked like that. Dancing wasn't violent and fighting, it was lovely and light and full of happiness. Why did they want to bring fighting in?

Dad was training Billy to be a boxer. I don't know where he got the idea that he could teach anyone to box, but Billy was taking it all very seriously. Every morning before he went off to his job as a pageboy at the National Sporting Club, Dad would take him for a run round Regent's Park. War or no war,

Dad was determined that young Billy would one day be feather-weight champion of England. Or else!

My mother had her twins, a boy and a girl. The girl died and only Harry the baby boy came home with her from hospital. I remember that she cried a lot these days. It wasn't because of the dead baby, it was because Georgie had run away and joined the army. Georgie, the sweet one, who looked after us all, had found a recruiting office where no one knew he was the son of George Matthews from the Market, and that he was under age to boot. Eventually we had a postcard from France. A picture of Boulogne Harbour and on the back was written, 'Love and kisses from Georgie.'

Dad had agreed to pay for two lessons a week at Madame Clare's. It was a sacrifice and I was always grateful to him for finding the money, for it wasn't just lessons, it was dancing shoes and practice clothes and a special white tutu and tights. Before I set off for my first lesson, Rosie admonished me, 'Watch that Audrey Betts. Find out how she does those spins.'

When Audrey executed a fouetté, each step was imprinted on my mind. It is a difficult step for the spins must be executed on the same spot without travelling. But if Madame's star pupil did five fouettés, I had to do six. The French words Madame used to teach us were much harder to learn than the steps: *Jeté . . . Bourrée . . . Entrechât.*

Every night after school Rosie sent me upstairs to practise for two hours. She even bored a tiny hole through the wall that divided my mother's room from ours so that she could watch me practise unobserved. I found out about that hole by accident when I came downstairs early one evening and heard Rosie say to mother, 'She's a good kid. I just had a look through the spy hole and she's hard at it.'

Dancing came to me naturally, I loved it, but the next part of Rosie's campaign was very painful. And it was all through a chance remark I made to Rosie.

I'd left the class of the severe Miss Steel and graduated to another teacher who, although she didn't turn me into a scholar either, did make her lessons more interesting and managed to excite my imagination. She told us about this teeming village we lived in. How years ago Soho had been open fields where horses and hounds hunted. 'So! Ho!' was the cry the huntsman used to draw off the hounds. She told us of the artists and physicians who used to live in these narrow streets, of the first foreign immigrants who moved here, the aristocratic French Huguenots, then came the Italian artisans, the Greeks and then the Jews fleeing the Russian pogroms. The Swiss opened restaurants and Soho finally became what it is today, the foreign quarter of London.

We took turns to read aloud from our story books and one day my teacher halted my rendering: 'Jessie, you're a dancer and you're going on the stage, but what will happen when you open your mouth and all that "Gawd Blimey" pours out?'

What a funny thing to say, I thought. I wasn't at all hurt by her criticism, after all everyone in Soho spoke that way. We all yelled and shouted at each other, we dropped our aitches, tortured our vowels and forgot to sound our consonants, but who cared. I told Rosie about teacher's remarks and discovered that Rosie cared. Being Rosie, she had to do something about it. She joined a girl's club in Argyle Street to learn elocution and drama.

Rosie became overnight my elocution coach, determined that I was going to learn to talk proper even if it killed me. We started with poetry. Rosie liked heroic poems.

'He is dead, the beautiful youth,' I declaimed.

'No, No, No!' Rosie cried, 'Not *bewtifoo*! Look, make your lips shape like mine . . . *bee-you-tee-full*! Make it come out all round. See!'

Everything Rosie learned at the girl's club was passed straight on to me. The odd thing was that Rosie got everything right. She was a natural teacher. Years later, when I was paying large fees to drama teachers, I remembered those long weary hours in the bedroom at William and Mary that always ended in flaming rows or tears, and I realised that Rose's groundwork had been very good.

At school I lorded it over the other little girls. I was becoming a proper little show-off. At dancing class, however, the iron discipline of Madame Clare put me in my place. Once, unbidden, I executed what I thought was a superb series of cartwheels from one end of the long room to the other. 'Jessie Matthews!' Madame stood in the doorway. 'Come here! I am training ladies to dance,' she said severely, 'not cheap acrobats. You are dismissed from class.' She swung her stick and I received a cut across my behind.

For three weeks she would not allow me back to the class. I stood at the door in my practice clothes weeping copiously, but she wouldn't let me dance. It was a lesson in discipline that I was never to forget.

But Madame took a real interest in me. Before the next Christmas show I was given many free lessons, and now with Audrey Betts, I was singled out to perform speciality dances. The show, *Bluebell in Fairyland* would run, for matinees only, at the Metropolitan Theatre during the school holidays. But first of all I had to get a licence from the London County Council.

Rosie took me along to County Hall. For all her twenty years, Rose didn't come much above the high counter and I, at ten, was a little shrimp.

The elderly clerk peered at me disapprovingly. 'A licence to perform for *this* child?' From the tone of his voice Rose might have been selling me to a chimney sweep.

'She's ten.'

The clerk adjusted his pince-nez. 'That's all very well,' he grumbled, 'but who's going to look after her when she's at the theatre?'

'I am,' said Rosie gruffly. This was her first brush with bureaucracy.

He leaned over the counter and examined Rosie. 'Impossible, you're not old enough. An adult must accompany the child.'

Rosie drew herself up, till her chin was over the counter. 'I beg your pardon,' she said in the ringing tones she had learned at the Argyle Street girl's club, 'I *am* an adult,' then with a bit of her native Cockney cheek, she added, 'And I can blooming well show you my birth certificate to prove it. So there!'

Most of the Matthews family, together with curious friends and neighbours from Berwick Market, came to the first matinee of *Bluebell*. They very nearly filled the front row of the Gods. My mother wore a new hat with an ostrich feather round the brim and baby Harry, in her arms, wore a long white robe. Dad, of course, refused to wear a collar and tie but he did put on a muffler, and my brothers and sisters were groomed to the eyebrows by Rosie.

The show opened with a snow scene. At a signal from the stage manager all the children ran onto the stage ready to

34

snowball each other. Just like we'd been told at rehearsals, I sped towards the footlights. I stopped abruptly, rigid with shock. In front of me, as black as hell yawned a deep pit and in it, heaving, breathing, reaching towards me, was a great monster. I couldn't move. I was petrified. And then a snowball hit me on the cheek and jolted the terror out of my head. I remembered what I had to do. But if that snowball hadn't hit me when it did, stage fright might have ended my career for ever.

From then on, stage fright often attacked me. I would step onto the stage and look out at, what seemed for a first horrifying moment, a black heaving monster. Only when the applause started would the monster turn into a mass of warm and friendly humanity.

Audrey and I did a speciality dance together in *Bluebell*. I was the Goose who was bitten by Audrey the Fox, and I died very delicately every matinee to rounds of applause. I don't think I earned much money, but Rosie did buy me a pair of brown leather laced boots to protect my money-making ankles.

At eleven I was chosen from Madame's class to dance in a real pantomime. I was billed as principal child dancer, 'Little Jessie Matthews', in *Dick Whittington* at the Kennington Theatre. At last I was a real professional, evenings as well as matinees. The cast rehearsed for two weeks in separate groups, child dancers in one and adults in another.

At dress rehearsal the whole company met for the first time. Rosie, in her capacity of 'child minder', stood hawk-eyed in the wings. A set depicting a cornfield was erected, and then, to Rosie's bewilderment, a tiny ballerina and a uniformed Nanny were escorted into the wings. The little girl fluttered out onto the stage and performed a dance as a cornflower.

Bristling with anger, Rosie rushed out front and found the dance director. 'What's this new girl doing here?' she demanded. 'Jessie's billed as principal child dancer.'

Slightly embarrassed, the director explained that Miss Alice Marks, the ten-year-old ballerina, was a cut above everyone else, the product of expensive tuition trained by world famous danseuses. He also explained that it was no business of Rosie's whom he engaged and she'd better go back to her child minding.

I thought little Alice Marks was the sweetest girl I had ever seen. I longed to make friends with her but what with her entourage on one side and an infuriated Rosie on the other, we were kept well apart. I followed Alice's dazzling career with interest, and four years later she appeared at the London Palladium billed as the Child Pavlova.

Chapter Five

They told us the news when we went round to Charlotte Street to welcome Madame Clare home from her holiday in America. The curtains were drawn and the house looked desolate. I sat on the stone steps and wept. A waiter sweeping the pavement outside his restaurant stared at me curiously.

Rosie said in a subdued voice, 'Don't make an exhibition of yourself.' She took out a hanky and blew her nose. 'I'm just as upset as you are.' As we walked down Charlotte Street, she kept saying, 'Why did she have to die now? Just now? Just when we were really beginning.'

Madame Elise Clare had died while on holiday in America and Rosie's hopes of making me a great ballet dancer received a crushing blow. It wasn't that she was disheartened, but for the first time Rosie didn't know what to do next.

The two hours of ballet practice went on daily but without Madame's wonderful classes, the impetus that thrust us along seemed to have gone. We still kept up the elocution lessons and Rosie entered me for a poetry contest. I stood on the platform, my arms behind my back, solemnly enunciating:

> 'He is dead, the beautiful youth,
> The heart of honour, the tongue of truth,
> He, the light and life of us all . . .'

I won a certificate but Rosie declared it should have been a medal. 'You know why you didn't get it, don't you?' she said bitterly. 'You said *loyght* instead of *light*.' Ah, those cunning cockney vowels!

We chased all over London to attend auditions. I came home early from school and Rosie took time off from her long-suffering button shop. On the day I auditioned at the Kilburn Empire she changed me out of my school clothes in the ladies' lavatory of the underground, and as she combed my hair she admonished, 'Watch all those girls who go on before you.'

I did, and none of them were ballet dancers, they all did musical comedy routines. 'Sorry,' the manager told us, 'we don't want ballet, we're taking one of Miss Terry's girls.'

This name, Miss Terry, was beginning to irritate Rosie. A girl from Miss Terry's had won a medal at the Elocution Contest. Rosie sought out the girl who had been taken on by the manager. 'Miss Terry? That's the school I go to, she's Terry Friedman, drama and dancing. Every Saturday morning at Stamford Hill. Can't stop now.' She raced off to join her friends.

Next Saturday morning we trekked into the wilds of North London. As Rosie kept saying, our expedition was a bit tricky. It was very tricky trying to find this elusive theatrical school in Stamford Hill. Someone eventually gave us the right directions and, hot and tired, we finally arrived at a three-storeyed suburban house in a quiet road. The hall door was open and the girls were coming out.

'We're too late,' said Rosie, in a voice of doom, 'and after coming all this way, too.'

Waving goodbye to the girls and ready to close the front door was a tall, lively woman about thirty with bright red hair. She couldn't help noticing the odd couple who stared up at her so mournfully. For one of the rare times in her life, words failed Rosie. I piped up, 'We've come for a lesson, please.'

'Sorry, dear, it's over. Come along next Saturday morning.'

Promptly, and on cue, I did what has always come very naturally to me. I burst into tears.

Terry Friedman had a very warm heart, her bright blue eyes were sympathetic and she didn't turn us away. She watched me dance and accepted me for her class. 'We haven't much money,' said Rosie awkwardly when the question of paying for the lessons came up. Terry gave us one of her warm smiles, she loved children and teaching them was a work of real dedication. 'Money's not that important, my dear. From what I've seen, Jessie will be earning money herself before long.'

The Friedman sisters became famous all over the entertainment world: Terry, for her theatrical school, her troupe of dancing girls, and her pupils who became stars; Flossie, who was a voice coach and taught the silent stars of Hollywood how to talk, and Dolly who became a theatrical and film agent.

Madame Elise Clare would have turned in her grave to see me jazzing it up in Terry's classes. But I didn't neglect my ballet exercises. I even did my exercises in class and before I knew where I was, Terry asked me to show the other girls the rudiments of classical ballet. Eventually, Terry asked Rosie to bring me along to classes she held at Marlborough Street, St John's Wood on Tuesdays and Fridays. I helped with the class, taught my ballet exercises and in the end I was getting three free lessons a week.

All the dancing I did made me perpetually hungry and I never seemed to find enough food to eat at home. Feeding twelve people took more money than my father ever brought home. Rosie said he made a good living in the market but he stood too many rounds of drinks to his mates. Billy, Rosie and Jenny were all at work, but their wages were minuscule, and most of Rosie's salary was spent in pursuit of my dancing career. I was the one with the big hungry eyes who was often sent next door to borrow half a crown from the Phillips to get some bread and sausage for supper.

I often wished we weren't so poor. For Beattie Joel, who lived with her parents, the landlords of the Blue Posts Pub, I often felt envy. There were curtains at their windows, a red plush cover with bobbles over the table and a velvet sofa and chairs. I could never understand Beattie saying, 'Let's go and play in your yard.' How could she bear to leave such elegance to play amongst a lot of old vans and ladders?

Mrs Joel, Beattie's mother, was always kind to me. She'd look at my skinny frame and ask me to stay to dinner. In many ways the Jewish community of Soho helped to stifle my hunger pangs. Humble Jewish families would impoverish themselves for years over a major event like a wedding reception. Little Jessie Matthews 'the ballet dancer', accompanied by one of her Jewish friends who knew where it was all happening, would be glad to attend and do a little dance, after which they would be rewarded with as much food as they could eat. I used to go to all the Jewish receptions, the barmitzvahs, the circumcisions, any event where there was food around.

Billy was now being entered for fights. He had a mean right hook. Once when he was shadow boxing against his blanket, his fist came through and knocked Rosie out stone cold. He now had a real trainer called Acky whom Dad had encountered in a pub. Dad had upgraded himself to manager.

My mother hated boxing. She wanted no part of it. When Billy had a fight we would all gather in the kitchen, close the door, and huddle together as if waiting for news of an imminent death. Mother would rock herself back and forth, gazing into space. No one would speak to her.

Then later, there'd be a great hammering on the door and Acky would rush in with news of how the fight had gone. Whether Billy had won or lost we knew it would be hours before Dad came home, up in the air if Billy had won, bad-tempered if he'd lost. No wonder mother hated boxing.

She was the one with the book learning who looked after the market accounts—my father couldn't write—so if ever she did get her hands on Billy's winnings, she made sure he got something. Once when Billy had won ten pounds, I saw her hand him a pound. 'Right, son?' she asked. 'Yes, mum,' said Billy with a grin.

Caw, I thought to myself, all that battering, having to run round the park every evening then come home and be wrapped in blankets before a roaring fire to lose weight, and then only getting a quid for it all! But like every one of us, Billy idolised his mother and he wanted to give her everything he could.

Armistice Day came. Berwick Market was en fête. The flags came out and the bunting was strung across the narrow streets, but my mother sat at home weeping. We hadn't heard a word from Georgie for six months. 'He's been taken prisoner,' said Rosie staunchly, 'that's what's happened, Mum.'

Oh, the joy in William and Mary when a postcard came. Another enigmatic message with a picture of the Eiffel Tower on one side and on the other, 'Alive and kicking, love Georgie.'

Georgie had received a headwound, serious enough for them to have fitted a plate in his head. He'd spent the last six months in hospital and for the rest of his life he suffered from appalling headaches. But he came home the same sweet Georgie, the darling of us all.

We were all growing up. Carrie was the one at home now doing the chores. By rights, I should be next, but I was one of

Miss Terry's girls and getting ready for the Christmas Pantomime, *Babes in the Wood* at the Alexandra Theatre in Stoke Newington. I'd been promised two solo dances, but there was a financial crisis in the company and it looked as if I should only get one.

'She could have the flower girl dance,' said the harassed ballet mistress, 'but there's no costume for her, and they won't give me the cash for another.'

'I'll make her one,' said the resourceful Rosie. With coloured cotton remnants from a stall in the market, she put together exactly the right dress. I shall always remember my dance as the ragged flower girl. The applause was loud as I ran off to where Rosie waited for me at the side of the stage. The stage manager told me to take a curtain call. The applause grew. I took another curtain call. The conductor raised his baton, the music started and I suddenly realised I must dance again. When I finally ran off I saw to my horror that Rosie was crying. Rosie, crying! What had I done wrong? 'Oh Jessie,' she wept, she didn't put her arms around me, we weren't used to emotional hugs and kisses, 'I'm so *proud* of you, Jessie.'

I couldn't get over it. Strict, authoritarian Rosie, using a word like that. Proud of me! After that I strained every fibre of my being to dance my very best as flower girl. I had to have curtain calls, the more curtain calls I got the happier Rosie would be. I loved Rosie, but it wasn't for love of her that I worked so hard, it was to have again this extraordinary feeling that I had power over Rosie.

I was now billed as 'Jessie Matthews, your favourite dancer', and in *Red Riding Hood* at the Kilburn Empire, Arthur Rigby, the producer, asked me to recite some lines. I brought out the well-tried, 'He is dead the beautiful youth . . .' and won the role of Red Riding Hood. 'I'm a real actress,' I shouted excitedly to Rosie, 'I've got a piece to recite. It's called, "I wonder if the Goblins know." '

George married a French girl called Lucienne. She had always lived in Soho, but came from a different background; her parents kept a chemist's shop. Somehow none of us thought Lucienne would fit in too well. Georgie still worked on the barrow in Berwick Market, but after he and Lucienne rented a flat in Old Compton Street, we didn't see so much of him.

Jenny, Carrie, Lena and little Eve went round to pay a call. For a couple of hours the girls sat in a solemn row in the parlour watching their new sister-in-law's every move. No doubt Lucienne found them more than disconcerting.

'You know what?' Carrie told us. 'She takes the cream off the top of the milk and drinks it. She says it makes her skin white. Fancy that?'

'Doesn't she save any for Georgie?' asked my mother.

Now that Georgie was back at the stall my mother could spend more time at home. Just her presence in the house was enough for us children. She'd never been much of a house-keeper, what with her brood of children and working at the stall, she'd never had the time. But her talent for loving was enough for us. Never a cross word from her, never a smack; if we had any aches or pains, round to the Middlesex Hospital she'd take us. Cuts were stitched and ointment for impetigo doled out in the out-patients' department. Everyone knew her. 'Hello Mrs Matthews,' the sister in charge would say, 'which one is it this time?' and my mother would produce a bunch of grapes or a bag of apples as a thankyou. We'd always wait till Dad was out of the way before we approached our fruit stall, we knew Mum would slip us an apple or a halfpenny for sweets.

We weren't neglected at home. As usually happens in a large family the older ones looked after the little ones. Carrie, the sister above me, was doing her 'daughter at home' sentence, and often grumbled because although I too had left school, Rosie frowned on me doing rough housework. A ballet dancer must not have red, wash-tub hands. Naturally there was a certain amount of feeling between my sisters about this. 'Jessie gets out of everything,' complained Carrie. 'I want to be a dancer too.' As it turned out three of my sisters did become dancers—Carrie, Lena and Eve.

We had more furniture in the kitchen/living room now. Dad salvaged an upright piano to sell then decided it was too much trouble to move so there it stayed. Rosie had a secondhand treadle sewing machine on which she was hoping to extend my meagre wardrobe. Lena was the only sister who didn't seem to mind the privileges that came my way. She was a quiet, gentle little creature, who hated wearing steel-rimmed glasses and being called 'four-eyes' by the neighbourhood boys. She'd inherited Dad's love of animals and birds. There was always a disabled city sparrow in a cardboard box on the window-sill.

Dad often looked after animals, such as the occasional horse, appearing in acts at the London Palladium. Once he was asked to take an elephant but it wouldn't fit into our stables. Then Dad had to mind two black monkeys called Trixie and Jacko. They hopped into the house and we treated them as pets until one afternoon they went berserk and started throwing things. One of them climbed on to the table and picked up a slab of cheese.

'Put it down,' I screamed. Trixie took careful aim and got me right on the jaw. 'Fetch Dad,' Lena yelled. By the time I brought Dad back from the market stall, Jacko had found an open window and was throwing the cups and saucers into the yard below. Dad quietened them down right away. They rushed to his arms, jibbering with delight, but were then banished down to the stables with their cages.

Another excitement was going down to Brighton. Terry Friedman tried to get me as many dancing jobs as she could, she knew that money was tight at home. Together with nine other girls off we drove in a charabanc to do a cabaret at the Albion Hotel and then stay overnight in the hotel. I'd never seen the sea before and my first paddle in the grey waters of the English Channel was a highspot in my life. After that, like most Londoners, the name Brighton was always linked with the glorious seaside for me. I shared a bedroom with four other girls and immediately became a social outcast. I sat down too hard on the chamber pot and broke it. I hid the pieces in the wardrobe and spent a sleepless night worrying what would happen when the management found out.

Terry Friedman was more than my dancing teacher, she was a good friend and one of the people who started my career. She had a brother called Sidney Jay who was a film agent and he promised to let me know if the film people ever needed a child dancer. He was the one who suggested to Rosie that we go along to the London Pavilion when Mr C. B. Cochran was holding auditions for his *Music Box Revue*; he'd heard they were using children in the show. Rosie was completely unimpressed. In our small world, chasing a dance date here, a concert piece there, with pantomime as the yearly goal, what did we want with the London Pavilion? They didn't have pantomimes, did they? And we'd never heard of Mr Cochran. Even had Sidney Jay told us that Mr Cochran with his revues at the Pavilion was just as famous as Ziegfeld with his Follies in New York, we should have remained unimpressed.

However, a job was a job, and off we marched with our carpet bag round the corner to Shaftesbury Avenue. I sang my usual audition song and did my musical comedy routine, and then the manager asked me if I could do any other type of dancing.

'Ballet,' I told him.

'Let's see it,' he said.

When I had finished and changed back into my outdoor clothes I found Rosie at the side of the stage arguing with the manager. 'Odds and ends, you say, that's not enough.'

'Well, she can have a bit as a page boy.'

'How much?'

'Four pounds a week.'

'What!' Rosie's voice rose high. 'She was getting more than that in pantomime.'

A thin, almost reed-like voice called out to the manager from the darkened stalls. The manager nodded back respectfully. 'Mr Cochran wants to have a word with you.'

We went down into the stalls. Mr Cochran was portly and round-faced; next to him sat a small dark man who was introduced as Hassard Short over from New York to supervise the show.

'Now, what's the trouble, my dear?'

'It's not right that Jessie should only get odds and ends to do. It's a come-down. She was Red Riding Hood at the Kilburn Empire.'

'Suburbs, my dear, suburbs. This is the West End, but Jessie shall have a song and dance.'

'Give her the *Down on the Farm* number,' said Hassard Short, 'The kid's got what it takes.'

'But only four quid.' Rosie wasn't convinced. 'Not much, is it? I'll have to ask my Dad.'

She marched me backstage where we met the manager. 'God Almighty,' he said despairingly. 'You've been offered a part in a Cochran show! Don't you know there are hundreds of girls who would pay for the privilege?'

In his book, *I Had Almost Forgotten*, C. B. Cochran wrote:

'Jessie was an interesting looking child with big eyes, a funny little nose, clothes which seemed a bit too large for her and a huge umbrella. It may have been an ordinary sized umbrella, but it seemed to dwarf her. "You're engaged, my dear," I said when she had finished her song and dance.'

Rosie has always been annoyed about that description, 'clothes a bit too large for her', indeed! That good brown coat had been painstakingly put together on the treadle sewing machine and I was wearing the famous sable tam o'shanter, just like Queen Mary used to have. I suspect that the clothes were too big for me, for everything Rosie made was on the big side so that shrimp-sized Jessie could grow into them.

Rehearsals for *Music Box Revue* were different. To begin with Rosie was not welcomed as 'child minder'. The other children in the show from the Italia Conti school had a proper matron to look after them. This lady refused to allow Rosie to lurk in the wings. Rosie sought out Mr C. B. Cochran himself. 'But of course, my dear, I know you want to look after your little sister.' He gave my head a fatherly pat. 'And how's my little chicken today?' Dressed as a chicken I was supposed to hop out of a casserole in the restaurant scene and do a song and dance. Nightly I sang Irving Berlin's famous verse *I want to go back to the farm* and performed my little dance.

I was not allowed to mix with the children from the Italia Conti school. 'You're better than any of them,' declared Rosie, and my corner of the dressing-room was prudishly isolated from the rest of the laughter and noise. Rosie watched over me like a tigress to make sure my fifteen year old innocence remained unblemished. Looking back I think that Rosie was over-protective. I shouldn't have had so many miserable moments if I'd learned how to adapt easily to the bawdy life of the chorus dressing-room. Rosie isolated me completely, walking with me to the wings, walking back to the dressing-room with me when I came off.

Rosie was very unworldly herself, and it was probably her fear of the terrors that lurked backstage that made her so prudish. However, my first West End Revue didn't last very long. After three months closing notices were posted. Rosie

45

was bitterly disappointed for Cochran had seemed so interested in me. Later we learned that he was going through a financial crisis and had lost £8,000 on *Music Box Revue*.

Sidney Jay did get me some dancing parts in films but you had to watch very carefully or you'd miss little Jessie Matthews toe-dancing across the screen. I was in *Beloved Vagabond* with Carlye Blackwell and Maggie Stuart, *Straws in the Wind* with Queenie Thomas; it was the film *Young England* that made Rosie finally decide there was no future for me on the silver screen.

I had only a short scene to do at the Isleworth studios, but the day before it was shot Terry told us to go to two auditions. One was for the chorus in a Charlot revue, the other was to dance in ballet at the Hippodrome. Naturally, Rosie favoured the ballet.

After *Music Box Revue* our status demanded that we do better than the ladies' lavatory in the underground and we used an occasional taxi as a changing room. With two auditions, one in ballet costume and the other in shorts for chorus work, this was a necessity.

'Not much good hanging around here,' said Rosie impatiently when we went backstage at the Duke of York Theatre. Every chorus girl in London seemed to have turned up. After all, it would be a good job. Charlot's *London Calling* with Noël Coward and Gertie Lawrence needed replacements as the stars and the cream of the chorus were off to New York. We were about to leave when Rosie spotted a face we knew by sight. Danny O'Neill, the stage manager, a tall good looking young man, stood surrounded by hopeful chorus girls. Danny came from Soho and, although we'd never spoken to him, Dad and Georgie knew him well. He was already making a name for himself as the kind of man Noël Coward and the other stars wanted to stage manage their shows.

Rosie grabbed my hand and we fought our way to his side. 'You're George Matthews' girl are you.' He took a critical look at me. 'I'm not sure if you'll be up to these routines. Still, you hop off to your other audition at the Hippodrome and I'll tell our ballet mistress Miss Graham to give you a chance when you get back. Take some time to weed through this lot, but get a move on,' he called. 'Don't want to miss a chance for a Charlot show.'

On the way to the Hippodrome I changed into my ballet skirt in the back of the taxi. But it was wasted effort for when we got there the audition was over. Into another taxi, and Rosie produced the chorus shorts. 'Come on, don't waste time.'

I could see the driver taking an interested look in his mirror. Suddenly I felt rebellious. After all I wasn't a little girl any more, I was nearly sixteen. I knew perfectly well how old I looked, about twelve. Rosie deliberately kept me in white ankle socks and black barred shoes. All those other girls this morning, in cloche hats and silk stockings, that's how I ought to look. 'I'm fed up with being treated like a kid,' I said sullenly.

Rosie's lips tightened. 'Put your bloomers on.'

I put my hands under the seat of my tarlatan tutu and sat on them, 'No!'

Carrie Graham, the ballet mistress at the Duke of York's, was small, fair and determined. She'd subdued a thousand chorus girls in her time. 'You can take that ballet skirt off for a start.' I climbed obediently into my shorts. 'Can you kick?'

Rosie answered for me, 'Of course she can.'

I raised my leg tentatively.

'Higher,' said Miss Graham.

Rosie glared, and my leg flew right up in the air to the side of my head. I was amazed. I'd never done that before.

'Good! Loose joints. Now if she wants a chance she'll have to get on the end of that last line going on and try and pick up the routine. Can she?'

'She can,' said Rosie grimly.

I grabbed the last girl round the waist just as she moved out onto the stage. It wasn't too hard to pick up the routine. One, two, three, kick. Coo! That was a lovely kick!

'Little dark girl on the end,' said a voice from the stalls. It was me! I was put on the short list and asked to dance again.

Miss Graham said she'd let us know. Rosie's expression was dour. I was blamed for being so difficult in the taxi and wasting time. But I did get the job. Next morning there was a telegram asking me to report to the theatre at seven that evening. Panic! We were booked to go to Isleworth that day to film *Young England* and certainly didn't want to lose the money. 'We'll have to go,' said Rosie. 'Shouldn't take long. All you have to do is be one of the young princes in the tower and walk down a flight of steps.'

This was the day when Rosie turned away from the film industry. They didn't start shooting our scene until the afternoon and it looked as if it would never be finished. The other Prince, my little brother, was a girl who was filming for the first time. Dressed in jerkins, tights and velvet hats adorned with a feather we held hands and walked down a long flight of steps towards the dungeons and death.

'Camera! Action!' called the director. My little brother blinked his eyes.

'Cut! Now this time, dear, don't blink. And for God's sake look sad, you're gonna be killed.'

We did it again. Blink! And again. Blink! Every time the director pointed his finger at us, my brother blinked. The long afternoon wore on. Rosie was biting her finger-nails. We should never get from Isleworth to the Duke of York's Theatre in time.

'Break for tea,' cried the director.

Down the long flight of steps we walked again. I felt like pushing my companion down to the bottom. 'Got it!' cried the director. 'Pan on to Jessie's face. Jessie, take your hat off. Now look sad!'

Sad? I was desperate. But it worked, my brother looked at me and forgot to blink. 'Print it.'

Out of breath and dishevelled we raced through the stage door of the Duke of York's. 'Ah,' said Miss Graham, 'we're not using you tonight. Just sit out front and watch the show. Tomorrow night we'll push you into the line.'

The chorus girls I shared a dressing-room with couldn't stand me. 'Get out of the way, brat. What the hell does the Guv'nor want sticking a kid in the line?'

The protective atmosphere of *Music Box Revue* was gone. Although Rosie waited for me outside the dressing-room after the show, even she was startled by the language of some of the chorus ladies if she tried to get in.

After two weeks, Miss Graham said, 'Mr Charlot wants to see your birth certificate.'

Mr Charlot liked the way I danced. I'd been picked to go to America with the cream of the chorus. America? What about

48

Rosie?

'Who's Rosie?' said Miss Graham. 'You'll be sixteen soon, won't you?'

Like pushing my way out of the shade into the glorious sunshine the whole wonderful situation opened up before me. I was old enough to travel. I was considered to be grown up. I was going to America. *Alone!*

Chapter Six

Christmas was coming again. Dad's stall in Berwick Market was piled high with toys and there was a goose growing fat in the stables of William and Mary Yard. Rosie's sewing machine whirred late into the night and everyone in Brewer Street stopped me and said, 'Aren't you a lucky girl, going to America.'

Dad had flatly refused to let me go at first. 'A kid of her age, on her own! She'll go wrong.' Danny O'Neill came round to explain that New York wasn't all that different to Soho, and Carrie Graham told my mother that I'd be well looked after.

Rosie wanted me to go. Looking back, I can see now how hard it must have been for her. The child she had turned into a dancer, the kid around whom her whole life had revolved for so long, was leaving her. She threw herself into the hard work of getting me properly outfitted, buying yards of material from the market stalls, standing over me, mouth full of pins, ripping out basting thread, cutting hemlines straight. 'Now this dress is for best, mind. Don't go messing it up on that dirty ship.' Rosie's idea of a transatlantic liner was coils of rope and the rusty hull of a tramp steamer with smoke belching from the funnel.

The two people I loved most in the world and my father saw me off on the boat train at Waterloo. Rosie gave me a quick peck on the cheek. None of our family were used to emotional farewells, but I sobbed loudly as I climbed into the compartment and I saw my mother brush away a tear with the back of her hand. The whistle blew, the guard waved his green flag and the train steamed out of the station. I clutched my comic and the paper bag of sandwiches Rosie had made for me. The other ladies of the chorus turned the pages of *Nash's Magazine* and *Vogue*, and raised their eyebrows as I wept into the cotton fur of the stuffed Bonzo dog my sisters had given me for luck.

I was luckier than I knew. I had joined the company of a man who created artistes of the theatre. André Charlot's greatest satisfaction was to find and polish rough talent until it had star quality. This French producer, who had once been business manager to the Folies Bergère, had become a cult in England and his revues delighted London audiences.

Charlot was now to present a revue in partnership with Archie Selwyn in New York. This was to be a conglomeration of all the best numbers and sketches from the Charlot shows of the last few years. *London Calling* had been a tremendous success, but now it was sadly depleted. Jack Buchanan, Beatrice Lillie and Gertrude Lawrence were going to New York with the best of the chorus, and small part girls were going too, as well as Danny O'Neill and Carrie Graham. Joyce Barbour was taking over from Gertie in *London Calling*.

I did not fully understand any of this when I boarded the *Aquitania* to sail to America. To me, 'the Guv'nor', as the company called him, was a big frightening producer, a man with a funny French accent who when he noticed me, which wasn't often, called me 'la petite', or 'babee'.

Carrie Graham, the ballet mistress, looked quite stunned when I told her that I hadn't any stockings with me for I had always worn white ankle socks. 'You can't walk around dressed like a child,' she exclaimed. 'I'll find you some stockings.' I shared a cabin with a pretty American girl called Marjorie Martin, who was returning from a convent school outside Paris. Marjorie was just as immature and innocent as I was; she was also the sister of Mary Martin who became one of America's brightest stars.

I couldn't get over the sheer beauty of our cabin with its two little beds, the running hot and cold in the basin, the wardrobes, the fluffy towels, and the steward who brought early morning tea on a tray. In fact, the only people I dared speak to for the first day or two were the stewards. That was how I became involved with Jorge.

51

Jorge was South American and handsome enough to have come straight out of the pages of Miss E. M. Hull. He reminded me of the Sheik, but was much better looking than Rudolph Valentino. He came over to me when we were in the lounge, corrected me for speaking to the stewards and told me I wasn't using my knife and fork correctly. I told him I was English and would eat in the English way. Would he please go away as my mother had told me I must never talk to strangers?

On the third night out Charlot invited all the members of the company to eat with him and the stars at a big table. Miss Graham came down to my cabin. 'The Guv'nor thinks the dresses you've got aren't quite right,' she said crisply. 'They're too young, so I've borrowed something else for you to wear.' I was bitterly hurt. I knew that Rosie liked me to look like a twelve year old, but even so I couldn't bear to have her works of love scorned.

Gwen Edgell, one of the most beautiful and sophisticated of the chorus girls, was nearest to me in size and she had kindly gave me a dress and shoes. Marjorie did up the hooks and eyes of a pale pink chiffon dress with silver bugle beads on the bodice and lent me her pearl necklace to go with it. I slipped on the high-heeled silver shoes and looked in the mirror. Oh, if only Rosie could see me now! All my life I'd thought I was funny looking: a scraggy little thing with eyes that were too big and a nose that turned up, but these clothes transformed me.

The array of knives and forks at the big table was devastating. What was I supposed to do with them? I watched the others desperately but couldn't catch on. I found a spoon for my soup but after that it was a nightmare. Beatrice Lillie laughed with Jack Buchanan and held a fork daintily in her fingers, but which one was it? Glamorous Gertrude Lawrence didn't seem to eat at all, she smoked continually. I wished with all my heart that I was back in William and Mary eating stewed eels and throwing the bones down for the cat.

The evening improved after dinner when I met Jorge. He took one look at me and murmured, 'Muy guapa!' then led me to the ballroom where he taught me to tango. On the boat deck, wrapped up against the cold wind of the Atlantic, we watched the winter moon. He put his arm around me and kissed me. I was very shocked. This was the first time I had

Jessie's adored mother, Jenny, at the St John's Wood house.

sie's father had a great love for ani-
ls—Jessie herself gave him Rival, the
dog pictured.

Mrs Matthews, for once relaxing, in the
garden.

Elder sister, Rosie, helped and
supported Jessie along the road to
stardom.

Birthday celebrations for Rosie.
Top: Eve and Eddie, brother and sister, w
followed Jessie to a stage career.

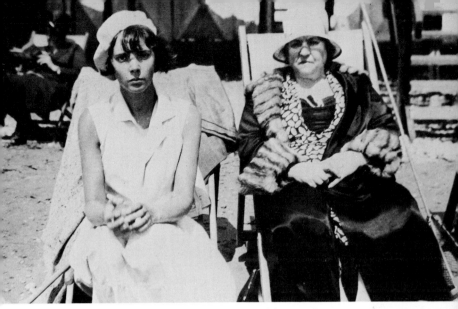

A day at the seaside: Jessie and her mother.

osie and George Galletly on their wedding day.

Jessie came from a large family of seven sisters and three brothers. From the top, Jenny, Carrie, Jessie, Lena and Eve.

Terry Friedman, Jessie's theatrical dancing teacher, and some of the many young hopefuls in her troupe.

Jessie, like any other teenager on a picnic.

Twenties-style Jessie with the famous bob and fringe.

Right: At the beginning of her career—a wistful gaze into the future.

To Rosie — Love darling Jamie

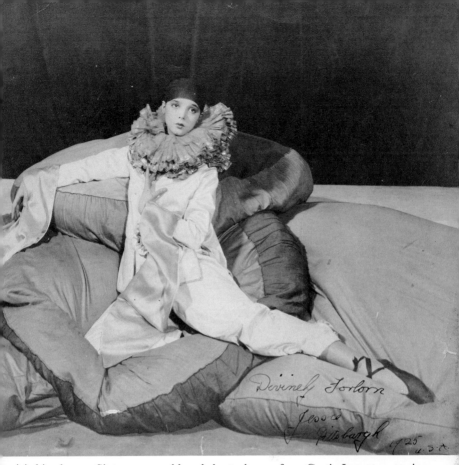

Divinely Forlorn
Jessie
Pittsburgh
1925
U.S.A.

essie's big chance. Sixteen years old and she took over from Gertie Lawrence to sing *Parisian Pierrot* in America.

Off-stage, as gamine as ever.

Next page: Charlot's Revue 1925 and Jessie moved out of the chorus.

Far Left: The look and line that caught the eye of impresario André Charlot.

been kissed, it was a suffocating experience. And who knew where it might lead?

I woke Marjorie up and told her what had happened. 'It's a sin all right,' agreed the convent bred Marjorie. 'But he kissed you, didn't he? You didn't kiss him? So I guess that's different.' She turned over and went back to sleep.

A sea of hands stretched out to meet us as the ship docked in New York. Cameras flashed at Gertie, Jack and Beatrice. There were bouquets of flowers and telegrams, for everyone it seemed, but me. Jorge patted my cheek, said he'd come to the first night and went to collect his baggage. Marjorie had her family, every girl in the chorus had an admirer waiting. In all the excitement I was overlooked.

I sat on my trunk in the customs shed and wondered what had hit me. It was nine o'clock on Christmas Eve and no one wanted me. After all the excitement and joy of the voyage I had been deserted. Even Miss Graham, who had promised to look after me, had vanished. The burly customs guard said, 'You can always spend the night on Ellis Island, kiddo.'

This was my first sharp lesson in something every actress has to learn—the art of self-preservation. Show business is not always a soft-hearted business. But Jorge, of course, came back at the same time as Olive Lindfield, one of the girls in the show, returned to search for me. He packed us both into a taxi for the Martha Washington Hotel.

But even Olive couldn't spare much time, she had a party to go to. She deposited me in my steam-heated room on the fourteenth floor, told me to ring for room service if I was hungry and then wished me 'Merry Christmas.' I put on my flannelette nightie, cuddled my Bonzo dog and sat by the window watching the electric advertisements switching on and off. Tomorrow was Christmas Day and I wouldn't even get a stocking.

Next morning everything was different. Charlot invited all the company to Christmas Dinner at the Waldorf Astoria, and it was just like going to Buckingham Palace. After that the hard grind of rehearsals began and there wasn't time for anything else. Charlot was a glutton for work. He demanded perfection both from his principals and his chorus. Only one part of my new life worried me, sharing the dressing-room with the other chorus girls.

I was completely out of place. The other girls had all travelled with Charlot before, they were older and experienced women. They refused to guard their tongues just because, 'that kid's here with her ears flapping!' I didn't understand half of the smutty jokes or the gossip about the principals. I'd much rather have been playing with the other kids in William and Mary Yard. And Charlot himself was a reason why some of the girls couldn't stand me. Lately in rehearsals he'd begun to single me out, calling me the baby of the show, and telling one of the girls when she pushed me out of the way, 'Be kind to her, she's only a child.'

'What the hell does he think this is?' she demanded angrily in the dressing-room, 'a bloody nursery?' She caught my wide-eyed look. 'Go on, run and tell him, you nasty little sneak.'

I told myself that if they didn't want me in the dressing-room I'd stay out of it. I hated the atmosphere anyway, cigarette smoke, face powder, French perfume and sweat. I preferred to stand out in the darkened wings watching Gertie Lawrence rehearse a number. She was as lovely as a dream in her satin Pierrot costume, and I'd never seen such a beautiful stage picture as the set for *Parisian Pierrot*. There were black velvet hangings and on the stage were masses of huge coloured velvet cushions. I could imagine Rosie whispering, 'See how she moves, Jessie, she's like silk. You try to move like that.' In my room at the Martha Washington Hotel I'd scrape my hair under a tight handkerchief and pretend it was the little black skull cap that Gertie wore. I'd pull the pillows from the bed and lie on the floor like she did and sing *Parisian Pierrot*. Every gesture that Gertie had made I practised, every movement I copied. By the time opening night arrived I was a little, undersized, immature carbon copy of Gertrude Lawrence. I knew every song, every dance, every nuance with which she held her audience in thrall.

Opening night at the Selwyn Theatre on Broadway was a huge success. Society with jewels and sables came, the bookings were terrific for the press had really splurged on this new English show. The simplicity was new to American audiences backed by the clear uncluttered stage where Charlot encouraged his magnificently dressed artistes to show their talent to perfection. With every set beautifully lit, first class material

54

to work on, the stars bowled the audience over with their sophisticated comedy, and Gertie Lawrence had a standing ovation when she sang *Limehouse Blues*.

Beatrice Lillie sang *March with Me* as a scout leader with us girls dressed in shorts and shirts. Her clowning was brilliant but, as the chorus exited, I almost ruined her number. I slipped and fell, my foot catching in the wire where the curtain comes down. Beatrice Lillie gave me a lively kick in the back-side to get me moving, but I was hopelessly tangled. The more Bea kicked, the funnier the audience found it. I was very sore by the time I crawled off stage. Bea was furious. I pleaded with her, 'I swear, I didn't do it on purpose, Miss Lillie.' I didn't either, I wasn't up to such tricks—yet.

As soon as the show had guaranteed bookings, the management found us apartments off Broadway. Olive Lindfield, whom I adored ever since she rescued me from the customs shed, said she'd share one with me. I don't think she realised what she was taking on. My complete lack of house-training appalled her. I'd never hung up a dress in my life. A nail on the wall or the floor had always been good enough. Olive was patient and kind, she taught me about coat hangers, how no lady leaves a ring around the bath and that towels are meant to hang on rails.

I was overcome with the wonder of living in this apartment. There was a kitchen with a shining ice-box, a dinette padded in red leather and the bedroom, with a dressing table and two single beds, was like paradise. I was glad I had someone to sleep with again. I would often wake in the night and for a moment think I was back in William and Mary listening for my father's heavy footsteps. I would tremble with fright again, worrying lest he should raise a hand to my mother.

All my life I would re-live the fear of my father's home-coming. My sisters always seemed to accept and understand his violent temper. I never could. In some corner of my being there remained fear joined with contempt that a man should hit a woman.

Just as he'd promised Jorge came to the opening night. Although in a few short weeks I hadn't grown up much, I did have the glamour of working in a hit Broadway show, so Jorge asked me out to supper after the performance. Jorge was twenty-eight but he was still a student. His father owned a

silver mine so Jorge didn't have to take his studies too
seriously.

We went to the Ritz Hotel which with its impressive decor,
frightening table settings and gigantic menu had me over-
awed. I sat there in my coat and, when the waiter tried to take
it from me, clutched it closer round me ashamed to let anyone
see my 'little girl's' dress underneath. Jorge realised my feelings
and suggested we leave. After being driven around town, I
ended up completely famished. The first place we stopped was
at a Child's Restaurant—rather like Lyons Corner House.

Bemused, Jorge asked me 'Do you really like eating in places
like this?'

'Yes, don't you?' I countered.

But gradually Jorge educated me and I did finally end up
at the Ritz.

My social life, apart from meals with Jorge, had none of the
glamour of the other chorus girls. Olive watched over me like
a mother hen. However, once she relented and took me to a
party at a house on Park Avenue. A very nice man, about my
father's age, made a fuss of me and called me, 'his little pansy'.
He accompanied me back to the flat in his chauffeur-driven
Cadillac. He looked at the building where I lived with scorn.

'What would you say to an apartment on Madison Avenue?
I've got a little duplex you could have.'

'Really!' Such generosity from a complete stranger. 'How
many bedrooms?'

He gave my hand a squeeze. 'Cute little pansy. Couple of
bedrooms and a wardrobe filled with lovely gowns.'

'Ooh!' I squeaked with joy. 'Then there'd be a bedroom
for my mother, too. I'm saving ever so hard. How much would
her fare cost?'

He gave me a hard look. 'I'll give you a ring in a couple of
days.'

I had to tell the other girls in the dressing-room. At last I
could match their exciting stories of the generous gentlemen of
New York. 'What do you think of that?' I demanded with
pride.

'Take her away,' groaned Gwen. 'Someone tell her the facts
of life. If that guy telephones, I'll eat my bust bodice.'

I was completely unequipped to make friends with them.
I had come to New York with the mentality of a child. Now I

was thrown into the sexual hot-house of a Broadway show where the girls had been specially chosen for their allure. God knows why Charlot had brought me along. No doubt I was really lucky not to be accepted by these gorgeous creatures, not to be invited to the lavish parties their admirers gave, not to be spoiled by men too soon, but in those days I would have given anything to be allowed into their charmed circle. By the time the show had been running for a few months, I had spent so much time in the wings I had learnt every part in the show off by heart. I could even do a fair study of Jack Buchanan.

I wrote home to Rosie in my laborious scrawl. I still tried to use my right hand as I'd been told to—years later I gave up, used my left and my writing flowed from that moment.

> 'I'm saving hard, Rosie, and I've found a dancing teacher like you told me to. I do two hours' ballet practice every day. Give my love to Billy. I hope he'll soon be well again.'

Billy, my brother, was still in hospital after his disastrous fight with Eugene Criqui, the European feather-weight champion. All my father's ambitions had been realised when Billy became feather-weight champion of England. But Billy's next fight nearly killed him. Dad had arranged a fight against a man years older and with much more experience. Criqui had battered Billy almost unconscious but Billy refused to give in. In the end my father jumped in the ring and pulled Billy out of the fight. It broke Billy's heart. He never fought again. Rosie had written to tell me how Berwick Market had fêted their beaten warrior—a great banner with 'Welcome Home, Billy' had been hung across the street.

Rosie had a new job. She was now matron to Madame Terry's Juveniles, and went with them on all their concerts. Lena was now maid of all work in William and Mary, and Carrie was free to become a ballroom dancer.

In the early summer Charlot came over from London to see how everything was going, and to prepare for a tour when the show eventually closed on Broadway. He wanted to make sure that the original zip was still in the show and that the understudies were fit to take over if the stars fell ill. The first rehearsal call was for the understudies.

I'd recently been told to understudy one of the small-part girls who did a Russian dance, so I was there in the wings watching Danny O'Neill call the numbers. In his role of stage manager Danny was one of the mainstays of the show. If any props were missing it was Danny who found them; if there was a noise at the side during a quiet scene it was Danny who silenced it. Charlot sat in the stalls listening to Sylvia Leslie, Gertie Lawrence's understudy, sing *Limehouse Blues*. Halfway through her song, Charlot held up his hand and stopped her. 'You're singing flat, Sylvia,' he called.

'Flat!' Sylvia's pretty face crinkled with horror. 'I'm certainly not.'

'You're singing flat, Sylvia.'

It was hot in the theatre that morning, the oppressive heat of the New York summer was beginning to exhaust us all. Everyone was perspiring. There was no air-conditioning in those days. Perhaps the heat sparked it off, but for some strange and ill-judged reason, Sylvia completely lost her head. She raved and ranted. She was not flat. How dare anyone say she was flat?

Charlot cut her short and ordered her off the stage. 'Let's hear Gertie's second understudy, Danny,' he called.

Danny O'Neill's face was a picture. He was in deep trouble. For some unknown reason no one had bothered to appoint a second understudy for Gertie. But this was neither the time nor the place to let Charlot know.

'Come on, Danny,' cried Charlot impatiently, 'who's second understudy?'

I didn't intend to do it. I don't know why I did it. It must have been Rosie's voice in my subconscious calling, 'You can do it better!' I brushed past Danny. 'I am,' I shouted.

Danny caught my arm. 'Don't be such a little fool.'

I was mad, I couldn't stop. 'I'll sing *Limehouse Blues*, Guv,' I called down to the stalls.

Charlot laughed. He knew very well that a chorus girl, the baby of the show, wouldn't have been made any kind of understudy to the star. 'How many numbers do you know, babee?'

'All of them.'

The theatre became a great well of silence. I could hear my heart thumping in my chest and the blood beating in my ears. I was petrified, suddenly aware of my devastating cheek. Charlot's face seemed to be growing enormous, his dark eyes glaring at me. I saw his mouth open, he was saying something . . . 'Go ahead, babee, *Limehouse Blues.*'

I breathed deeply just as Rosie had always told me to. I must think of what I was doing. I was Chinese, I wore a wig with two earphones . . . my white lover had gone . . . I kill the Chinese boy . . . my heart is broken . . . I am alone . . . they all hate me . . . they do!

By the time I heard the first bars of the piano music, I was really crying:

> 'Oh Limehouse kid, oh, oh, oh limehouse kid,
>   Going the way that the rest of them did,
>   Poor broken blossom and nobody's child,
>   Haunted and taunted, you're just kind of wild . . .'

My voice was coming out true and clear, and I was remembering every movement that Gertie made, every turn of her head, every sob in her voice. It was a strong dramatic number, way over my head really, but it was a good copy of Gertie's performance. I sank to the floor sobbing with despair.

The quietness came back to the theatre, and I felt very alone and inadequate on the big stage. 'Very good, babee,' Charlot's voice cut through the silence. 'I'll let you know my decision later.'

I was afraid to go to the theatre that evening. Everyone would have heard what I'd done. Olive, my flat-mate, could see how worried I was and tried to brush away my fears about Charlot's reactions. After all, she assured me, I had helped Danny O'Neill out of a tight corner, hadn't I? She was sure Charlot wouldn't be angry.

'But I don't think the others will like it, duckie,' she told me.
'Why?'

She shrugged, even Olive didn't like to tell me that I'd committed the unforgivable sin: trying to step out of the chorus.

A crowd of girls were clustered around the call board when I walked in. I heard someone say: 'My God, wait till Sylvia sees this.'

One of the girls turned her head and saw me, she nudged the girl next to her. 'Here comes Lady Muck herself.'

I felt like running then, but I mustered all my courage and pushed my way to the front. Pinned to the board was a notice:

First understudy to Miss Lawrence: Jessie Matthews.
Second understudy to Miss Lawrence: Sylvia Leslie.

It hardly registered at first, then I blushed scarlet. I could feel the hostility from the girls around me.

'What a bloody nerve,' someone said in a deliberately loud voice, 'pinching Sylvia's job.'

I pushed my way through them and got to the stairs. I heard the same loud voice say, 'You have to be dragged up in the gutter to do a thing like this.'

Another voice said very clearly, 'Little guttersnipe!'

I was still trying to brave it out when I got to the top of the staircase, 'Don't cry,' I was ordering myself, 'don't cry.' Inside my head were ringing the words my mother used to say, 'Sticks and stones may break your bones but words will never hurt you.'

Oh, but they did. Oh, how they hurt!

Chapter Seven

On a wave of heavenly perfume, Miss Gertrude Lawrence swept up to make her entrance. 'Little girl,' she said in her most regal way. 'Do you mind letting me go on?'

I must have been a pest standing there in the wings, watching her with keen young eyes, assessing every movement she made. It was nice of her not to make a fuss for I'm sure she was perfectly aware of what I was doing and of the words I was whispering under my breath. Gertie must have used them herself once, the classical prayer of every understudy:

'Just a slight touch of laryngitis or a vague sneezy cold. Nothing serious like a broken leg or a sprained ankle. Only one performance, God, that's all I ask for. A matinee would do. Just enough to show everybody that I can keep the curtain up.'

One very hot summer afternoon God answered my prayer. In spite of the whirring fans, the matinees in the stifling heat of the theatre were an ordeal for the company. And for the stars who really carried the show they were almost unendurable. Gertie's dresser marched into our dressing-room. Over her arm hung the beautiful costume that Edward Molyneux had designed: a white satin pierrot suit with green linings to the wide sleeves, a tulle ruff and a black skull cap. 'Matthews!' she signalled to me, 'Miss Lawrence is feeling the heat. She wants you to do the Parisian Pierrot number.'

My insides melted, my courage vanished and I felt as limp as a lettuce leaf. 'Look sharp about it, Matthews. I haven't got all day.' Now I was ice cold and then burning hot in alternate waves. 'Hold your head up,' she ordered as she pinned the tulle ruff around my neck. 'And take care of this costume.'

It was like listening to Rosie, 'Hold your head up, you look like a long drink of cold water,' but there wasn't Rosie's love behind the chastising words. Oh, Rosie, if only you were here!

The curtain went up and there I was lying on a bed of vivid velvet cushions. It is never very easy singing a song when you're lying on your back and trying to make your voice project to the back row of the stalls—this was long before microphones—it is never very easy when your voice sounds to you like a peep out of a tin whistle. The chorus dressed as dolls in crinoline frocks came on. I danced with them, there was a lot of work to do, it was, as Charlot had told me, a very artistic number. I did my best. I was so exhausted with the sheer effort of remembering all I must do that I hardly noticed the applause. Danny O'Neill gave me a thumbs-up as I came off and Olive gave me a quick hug. Oh, Rosie, if only you were here! I sent a cable home to the family that evening: 'Played Parisian Pierrot.' And I tried to imagine what it would be like in the kitchen of William and Mary when the telegram boy rode up on his bike.

At the next matinee down came the costume again and I went on in Gertie's place. At the evening performance Gertie's dresser walked in with the costume once more. I put on the make-up, dead white face, black eyeliner, red lips and dressed, when a message came that Gertie had changed her mind. She was going on after all. Send the costume back. Angrily I undressed and creamed off the make-up, but it was too late for me to put on my Crinoline Doll costume and lead the chorus on stage.

'Poor old Lady Muck,' called one of the girls as they trooped out, 'all on her own-ee-oh!'

Gertie became very capricious in the hot weather. I'd be dressed and made-up ready to go on when Gertie would change her mind. At one matinee she changed her mind twice. That evening down came the dresser again with the costume over her arm. 'Tell Miss Lawrence,' I said angrily, 'if I put that costume on, it stays on.'

I knew I was making an idle threat. Gertie was the star and only stars get away with temperament. But when I hung the costume on my rail that evening, it stayed there. Gertie's dresser didn't come back for it. Until September, the end of the New York run, the understudy played *Parisian Pierrot*. To give Gertie her due, it was a very nice thing to have done.

In October we began our six month tour of the main cities of North America and Canada. I was sorry to leave New York. In the year and a half I'd lived there I'd grown to know the Chinese laundryman at the corner of the block, the Italian grocer who gave me bits of mortadella sausage to eat when I bought the groceries, the cheapest cafeteria, Schrafts soda fountain on 5th Avenue. Eighteen months in the life of a seventeen year old is a long time, and I sometimes felt I'd lived in New York for ever.

I was more than sorry to leave Jorge. I was in love with him. A blissful idyllic first love affair that so far had gone no further than hand-holding and careful kisses. 'Oh, no, Jorge, I couldn't.'

'Why not, mia preciosa? We're going to be married.'

'When?' I asked with eternal female practicality.

'As soon as your show is over and you are free.'

Jorge, the rich carefree student, promised to come to every first night of our tour. He was there in Toronto, sitting in his seat in the stalls on the night the management announced that Miss Gertrude Lawrence had pneumonia and her part would be taken by her understudy. If anyone wished to leave their money would be refunded at the box office. The management did not divulge that the understudy was sitting in the star's dressing-room shaking with nerves and praying that Miss Lawrence would make a lightning recovery and arrive at the theatre just as the orchestra were tuning up.

The only number of Gertie's I had performed in public was *Parisian Pierrot*. Now I had all her numbers and my seventeen year old shoulders didn't feel strong enough to carry the burden. I had rehearsed all day and when I came off from *Limehouse Blues* I heard Danny O'Neill say to one of the stage-hands, 'She's too young for that number. Wait till she's had a man, then she'll understand what it's all about.' For one wild moment I wondered if, in the interests of the theatre, I should shed my virginity before the performance.

The stage was mysteriously lit, the soft silken hangings parted as I came on stage. There was a polite round of applause.

A few people had left when they knew Gertie was ill, but the majority stayed out of curiosity. *Limehouse Blues*, my first number, was a Chinese *East Lynne*, an old-fashioned theme of the broken blossom of Limehouse falling in love with a good man. There was a touching scene where I serve my white lover tea, but my dream of happiness is shattered by the entrance of a chinese boy who tries to rape me and whom I kill rather than have my perfect love tarnished. It was real heavy dramatic stuff, loaded with heartbreak, as I wept: 'Rings on my fingers and tears for a crown . . .'

The reporter from the Toronto paper who was there wrote: 'The understudy commenced just a little timidly . . . but the house rose to her. I've never seen anything like it before. We stamped, we waved our programmes, we shouted ourselves hoarse . . .'

That was how the audience were all evening. They drew me through each number on a great wave of enthusiasm. I could do no wrong, and I did no wrong. Roars of welcome when I came on and thunderous applause when I exited.

The reporters came backstage, 'Hi, honey! You're a hit!' The photographers flashed their cameras my way. I had hit the headlines in a big way: 'Cinderella's rise to fame!' was one, 'Seventeen year old wows Toronto!' was another.

Gertie's influenza turned to pneumonia and when the company left for Philadelphia, Gertie stayed behind in hospital. I prayed that she would get well, be restored to perfect health, but that she would convalesce slowly. 'Please, God,' I prayed, 'let Gertie take her time. Just a few weeks more.'

In Philadelphia I had the overwhelming joy of seeing *Jessie Matthews* across the billboards, and the sublime satisfaction of having my own dressing-room far away from the caustic comments of the ladies of the chorus. I was only an embryo star, it is true, but I was getting all the perks. Bud, the stage-door man, saluted me when I tripped past his den, and every evening he would tap politely on my dressing-room door to say there was a gentleman outside who would like to take me to supper. I always told him to thank the gentleman but I was practically engaged to a gentleman called Jorge in New York, who was rather jealous.

Our next town was Boston and we were getting to the end of the tour. The day after we opened, Danny O'Neill came to my dressing-room while I was making up. I could tell by the look on his face that something was wrong. He asked the dresser to leave us for a moment, then pulled up a chair next to mine.

'You're not going to like this, kid,' he said gently. 'The management have heard from Charlot. They asked me to come and tell you.' He gave my shoulder a little squeeze. 'We're old pals, aren't we kid, both from Soho?'

The lips I was trying to cover with lip salve felt strangely stiff. Danny picked up a towel and rubbed off a smear of lipstick on my chin. 'Joyce Barbour's in New York. Charlot wants her to take over the part.'

The terrible disappointment almost stunned me.

'As a matter of fact,' Danny went on, ' she's here, kid.'

I said the first thing that came into my head, 'Does that mean I have to go back with the other girls?'

Danny nodded. 'Be a good kid, don't make it more difficult for me.'

I spent the next day rehearsing with Joyce Barbour. The American Charlot Revue had other numbers besides the ones she knew from *London Calling*. Joyce was a very sweet person. It wasn't her fault that she had been asked to take over. She didn't know the situation.

Going back to the chorus was, to put it very mildly, a living hell. In all probability I had behaved like a snooty little beast when I'd been rapidly elevated to stardom, but I was now made to suffer for it by two or three girls in the chorus who hated my guts.

'Out of the way, Lady Muck,' one would say as she tripped me up. My make-up would find its way into the trash can, my costumes would be kicked into a corner. When a group of women band together against one of their own sex they can be completely ruthless. After a couple of days I was not merely cut down to size, I was whittled away to nothing.

'Why don't you leave me alone?' I turned on my tormentors after the evening show.

'Hark at Lady Muck!'

'You've had your fun. Now leave me alone.'

'Leave you alone? What a bloody nerve. Who said she was worth two hundred quid a week? So you wouldn't go on unless they upped your salary. Why, you're not worth two hundred bob.'

'That's not true. I never did.'

A loaded powder puff sailed across the room and hit me full in the face. 'Go peddle your wares in Berwick Market. Go back to the gutter.'

This old taunt was the end. All right, so I was born in Soho. I'd show them how we act in Soho when we're baited beyond endurance. I picked up my box of powder and got one girl right in the middle. I slung my hairbrush to hit another, towels, tins of cleanser, everything I could lay my hands on went straight at my tormentors. The missiles flew back and forth. The language was shocking.

There was a thunderous banging on the dressing-room door. We all stiffened. The door opened a fraction. Bud's head poked round cautiously. 'When you dames quit yelling there's a gentleman out here who wants to take Miss Matthews to supper.'

'Tell him to . . .' I screamed.

'It's Mr George White of the George White Scandals!'

At the mention of that magical name a complete hush descended. Covered in face powder, tears making dirty rivulets down my cheeks I sat on the floor and wailed. Carrie Graham came in and started cleaning me up, but I was still rather bedraggled when Mr George White drove me to a quiet restaurant for supper. Fortunately the lights were dim and the waiters were obsequious and he acted as if he was used to taking tearful teenagers to supper.

'I caught the show in Philadelphia,' he told me, 'when you were playing Gertie's part. I thought you were a very talented little lady. I watched it again tonight and there's Joyce Barbour in the part. What's happened?'

A tear rolled into my glass of iced water. 'I wish I knew.' I told him all about Gertie's illness right up to this evening when the girls had accused me of demanding £200 a week. 'Of course it isn't true,' I said. 'Why I'd pay anything just to get away from them.'

'I can't understand why Charlot took you out of the part,' declared Mr White, 'but he's making a big mistake and I'm going to cable him tonight.'

I thought he was just trying to comfort me, but next evening Danny O'Neill came round and said there was a cable from Charlot and I was back in the leading role again.

This time I was really in trouble. Not only the chorus girls hooted in dismay, but the principals, too, didn't care for the decision. Beatrice Lillie declared that Joyce Barbour had been badly treated; why should a seventeen year old chorus girl be given preference over her? Thank goodness Joyce herself didn't take that attitude. Although she was the leading lady of *London Calling* and a star back in England she was as sweet and as nice to me as ever. For the rest of the tour she was the only woman in the company who was.

Much later I discovered why Charlot had acted so strangely. In Pittsburgh the manager of the company had started to pay attention to me, asking me to come to his hotel room and hear the latest gramophone records. Although I was pretty silly and innocent, I turned all his invitations down because I was in love with Jorge and had promised him never to date other men. Perhaps his wounded ego was the reason the manager sent word to Charlot that I was becoming big-headed and difficult and should be replaced. Only George White's kind intervention saved me. Although I had been in the theatre for years, Rosie had protected me from management and managers, and I was too inexperienced to know how to refuse men gracefully. I was also too young to understand that success brings problems, not the least being the amount of envy it arouses.

The tour was over. I had a few days of freedom before the company sailed home, and I spent them with Jorge.

In the two years since I had arrived in America, this tall, dark-haired young man had become the pivot of my world. He was all people to me, a gentle father-figure to tell me how I should behave, a loyal friend who would listen to my tales of triumph and applaud me, and now, because I placed my trust in his promise to marry me, my lover. Love was my new discovery; I gazed into a happy future that would last for ever with eyes untinged by disillusionment.

With most of the dollars I had saved I bought a trunkful of presents to take home to my family and then Jorge and I went on the town. We went to Harlem and danced to wonderful rhythms, to Coney Island and bumped over canvas mountains and whizzed through terrifying tunnels. We went down to the river and watched the ferry boats and glimpsed the great liners festooned with fairy lights. For the rest of my life, these few days would always seem the ultimate in happiness.

March 1925 was bitterly cold and Rosie told me that she felt frozen to the bone as they waited for the ship to arrive at Liverpool docks. The train from Euston drew into Lime Street at 4 am and there was nowhere for them to keep warm. Rosie wanted to wait on the station until the buffet opened and they could have a hot drink. 'We'll miss the ship,' Dad shouted, 'and all because of you and your hot drink.'

Dad, who prided himself on being a dab hand at everything, didn't know much about ships and tides and poor Rosie and my mother nearly perished with the cold while they waited on the dockside for the ship to sail in with the tide at 7.30 am.

As soon as the great ship slid into its moorings, Dad started to whistle. He had a special signal whistle that all us kids had had to jump to. The Matthews whistle, one long blast and then a short one. Dad whistled and ran up and down the docks and no one took a blind bit of notice. Eventually Carrie Graham came on deck, recognised the shivering trio and went in search of me.

Rosie says she can remember it perfectly. 'I can see you now, leaning over the side wearing a lovely woollen dress with a full skirt.' I don't remember much about that March morning, but Rosie declared: 'You went away a little girl in socks and came back a sophisticated young lady.'

As soon as I was allowed, I was rushing down the gangway, the revue star to my very fingertips. Gertie Lawrence couldn't have done it better. 'Darlings!' My arms opened wide 'Darlings!'

The three of them looked stunned. Rosie was the first to recover. She could impersonate anyone and she got my accent perfectly. 'Oh, darling!' she mimicked. 'Oh, hello, darling!'

It was my turn to look stunned. I knew she was taking me off and making a good job of it. But why? If I'd known of the hours they'd spent on an icy wharf I might have understood. My father was ready to take umbrage when he discovered I had a first-class ticket for the train—all the company had. 'Where the bloody hell do you think I can find the money to travel first? You're coming third with us, me gel.'

Only my mother was living up to my rose-coloured expectations. 'Don't take any notice of them, my darling. They've got the pip. Give me a kiss, love.'

As the wheels ground out every long mile on that train journey back to London I was remembering how it would be in William and Mary. All the bathroom I would have from now on was the cold water tap in the kitchen. Where would I hang my beautiful American dresses? I knew the answer—over a chair in the room I would share with my sisters. Foremost in my lovesick mind was Jorge. How could I introduce Jorge with his impeccable manners to my father who'd said 'Shove off,' to the porter who tried to carry my bags? What would Jorge think when he saw the home of his beloved?

Oh, they'd all tried. It touched my heart to see how my mother had tried. The kitchen was festooned with streamers, there was a big birthday cake for my eighteenth birthday, but gloom was just round the corner. I wasn't old enough or wise enough to laugh and say, 'We may be poor, we may be rough, so what? Home is where the heart is.'

Of course I soon got used to it again. I'd avoid my mother's anxious eyes when I carried another kettle of hot water and a bowl upstairs. She'd say, 'But you had a wash this morning, darling.' My father would wake me at two in the morning and shout, 'Come down, I've got some lads from the market who want to hear you sing that song about Limehouse.' I wasn't sleeping very well anyway so I didn't care, and as I strummed my ukelele, every sad song was from the heart.

Worst of all was what happened at the theatre. Charlot decided that my rise to leading lady had been too rapid. The principals of the show may have offered their advice, but whatever the reason, I was ordered back to the chorus.

There was a stand-up row between Charlot and Carrie Graham. 'How can you put Jessie in the back row of the chorus after she worked so hard in America and did so well?'

'It will do her no harm to come down to earth,' declared Charlot. 'When I think she's ready I'll give her parts.'

A month before I had returned, when I was seventeen and still under-age, Rosie and my mother had been asked by Charlot to sign a contract on my behalf. 'How could you do it?' I groaned to my mother. 'Why didn't you wait till I got back? Look what he's done to me now.'

'He promised faithfully he'd look after you. Oh, Jessie, please do what Mr Charlot says,' pleaded my mother.

Rosie wasn't around too often to hear what I thought of her part in the affair. A few months before, she had married her faithful George and gone to live in Shepherd's Bush.

In the middle of all this unhappiness Jorge arrived in London. It wasn't quite the same for us now. We had nowhere to go. I was too timid to walk past the hall porter in Jorge's hotel, and no longer did I have a little apartment off Broadway where we could open cans, make supper and afterwards listen to records, entwined in each other's arms. Every night I had to return to William and Mary or my father would have demanded the reason why, and over my dead body would I take Jorge home.

Something awful had happened in New York and now memories of it crowded in upon me. It had been the result of our blissful days together. I wept when I found out. 'Oh, Jorge, what shall we do?' I had asked.

I expected him to wipe away my tears and produce a special licence for us to marry. Instead he took me in a taxi to see a doctor whom a friend of his had recommended. 'Just do what he says,' Jorge told me, 'and then everything will be all right again.'

These things stay imprinted on your memory for ever. I remember the doctor was a small dapper man, with smooth well-kept hands and dark hair brushed back from a bland face. 'You don't look eighteen,' he said to me. 'You're quite sure you are?'

Later he said, 'It won't hurt if you keep still.' In the next room someone put on a gramophone record, 'Valencia, land of orange groves and sweet content . . .' The music went round and round in my head. I didn't understand what the doctor was doing, except that it was the greatest indignity I had ever suffered in my life and through a miasma of pain it seemed that my life was ebbing away. I felt I was dying. I deserved to die.

Now, back in London, I was being punished. If Rosie or any one of the family found out, they would despise me. None of my thoughts made what was happening easier to bear. For Jorge, upset by not being introduced to my family and considering my behaviour unreasonable, was treating me coolly.

I went to the theatre; I danced in the chorus. Afterwards I would walk home alone to William and Mary. The streets of Soho might have been an alien wilderness I felt so alone. Was this love, this confusion of shame and pain? Solitary, I was prone to the fear that was crowding in, had I been deserted?

Even now I don't know what went wrong. Perhaps Jorge had never intended to marry me and this mishap frightened him off. Whatever his reason, he ended our love affair in an abrupt and cruel manner. The stage door keeper handed me a letter. As I had no intention of living with him again, Jorge said he was going back to New York and would not be returning.

Every grey morning when I awoke I clung to this hope. I was ill equipped to deal with this crushing blow. I felt I would never get over my terrible loss. One day he'll be sorry he left me, I wept, when I'm a great star of the theatre, then he'll be sorry.

Chapter Eight

Mr Harry Lytton, son of Mr Henry Lytton, the famous
Savoyard, is engaged to Miss Jessie Matthews, a charming
young actress in Charlot's Revue. A photograph of them
at Mr Lytton's home in Chiswick yesterday.

The photograph taken by the *Daily Graphic* showed a happy
young couple: the girl, dark bobbed hair with a fringe, and
the man, debonair, handsome with a cigarette held non-
chalantly between his fingers.

A few months ago I would not have believed this could
happen, that I could marry any other man but Jorge. Despair,
even eighteen year old despair, takes time to lift. Edmund
Gwenn, the character actor who was in Charlot's Revue,
finally jolted it out of my system. Teddy Gwenn, the kindest
of men, waited for me in the wings when I came offstage.

'There's a friend waiting for you in your dressing-room,' he
told me with a twinkle in his eye.

I rushed upstairs filled with glorious hope, I was quite sure
that Jorge had come back. I flung open the door, and there,
sitting on my chair, was a huge teddy bear. Teddy Gwenn's
parting present before I left on tour.

The intense disappointment made me almost distraught for
a while. I had to accept the fact that Jorge wasn't coming
back, that he didn't want me. The only way I could bring
comfort to myself was to swear that one day I'd make the
whole world want me. I was about to start a tour, an apprenticeship to prove to Charlot that I was capable of playing leads.

How I'd work, I vowed. I'd drive myself, I'd dance till I dropped. I'd get to the top even if it killed me. I'd prove that Jorge had been wrong.

Teddy Gwenn had been kind to me ever since the day Charlot first started to relent and gave me one line to speak in one of Teddy's sketches. 'You are wanted on the telephone, sir!' How I rehearsed and polished that line until Teddy used to hide when he saw me coming.

One morning Charlot called me to his office and handed me a script with my name on the hard cover. He had given me status at last. Even in America, performing song and dance numbers, my salary hadn't changed, nothing was official, I was only standing in for Gertie Lawrence. Now, although I had only a few lines here and there and one dance number, everything I did was my own, and my name was in the programme.

As a final gesture Charlot invited me to sit in the stalls with him and the principals while a new American dance director drilled the chorus girls and yelled, 'Pick up your feet!' or 'Put some guts in it!' Charlot knew very well about the rough time these girls had been giving me. Thank goodness it was over, and I'd been promoted.

Charlot had promised my mother a future for me in his revues. His plan was to give me a really tough going over on a provincial tour. Twice nightly, I'd have to dance, sing, act; I'd appear in twelve items, which would mean twenty-four changes a day, and thirty-six on matinee days: you have to be young and healthy to stand that. On this tour I'd gain experience, and if I came through the apprenticeship with glowing reports, then I 'might' appear in the West End.

For me, the most important factor in this tour was the company itself. In people of real talent there is often a willingness to help the beginners. Their attitude was very much like that of Maisie Gay who I had worked with on another occasion. 'Jessie,' Maisie had said to me, 'people won't pay to see a carbon copy of Gertie Lawrence. You must develop your own particular personality.' I knew quite well that I had too many of Gertie's mannerisms so faithfully copied in America. Maisie rehearsed me in her idea of on-stage behaviour. 'Now the way you stand with your arms behind your back, that's you. You're a little girl, and you look younger than you are. Act eighteen, not twenty-eight. Your face is round and cute—visualise it

73

when you're on the stage, roll those big brown eyes, and stop trying to act like a sophisticated woman of the world.'

I listened, I practised and with Maisie's help I began to mould an on-stage personality that was mine and no-one else's. The vow I had made to myself to succeed was always in the forefront of my mind. I polished my dance routines, until I could literally float through them, I learned about audiences, how to pick out the part of the audience where the applause and warmth is coming from and play to it with all your might. Timing, no one could teach me more about timing than Maisie Gay—it is instinctive to a certain extent but it also takes technique.

I worked very hard and I was scornful of others who didn't. One young man in particular, who danced and sang with me in some of the numbers, didn't take his profession half seriously enough. He was a bit of a dilettante. If there was a golf course near the town we were playing, he was on the course every afternoon, getting back to the theatre just in time for the first house. If there was a poker school backstage, he'd be part of it. Harry Lytton, I decided, was irresponsible and extremely conceited. Oh, he was good looking enough, but I thought his manner condescending and arrogant. It might appeal to other girls—and he had plenty of girl friends—but certainly not to me. My emotions were still numbed after Jorge and I had no time to waste on spoiled young men.

Because we didn't have to impress each other our working relationship in the easy camaraderie of a touring company was ideal. I'd pull his leg about his adoring fans and the mating calls from the gallery girls, and he'd joke about my dedication to hard work. His well-educated mind secretly fascinated me, and although I mimicked his public school drawl unkindly, I was very envious of his cool confidence.

Only once did I see him disconsolate and unhappy. He'd quarrelled with the particular girl of the moment he was in love with and was feeling let down. 'Come and have coffee and sandwiches with me after the show,' he said.

We were in Birmingham, and instead of going to a cheap café Harry took me to the Queen's Hotel. Only the best was good enough for Harry. In a quiet corner of the opulent lounge, deep in well-upholstered chairs, we talked about ourselves. I was more than a little curious about his background.

His father, Henry Lytton (he became Sir Henry in 1930), was the mainstay of the D'Oyly Carte Company. They were called the Savoyards, their popularity was enormous and each new production of Gilbert and Sullivan Opera was greeted with the fervour of a new religion. His way of life was completely foreign to mine, he'd been to boarding school in Brighton, and had never wanted for anything in his short life. He was a year or two older than I was.

I tried to compare him with Jorge, but Harry, with his cool clipped manner, had nothing of Jorge's warm intensity about him. He was a typical well brought up young Englishman whose parents just happened to make their money in a favoured spot of the English theatre.

However, we became friends that evening when he was down in the dumps and wanted sympathy, and if there was anything I needed in return, it was sympathy. We comforted each other, 'I thought you had a sad look about you,' he said when I told him about Jorge, 'but you're well out of it. If he'd taken you to South America you'd have had ten kids and grown fat.'

From that point our friendship grew. Sometimes we met after the show and had supper together and sometimes I paid, for Harry was always chronically short of money. With Harry, unlike Jorge, I did not have to worry about his reactions. I told him the truth about my childhood in William and Mary, of the grinding poverty, and my father's foul temper. He didn't seem shocked, and when I eventually told him how my love affair had ended and of my humiliation in the doctor's surgery, he didn't condemn me. At last I had found balm for my aching heart. Harry was unhappy over his broken love affair so we turned to each other in our mutual need for a confidante and a comforter.

It was curiosity more than anything else that made me agree when he suggested we go down to London one Sunday morning and spend the night at his parents' home. I wondered how these famous Lyttons lived. Their house at Chiswick impressed me enormously. A parlourmaid in a white cap with streamers opened the front door, there were oil paintings and antiques, thick carpets in the large hall and on the stairs, and in the drawing room waited Henry's parents.

Mr Lytton was on his way to some appointment or other but I saw he wore an eyeglass on a black cord and carried a gold-topped malacca cane, and Mrs Lytton was a sweet-faced grey-haired lady full of warmth and chatter. 'What a beautiful child,' she exclaimed when she saw me, and when she took me up to my room she told me how delighted she was that Harry had found a girl friend nearer his own age than the sophisticated young women he often brought home. She called Harry, 'Boysie', which I found rather strange, and I decided I could never call him that. But Boysie was the apple of his mother's eye. She'd had him late in life when her other children were grown up, and as the rest of the family soon told me, 'Whatever Boysie wanted, Boysie must have.'

When I left the Lyttons on Monday to return north with Harry, I thought they were a lovely family and Mrs Lytton an absolute darling. I'd glimpsed a way of life I knew nothing about, but it appealed to me very much.

In Cardiff, when the tour was nearing its end, Charlot sent up the writers of his new revue to watch my performance and see what they thought of me. Thank goodness I didn't know they were in the audience, but when Ronald Jeans and Rowland Leigh came backstage they were very encouraging and said they would write material for the new show to fit my personality.

Some time later Rosie and I stood outside the Prince of Wales Theatre in Coventry Street and watched the workmen putting up the names of the stars in electric bulbs. Under *Charlot Revue of 1926* was the name Jessie Matthews. Rosie and I held hands, 'You've worked hard for it,' she said, and we both had to pretend we had something in our eyes to hide our emotion.

Rosie told me that every night for a week, she went up to the West End and walked round and round the theatre to see my name in lights.

It was a wonderful revue, very good material and marvellous people to work with. Anton Dolin and I danced ballet, I did sketches with Herbert Mundin and danced musical comedy numbers with Harry Lytton. We all knew we had a success well before the final curtain fell. As we stood taking our bows at the end, Teddie Gerrard, one of Charlot's stars who was in the stalls, threw her corsage of flowers onto the stage for me. The audience stood up and cheered. Other women took off the flowers that decorated their gowns and tossed them at my feet.

I gathered up these tributes and thought my heart would burst with pride.

There was a party on-stage afterwards. Famous actors and actresses, whose names I revered, came up to me and complimented my performance. It was a heady feeling to be fêted by the greats of the English theatre. I was the belle of the evening.

C. B. Cochran took me aside and told me that he had always felt that he discovered me and how much he had regretted letting me go when *Music Box* had failed financially. 'As soon as you finish your Charlot contract,' he said, 'I'm going to make you into a Cochran star.' Cochran was already known as a great showman and a genius at publicity.

The evening ended on a supreme note of happiness at Cochran's words, and Harry eventually took me home to Rosie's little house in Shepherd's Bush. I had moved the week before to live with Rosie and her husband. It was my mother's idea. Although I was only getting £18 a week, in my mother's eyes I now had star status and it wasn't fitting that I should have to bathe in a tin bowl and share a bedroom with my sisters. So I bought a divan bed which we put up in Rosie's living room, and I could have as many baths as I wanted in Rosie's bathroom.

For a few days after my triumphant first night, photographers followed me around, even to St James's Park where I went to eat my lunchtime sandwiches. And for the first time I read the headline that was to follow me down the years: 'Chorus girl becomes star.' But very soon all the fuss died down and we all went back to normal living. There was, however, one change —Harry Lytton's attitude. I first noticed it when he became violently jealous of my dancing partner Anton Dolin. He started to send me flowers and ask me to the Ivy for supper, and every time we went to his home—where I loved going— Mrs Lytton would say, 'I hope you're going to be kind to Boysie, he's so much in love with you.'

If Harry was in love with me, I thought he had a strange way of showing it. I had no idea what his intentions were until one day when we were walking down Berwick Street we met my mother.

'Mrs Matthews,' he said as soon as I introduced them, 'I want to marry your daughter.'

'Marry her,' laughed my mother, 'but you're only a boy yourself. How are you going to keep her?'

'I have an allowance from my people,' declared Harry. 'If Jessie marries me she need never work again.'

I stared at him. If he had an allowance from his parents it didn't go very far, for Harry was always hard up.

My mother smiled at me. 'Do you want to get married, my darling?' 'Of course I don't,' I cried, 'not for two or three years. Not till I'm twenty-one, at least.'

But the pressures began to build up around me. Mrs Lytton, whom I admired very much, so obviously wanted me to marry Harry. And Harry's sisters, very sweet girls who had been educated in a Belgian convent, began to embroider linen tablecloths for us. 'Meet me in Debenhams one afternoon,' begged Mrs Lytton, 'and we'll choose some linen for you and Harry.' I began to imagine entering the charmed middle-class circle where a maid brought in afternoon tea, and where groceries were delivered to the back door by an errand boy who tipped his cap and called me 'Madam'.

The whole family went to the first night of the latest Gilbert and Sullivan Opera and the audience applauded as the Lytton family took their seats in the stalls. Afterwards we were introduced to admiring friends as 'Harry and his fiancée'. Almost without knowing it, we were engaged.

One person didn't approve at all of the engagement. Rosie didn't like Harry Lytton. 'I think he's a snob,' she said. When I produced my engagement ring she said bluntly, 'It's a bit large for a real diamond, isn't it? Are you sure it's not glass?' I knew she wasn't joking. But I was hurt when she said, 'You're trying to better yourself, aren't you, Jessie?' Was it so wrong, I wanted to ask her, so wrong to want to live in a nice pleasant atmosphere amongst cultured well-educated people? I said nothing, Rosie was fiercely loyal about William and Mary, and about every member of my family, including my father.

The wedding at Hammersmith Town Hall was a traumatic experience for all of us. Waiting at the top of the steps were the Lyttons with years of good living showing in their clothes and their bearing. Mother righted her new hat nervously and my father tugged at his unaccustomed collar. Rosie began to sniff back a tear; she cried relentlessly all through the ceremony.

Georgie, my eldest brother, drove up on his motor bike. I turned and saw him, and suddenly broke away from my family and ran down the steps to him.

'Oh, Georgie!' I clutched his arm, Georgie was my old protector from childhood days.

'Anything wrong, kid?' he asked.

Suddenly it was all wrong. I wasn't sure I wanted to get married. I wasn't sure of anything.

Georgie kissed my cheek. 'What say you get on the back of my bike, kid, and we drive off?'

I was very tempted. We stood clasped in each other's arms until I got my nerve back and then we walked up the steps together and I became Mrs Lord Alva Lytton. I never asked Harry why he was called Lord Alva. I wish I had.

Our married life began in a little flat in Earl's Court, and I remember that the first time my mother-in-law, Mrs Lytton, came to tea I was overcome with nerves, desperately afraid that I should do something wrong and shame myself forever in her eyes. An hour before she was expected I dashed out of the flat and caught a bus to Shepherd's Bush. I found Rosie in the park with her infant son in his pram. 'Please come, Rosie,' I begged. Just like old times, as if we were going to an audition, Rosie took over. We raced the pram back to Rosie's home, found someone to mind the baby and got back to Earl's Court just in time.

Rosie and Mrs Lytton didn't really get on. I could see Rosie bristling at any slight or imagined slight against me or my family, and when my mother-in-law left, Rosie said, 'Did you hear what she called Harry? Fancy calling a grown man, "Boysie!"'

After that I didn't like to bring my problems to Rosie. And I had one which was a constant worry. Harry's attitude to money was proving an unpleasant surprise. Bills, he declared, should never be settled at once, but tossed in a drawer and paid at one's leisure. To me, brought up in a society where you have to pay your way or go under, where, if you borrowed half a crown, it had to be returned or you'd risk getting a bad name, I couldn't accept this philosophy. And I knew very well that Harry's family wouldn't approve of his attitude.

'For God's sake,' said Harry, when we argued about it,

79

'we're in the theatre. What will people say if we keep counting the ha'pennies?'

Our arguments were forgotten when Charlot decided to take his 1926 Revue to New York. The arrangement Charlot made was that we should join forces with an American Revue company and perform together in their theatre.

The excitement of the crossing, the arrival in New York, suddenly evaporated when the Charlot company trouped into the theatre and there in front of our eyes was something none of us had expected. A catwalk, a long platform jutting out from the auditorium, the kind that burlesque girls use. The resident company, famed throughout America, certainly did revue, but it was hardly the kind we were used to. Earl Carroll and his Vanities were renowned not for wit and artistry but for the gorgeous nude show girls.

Opening night came round. My first song was a typical Charlot number, light and witty, in the Noël Coward manner, called *Carrie was a Careful Girl*. As I sang, round me swept the show girls, bare bosoms gleaming, long legs teetering on the highest of heels, feathers, spangles, just a breath away from the bumps and grinds of burlesque. As I floated back along the catwalk, a young man leaned over and pinched me where it hurt.

Charlot's Revue of 1926 flopped just as spectacularly in New York as we had succeeded in London. Sophisticated English revue linked with a brassy American girlie show was not what New York expected.

We went on a tour of the major American cities and I learned all about getting the American bird. They threw pennies at us in Detroit. In Pittsburgh they jeered and stamped, and in Philadelphia they opened their newspapers and read while the English actors and actresses performed. I don't blame them, they weren't going to be fobbed off with a fully-clothed Jessie Matthews singing a simple English song when they expected the bosoms and buttocks of the original New York show.

By the time the tour was over we were all so toughened up that there wasn't an audience in the world that could frighten us any more. Before we sailed for home I received a cable from C. B. Cochran, 'Don't do anything until you see me'. At least an English producer was still interested in me.

I felt very confident when I called at Cochran's office in Old Bond Street. He'd sent me a cable, and hadn't he told me that he had great plans for me once my contract with Charlot was over? Cochran sat at his desk smoking a cigar; he lived in a permanent aura of rich cigar smoke.

'What a hell of a flop you've been!' That was his greeting.

It took me a moment to catch my breath. I knew the American tour had been a disaster, but it hadn't been the fault of the company, we'd worked just as hard as we had in London. 'You mean the show flopped, don't you?' I said cautiously. I couldn't believe that the benign, fatherly Mr Cochran was being unkind.

'No, you!'

We stared at each other. This wasn't the welcome I expected when I got his cable.

'From what I hear you weren't worth the £18 a week they paid you.'

'£30,' I said stiffly. 'They paid me £30.' They had too, my increase in salary had been the only nice thing about the American tour.

Cochran raised his eyebrows unbelievingly. 'That's not what I was told.'

'Are you calling me a liar?'

I completely forgot that I was Mrs Henry Lytton Jnr, who didn't raise her voice. I was Jessie Matthews from Soho and ready to fight all the way. 'Don't you dare call me a liar, d'you hear?' I shouted and then I turned on my heel before I said something even worse.

'Where are you off to?'

I shouted the first word that came into my mind, 'Shopping!'

'What with? I hear you're broke.'

'Well you've damn well heard wrong.' Some sixth sense told me to get out of this office at once. Nineteen-year-old actresses don't tell powerful impresarios what they think of them and get away with it. 'Good afternoon,' I yelled and was through the outer office and half way down the stairs before someone came racing after me.

'Miss Matthews! Come back. C.B. was only pulling your leg.'

When I stalked back into his office I was very angry. No one was ever going to speak to me like that again. I'd had to stand it when I was a chorus girl, but not now . . . 'Don't you call me a flop again,' I said menacingly.

Cochran's red face was now as round and smiling as a cherub's. 'Would I offer a contract to a flop? What do you say to £60 a week to start with?'

'I'm not interested.' Oddly enough I wasn't. I hated bargaining about money. And if all that unkindness had been just a prelude to softening me up for an offer, he could keep his £60.

Cochran continued to beam. 'I think you will be when I say that your salary will rise with each show. £100 a week, then £150, and finally £200.'

No actress in her right mind would refuse such an offer. I did wish he hadn't baited me, but the attitude I took then became a pattern for our future relationship. He treated me with respect now and by the time I left his office we were good friends. In my handbag I had a draft contract for four Cochran shows. I had to take it home for Harry's signature as I was still a minor.

I stood at the bus stop in Bond Street suddenly aware that I was going to be very well off indeed. Sixty pounds a week in those days had many times the value it has now. Harry and I could have a little house, perhaps a little car . . . What was I doing here waiting in a bus queue? 'Taxi!' I cried. 'Taxi!'

Chapter Nine

The house came first. A dear little cottage in Warwick Close near Olympia. We furnished it well. The chairs from Maples, the bedroom suite from Heals, a pair of candlesticks from Partridges of Bond Street. I was learning fast. It was easy to have good taste when you had money.

I sometimes questioned the amount of money we were spending. 'What are you worrying about?' demanded Harry, 'you've got a marvellous contract.'

Harry was completely unworried himself and saving for a rainy day just wasn't his way of life. He was almost too easy going, he'd ring Daimler Hire and drive off for a day's golf quite unperturbed that he hadn't a job or one in view. I'd married Harry with the immature hope that at a stroke all my troubles would be over, every problem sorted out by a wise husband. Someone rather like Jorge who had treated me like a little girl and spoiled me, yet listened, advised and gently educated me. Harry wasn't prepared to take on that role, he wasn't so much older than I to begin with. His attitude was: if I was busy rehearsing that was my bad luck, but he was going to enjoy life.

Rehearsals for my first Cochran show, *One Damn Thing after Another*, began on the bare empty stage, in the dust sheeted gloom of the London Pavilion. We sat around the stage in practice clothes: Mimi Crawford, a dainty blonde beauty with breath-taking blue eyes, Douglas Byng and Morris Harvey, the comedy element, and a young man who was to be my dancing partner. His name was Sonnie Hale, he seemed rather shy and had an engaging smile.

Cochran handed us our various parts and introduced us to Richard Rodgers, the composer of the songs, and Lorenz Hart, the lyric writer. He had a special way of dealing with his stars at rehearsal. He laid down no cut and dried plans, no decisions were taken about which star would sing which song, or who would be better in this sketch or funnier in that routine. He tried us all out in turn, gave us our head and let us create what we would in an effort to get the very best from us.

With André Charlot, his players were his works of art, moulded to his direction, but not Cochran. He sat back and watched us use the material in our own different ways.

'There's a very nice song, here,' said Cochran, 'but I'm not sure which one of you should sing it. Shall we hear it first?'

Richard Rodgers went down to the orchestra pit and played the score.

'Jessie, you try it first,' said Cochran.

It was a song that seemed to wind around my heart the first time I sang it. A beautiful melody with simple but memorable words. I didn't know then just how important this song would be to me.

> 'I took one look at you,
> That's all I had to do,
> And then my heart stood still . . .'

'I like it,' said Cochran approvingly, 'but we've got to have a verse. Where's the verse?'

Larry Hart, who was sitting in the stalls with his hat on the back of his head, the inevitable cigar sticking out of his mouth, jumped up and rushed down the aisle and onto the stage. 'You wanna verse? You wanna verse, right?' He pulled an envelope out of his pocket and leaning against the proscenium started to scribble. 'How's this?' He turned to me. 'How do you like this, babe?' He handed me the envelope. 'Think you can read my writing?'

I held the envelope in my hand and read out an amusing little verse about hating boys in my Heathfield schooldays. 'Jolly good,' said Cochran, 'that song's going to suit Jessie.' To my immense joy I was chosen to sing 'My Heart stood still' and Cochran told me to work out some kind of movement and dance that would go with the song.

That was how he was. We were left to work out our own

Cheeri folks love

Jessie

Jessie sings *Limehouse Blues* in the Charlot Revue.
Previous page: Jessie as the innocent country maid, Pittsburgh 1925.

With her first husband, Henry Lytton, in the 1926 Revue. *Photo: Mitchenson and Mander.*

Jessie stars in Noël Coward's *This Year of G* 1928.
Right: Jessie plays a chorus girl in *Friday Thirteenth* 1933.

The Midshipmaid 1932.

Left: Pierrette this time for the film
Good Companions 1932.

There Goes the Bride 1932.

red Hitchcock directed her in *Waltzes from Vienna* 1933.

Again, in J. B. Priestley's *The Good Companions* 1932.

With her *Good Companions* co-star John Gielgud. *Photo: Mitchenson and Mander.*

One of the photographs of the star that fans clamoured for.

Jessie sings *La Seine* in *Sauce Tartare*.

Star chorus girl (second from left) in *Friday the Thirteenth*.

Left: A romantic setting in *There Goes the Bride* 1932, one of her early films.

Dance of a different kind in *It's Love Again*
1936.

It's Love Again—with sparkling costu
sparkling eyes.

Ralph Richardson starred with Jessie in *Friday the Thirteenth*.

dance routines with Buddy Bradley, the very talented American dance director he had brought to England for the show. It all looked easy, it seemed very carefree after Charlot's hand on a tight rein, but it wasn't really. *One Damn Thing after Another* was lovingly created by men of great talent who respected the tender egos of the actors and actresses that would expand and flourish under the right direction. Frank Collins, Cochran's right hand man, was always there in the background, working over the sketches with us, dealing with the cast, the stage hands, never raising his voice, but directing, advising and helping us all with quiet authority.

A week or so later Cochran would come to another rehearsal to see what we were making of our rough material. He would sit in the front row of the dress circle, puffing his cigar. At the end of a number he would call out, 'That's fine, just a little polishing, but don't add anything,' or else, 'It's half a chorus too short, Jessie, and you've got an anti-climax.' He had a magic way of putting his finger on the flaw.

Then he'd come onto the stage. 'I'm very thrilled with you, and thank you very much, children, for a lovely job.' Naturally we all worked hard until his next visit. He was paying us all a lot of money, but leaving us alone to create, and there is nothing more satisfying for an artiste.

After our first stormy interview in his office I had nothing but admiration for him. Of course I'd heard about his reputation, his well-known appreciation of beautiful women. I did notice that his eyes always wandered on to the next pretty girl. I think I am right when I say he was a man who delighted in beauty, but any girl he made into a star needed talent as well as looks.

The hard grind of rehearsals usually had me half dropping with fatigue by the time I got home at night. I'd come home and find the house filled with Harry's friends. Harry, as fresh as a daisy after a day's golf, would be organising a poker party. 'How about some sandwiches, Jessie?'

With bad grace I'd slice the bread and slap in some ham, and next morning we'd have another row. 'You know how tired I am when I get home from the theatre, couldn't you look after your friends yourself?' Those were the good old days when no husband worth his salt would wash up a cup or saucer.

'Oh, very well.' His look of contempt showed his impatience. 'If you're not capable of running a house, we'd better get a maid.'

Then there were nights when I came home and went straight to bed, worn out and exhausted. Harry, bored with no one to talk to, would play his jazz records until the early hours. The wail of the saxophone and the frenzy of the drums would bring me storming into the room, 'For God's sake, Harry . . . I have to sleep . . . I must sleep!' This was my first Cochran show, my testing time, I had to be fresh and alert at rehearsals. 'Turn that awful noise off!' I'd yell and when I got back to bed I was too angry and upset to sleep and the insidious pattern of insomnia began to take hold of me.

We were both young, self-centred and probably hopelessly wrong for each other. We were too immature to try to understand each other's problems and there was seldom enough love left now to kiss and make up.

When at last the first night was over and the press notices told us we had a hit on our hands, the whole company relaxed and we had time to take up our private lives again. Harry and I bought a little bull-nosed Morris two-seater, and we started enjoying the popularity that a certain amount of fame brings. We recorded songs for a gramophone company, had week-ends at Eastbourne and were asked to glamorous parties to meet celebrities.

Harry was offered work and went off on tour with Cora Goffin in *The Girl Friend*, and our uncertain marriage seemed to be settling down. However, when the tour was over, instead of doing what I thought he should, find another job, Harry went back to his old routine of playing golf, going to the races and having poker parties at night. We quarrelled constantly. Harry knew exactly where he could wound me with digs against my humble background but I had my own weapons, and women are rarely kind when they pay the bills.

Settling the household bills, an unpleasant chore at the best of times, took on new dimensions. I found I was paying for flowers I knew nothing about, and there in the chemist's bill was an explosive little item: a bottle of Mitsouku Guerlain perfume!

In the theatre where gossip hangs in the air like cobwebs, someone told me that Harry had a new friend who was dancing in cabaret at a well-known restaurant. Harry was often there, admiring her dancing from a table in the corner. 'What a pity you're working and can't go too,' added my well-wisher with a sweet smile.

I felt I needed advice badly. My mother wouldn't understand. Her philosophy was: 'A man's master in his own house and a woman has to make the best of it.' Rosie would be no help, she'd just tell me I'd been a fool to marry Harry, so I went to see Harry's mother. She was, and always remained, a staunch friend of mine. Torn as she was between love for her son and the desire to comfort me, she counselled 'Be patient, darling. Women have to bear these little affairs. It won't last long.'

'It certainly won't,' I sobbed, 'not when I have to pay for her perfume.'

If I was unhappy at home the friendship and family feeling I found at the theatre helped me forget. In the London Pavilion the principals' dressing-rooms are close together, and we were in and out drinking cups of tea, swopping gossip. Next door to mine, Fred Groves shared his dressing-room with Sonnie Hale. Although we danced and acted together in some of the sketches it had taken some time before Sonnie and I had dropped the formal, 'Good morning, Miss Matthews', 'Hello, Mr Hale', and used first names.

Not only was Sonnie married to a star but his family were big names in the theatre. Robert Hale, his father, was a musical comedy star, his sister Binnie Hale had also reached the heights and then there was his wife. Sonnie was a chorus boy of seventeen when he'd first met the beautiful Evelyn Laye, a musical comedy star. Sonnie and Evelyn's wedding at St James's, Spanish Place, some years before, had been a great event. Women had fainted in the crowd and the newspapers had played up the story of their boy and girl romance. Evelyn, golden-haired with the voice of a lark, was a firm favourite of the British theatregoer, and was then much more famous than Sonnie.

Rumour had it that competing against his brilliant family and talented wife had given Sonnie an inferiority complex, and I decided that this must be true when I saw how dejected he would become if he was criticised. 'Oh, God,' he groaned when the dance director corrected him, 'I'll never get it right.'

'Of course you will,' I declared, surprised at his pessimistic attitude. I'd realised very quickly that Sonnie had outstanding talent. 'Why d'you get so downhearted? You need someone like my sister Rosie to pump confidence into you. She'd have half killed me if I talked like you.'

'Then you were lucky,' he said ruefully. 'I belong to the kind of family where I have to compete. I can't just be good, I've got to be very good, top their performances . . . if I can.'

So the rumours were true, I thought. He needed someone to boost his ego; someone to inject confidence like an infusion into his veins. 'I'll help him,' I told myself, 'I'll give him the old Rosie-type patter when he gets downhearted.'

The beginning was slow, but that was how our friendship started. I tried to help him gain more confidence on the stage, and he, for his part, discovered that I needed more confidence in another area—my lack of formal education.

We were all backstage pouring over the notices of the show in one of the Sunday newspapers. Sonnie read aloud, 'The intelligent comedy of Mr Hale combined with the youthful insouciance of Miss Matthews . . .'

'My youthful what?' I interrupted.

'Insouciance?' Sonnie took off his horn-rimmed glasses and rubbed his eyes. They were light blue with the intense gaze of the myopic. He guessed that I didn't know what it meant. 'Insouciance . . . you could say something like, "Youthful carefreeness". How's that?'

'Thank you,' I said. Not many people bothered to explain the meaning of words to me. In fact no one had troubled since Jorge had gently corrected my failings.

Sonnie, with his horn-rimmed glasses and athletic build, looked a typical young Englishman who worked on the Stock Exchange or in the city, nothing like an actor. He was no Ivor Novello or Jack Buchanan, but I liked the way he looked, and when he was happy and relaxed his personality glowed. Cochran once wrote: 'Sonnie Hale is one of the best revue artists in the world.' I noticed that Sonnie polished his talent with real hard work, he was a 'watcher' as I was. I'd see him in the wings listening to the way another actor delivered his lines or watching the superb steps of the other dancers.

One of the partners I most loved dancing with was Anton Dolin, and our numbers in the Charlot Revue were always well received. But Anton, or as we all called him, 'Pat' Dolin, was a classical dancer, and for the musical comedy routines another style of dancing was needed. Here I found the perfect partner in Sonnie. As soon as I danced with him I knew I could follow his steps effortlessly. Some kind of fusion has to take place if people are to dance well together, and Sonnie and I were absolutely right.

At that time Cochran's shows followed each other at the London Pavilion. While *One Damn Thing* was still running preparations started for our next revue. We met in the Poland Rooms where Cochran always rehearsed. They were depressing, dusty rehearsal rooms with a battered piano, a practice bar and rows of chairs around the distempered walls where everyone flung their belongings.

We sat around, smoking and gossiping, waiting for the creator of Cochran's new show to appear. We all felt slightly apprehensive because even then Noël Coward was obviously something out of the ordinary. He'd been a child actor, written songs for revues, appeared with Charlot and Gertie Lawrence; his play *The Vortex* had been a sensation. At the moment he was acting in *The Second Man*, but somewhere along the line he'd found time to write the book and the songs for Cochran's new show. And he was only twenty-eight years old!

He walked in, tall and elegantly dressed and immediately he terrified me. He was so obviously everything I was not. Highly sophisticated, articulate and completely sure of himself. His voice was upper class to a degree, and unconsciously, when I answered his questions, my own voice took on an artificially refined accent. Rosie's elocution lessons had always leaned a little to refinement, and in my anxiety to iron out the cockney vowels, my accent was often unsure.

'Jessie!' Noël halted the rendering of a song I was trying out. 'Let's have that line again.' It was a lovely song called *A Room With a View*, and it was to be a duet with Sonnie Hale.

'High above the mountains and sea . . .' I trilled.

'*Mountaynes!*' Noël mimicked my ladylike pronunciation, 'Mountaynes? How d'you spell that word?'

Scarlet with embarrassment at being shown up in front of the whole company, I stumbled, 'M . . . o . . . u . . .'

'Mountains!' Noël's voice was clipped and curt. 'For God's sake, darling, stop singing *mountaynes*.'

It was never cosy working under Noël's supervision, but it was a wonderful experience. I knew this man was absolutely right in everything he decided. He was a hard taskmaster, he didn't give a damn about anyone's feelings, but the touch of genius was there in everything he did. *This Year of Grace*, as the new production was to be called, was exciting and new with wonderful songs and marvellous sketches. At the end of the first meeting the excitement had spread to each one of us.

Tension built up tremendously as the days went by. Cochran had brought over a beautiful Viennese dancer called Tilly Losch and we shared a dressing-room. Tilly was exotic, extremely feminine and rather touchy. I walked in one day wearing a new tweed suit of which I was inordinately proud. Lo and behold there sat Tilly wearing exactly the same one. 'Snap!' I cried gaily, rather pleased that my own taste equalled that of the continental star. Tilly stared, froze, then suddenly showed her displeasure. 'How dare you wear my suit,' she cried and promptly smacked my face.

We called each other names, we wept, and finally we dried our tears and forgave each other—until the next time.

After the three week try-out in Manchester *This Year of Grace* opened at the London Pavilion in March 1928. The atmosphere leading up to that first night was very different from the previous show *One Damn Thing*. Perhaps the electric current that Noël seemed to generate kept us on tenterhooks. I knew that I *had* to be good. I had much more to do in this show; it was going to be a proving time to see if I had real star quality. I worried constantly that I might not do justice to the superb material Noël had given me.

A Cochran first night was always a great occasion. All the big names of London society were there, all the celebrities. Silk hats and tails, furs and diamonds filled the auditorium and the atmosphere was charged with excitement. Sick with nerves, my insides feeling that they were about to drop out, I waited in the wings to step out onto the stage for my first number.

Cochran came up behind me, 'It all depends on how you put over this first number, darling,' he whispered.

He couldn't have picked a worse moment. The curtain rose, I stood there in a demure white georgette dress, a picture hat hanging from my wrist with cherry ribbons, and I was shaking so much that the prop book in my hands quivered as if it was a blancmange. The orchestra struck up, I stared out at the great black void, the monster that would devour me if I made a mistake, and my throat dried up completely.

The orchestra leader could see what was happening, he tried again. I opened my mouth. A tiny squeak came out, 'Mary . . .' I made a tremendous effort and the words of *Mary, Mary Makebelieve* began to squeeze past my larynx. God knows where the words came from, but I got through the verse and the chorus. I could hear the girls coming on behind me, the theme of the number was that the chorus girls seduce me away from my ballet movements with their rhythmic dancing. The cue for my dance came . . . I couldn't stop trembling, my arms shook, my legs shook . . . ready . . . now! I raised my right leg for the high sweeping kick I had made my own . . . Oh God! It collapsed under me. Down I went on my bottom.

The gasp from the audience had Noël Coward diving down in the box he shared with Cochran, his hands over his face.

'Is she up yet? Dear God, is she up yet?' Noël saw his wonderful show in tatters as I was wheeled off with a broken ankle.

But the sudden contact with hard solid wood knocked the nerves right out of me. My head cleared. I was up on my feet and dancing, smiling. That was the first and last mistake I made in a night filled with glory.

When the thunderous applause died down and the stalls emptied, the champagne flowed in the dressing-rooms. High society came backstage and kissed and hugged us. Cochran was ecstatic. There were cheering crowds at the stage door as each limousine drove away. My arms were filled with flowers as I stepped into my hire car and drove home.

Home for me now was a hotel in Bayswater, and when I switched on the light and walked into the empty room, it was hard to realise that just an hour ago I was delighting hundreds of people and their applause rang in my ears. Their warmth and love had enveloped me, but now I was alone and there was no one to welcome me home.

My marriage had broken down completely. Harry and I were living apart. After the last devastating row Harry had agreed to leave Warwick Close. He had packed his bags one Sunday morning and driven off in a taxi. Two hours later he was back, someone had advised him to return.

'Let's try again,' he said.

We talked endlessly all that day and half the night. In the morning I telephoned Harry's father and asked him to come round. Harry still refused to leave, so we decided that it was best that I should go. I paid the maid a month's salary, left a cheque for the rent of the house, and then Harry's father carried my bags to a waiting taxi.

We embraced each other. 'I'm sorry it had to end this way, darling,' he said. I was sorry too. I loved all the Lytton family except the one I was married to. I knew there would be no hard feelings from them, just sadness that two headstrong young people had parted.

I was twenty-one years old, young enough to be resilient but old enough to be deeply hurt. My own family did not take our parting with the understanding of the Lyttons. They were very angry with Harry. Some time later my father was given a couple of tickets for a show at the Metropolitan Theatre, Edgware Road. They had no idea who was in the variety show until they opened the programme. When they found out my mother wanted to leave.

At one point in the show Harry had to walk down the stairs from the stage into the main aisle. He recognised my mother and father sitting in the second row. 'Why, hello Mrs Matthews,' he said breezily.

My mother glared at him, 'Go away, Harry,' she said, 'I don't want to know you.' Then she held on to my father's jacket, for he wanted to get up and do battle there in the stalls. Harry cut short his act and returned to the stage.

Chapter Ten

Life was much more peaceful now that I lived in a hotel, and I was able to spend more time with my family. I'd finally persuaded my parents to leave Berwick Market and I'd installed them in a little house in Springfield Road, St John's Wood.

My father had grown easier to live with, but his strange sense of humour could still send shivers down my back. Sometimes he'd wait for me outside the stage door, deliberately wearing his shabby old market clothes. Making sure he had the riveted attention of the gallery girls, he'd swing open my taxi door, doff his battered trilby and cry, 'Make way for her Ladyship. Going my way, Miss?'

'Get in, Dad,' I'd hiss. One fine night, I decided, I'd hand him a tip, and tell the taxi driver to move off sharply.

He still hankered after the market and was really upset when William and Mary was pulled down and a Lex Garage built on the site. Jenny the horse had gone to end her days on a farm in the country. No longer could he hear her snorting into her nose-bag and sending up a shower of husks. Now he had a real back garden where he could keep his chickens and Rival, the dog, could bury his bones among the petunias. Every time I went round to see them, I'd hear Dolly, the parrot, croaking and swearing in her cage in the parlour and Dad's voice in the scullery groaning, 'Gawd! Is that Jessie? Where the bloody hell did I put my teeth?'

The little house seemed always full of children. The three young ones, Eddie, Ray and Harry, were still at school, and Eve, just out of her gym slip, was dancing with Terry's

Juveniles. Eve was the only one of us who never felt the lash of my father's temper. He adored her. She had grown from a pretty child into a beautiful young girl and in his eyes she could do no wrong.

Lena, the sister below me, was still the one who stayed at home and helped in the house although, to my father's dismay, a young man from Yorkshire, called Leslie, had begun to court Lena. He had my father well taped. 'He wants you round at his beck and call,' he told Lena, 'and he'll do his damnedest to stop me marrying you.'

All the older ones were married now. George and Billy lived with their wives in Soho. Dad had given Jenny away at the altar and told her nervous husband-to-be, 'You're getting a beautiful girl, but, by Christ, she's got a bloody awful temper!'

Only my mother remained unchanged, sweet and gentle and full of warmth. I knew she kept a special place in her heart for me and I was glad that my success had, at least, made her life a little easier.

This Year of Grace was proving a great success. The critics declared that Noël Coward was the most brilliant man of the theatre that England had ever known, and that the whole company was sublime. I'd made a close friend of an understudy. Marjorie Robertson was a very pretty talented girl who, as one of Cochran's Young Ladies, had started her career by doing a sword dance at the Trocadero. Marjorie stood out among the other Young Ladies—her eyes were just that bit more expressive, the way she danced had more verve. I was sure Cochran would pick her out sooner or later and her days in the chorus would be over.

One of Cochran's other Young Ladies had graduated from the chorus of *One Damn Thing* to parts in *This Year of Grace*. Sheilah Graham was a lovely blonde, her looks were really outstanding. At rehearsal one morning, before the show opened, Sheilah was told that Cochran had decided to give her a dance number. Naturally she was delighted. At the end of the dance her partner was told to lift her on his shoulders and spin her round. We all watched as the beauteous Sheilah was lifted in the air. He lifted her higher. She was on his shoulder. The spin began. Sheilah let out a little shriek. Round they whirled. Sheilah began to yell with fright and as she flew through the air she literally screamed the place down.

94

I knew exactly how she felt. I'd never liked high lifts very much. The hard wooden stage is an unkind place to break your fall, and it looks a long way down when you're being twirled on someone's shoulder. My years of training and dancing experience had taught me how to cope, but for Sheilah, whose ballet training had been minimal, and who through sheer nerve and guts had done in months what had taken other girls years to achieve, it must have been terrifying.

I remember thinking what a pity it was that Sheilah should lose this dance because she couldn't stand heights. She was a vision of loveliness and had great promise, but at the end of *This Year of Grace* she became ill and gave up the stage. Not that it stopped her rise to fame. She went off to America and started writing show business columns in New York and then Hollywood, and later she became the author of best-selling books.

Harry and I had not spoken to each other since the day I walked out of Warwick Close, and our only contact was through our solicitors. I had foolishly imagined that marriage would be like a magic wand with which I could open locked doors. That being a married woman would somehow make me into a different person. I had since discovered that only I had the key to locked doors and I was the only one who could change my life. Now that our marriage was over I wanted our parting to be legally settled, but although my solicitors had told Harry that I wanted a divorce, so far he had refused to consider it.

One afternoon someone told me that Harry was sitting in the front row of the stalls, and sure enough when I went on next time I recognised him. When the matinee was over I guessed that he might come backstage, and I waited apprehensively while Tilly changed and finally departed. Someone tapped on the dressing-room door. I called, 'Come in!'

Harry stood there, his own special smile, half enquiring, half arrogant, on his good-looking face. Again the thought flashed through my mind just as it had when I first met him, 'What perfect type-casting for a sophisticated man-about-town.' He was dressed immaculately, as always. Blue pin-stripe suit, silk shirt from his Jermyn Street shirtmakers with just the correct show of snowy white cuff, a corner of crimson silk handkerchief at his breast pocket, black shoes polished to mirror finish. He did what he always did when he wasn't quite sure what to say, he smoothed back his well-brushed brown hair with the palm of his hand and fiddled with his tie. He hesitated for a moment and said, 'Your solicitors tell me you want a divorce, Jessie?'

I nodded without speaking.

He sat down and crossed his legs. 'All right,' he said evenly. 'You can have one.'

This was so unexpected that I gasped with surprise. My solicitors had assured me that Harry would not give me grounds for divorce and I should hire a private detective to seek out the evidence. So far I had recoiled from doing that. 'So you've changed your mind,' I blurted out.

He reddened slightly and I wondered what was coming next. 'I have a proposition.'

I knew I shouldn't like his proposition when I heard it, and I didn't. A slow burn of anger started inside me when I heard how much it was going to cost. 'Go away, Harry,' I said stiffly. 'Go away.' And then the rage bubbled out. I called him names, I picked up the nearest missile at hand, a large box of face powder. But the door banged shut as the box of powder split against the wood in a peach-coloured cloud.

It took me about half an hour to clear up the mess. I knew I had behaved just as he often said I did, like a brat from Soho, but I was glad.

Even today, suing for a divorce makes you feel apart from the rest of the world, seems to be a mark of failure. But forty years ago when the moral attitude was very strict, people just didn't get divorced. It was scandalous, it might be splashed across the newspapers, gloated over at the breakfast tables. Divorce was a nasty business that nice people didn't get involved in.

My family with their strict moral and sexual code didn't approve at all. They didn't like Harry as a husband but they feared divorce even more. Only at the theatre did I feel a complete lack of criticism. Everyone went out of their way to be sympathetic. Theatre is more of a life-style than a job. This is partly due to the hours of work. There has to be total involvement with a job that demands possibly all-day rehearsals and then evening performances. People who are thrown together so much turn to each other for comfort, and a relationship that in the outside world would take time to develop, hastens in this hothouse atmosphere.

Sonnie Hale, who shared the dressing-room next to mine with Fred Groves, was particularly kind. One Saturday afternoon he and Fred took me to watch a rugger match. Prompted by Sonnie I yelled myself hoarse, and later when we drove back to London, red-cheeked and our lungs full of clean Surrey air, I knew I hadn't felt so carefree for months.

Then I had a chance meeting with a girl I had known years ago when I danced with Terry's Juveniles. Her name was Daphne Brayne and she lived with her family in a lovely house in St John's Wood. When Daphne's mother, Lizzie Brayne, discovered that I was living in a hotel she invited me to come and stay with them as a paying guest. It was an ideal arrangement. Daphne, who was younger than me, was like a kid sister, and with the outrageous energy of the young, we used to get up at six and have a run round Regent's Park to keep fit and slender.

Sonnie suggested that now I lived in North London I should buy a car to drive to the theatre and he would teach me how to drive. The empty streets of London were then a paradise for a learner-driver—no tests, no provisional licence, just get in behind the steering wheel and away.

Sonnie was a natural teacher, although not always of driving. He loved to talk and impart knowledge and often his mind would wander from the driving instruction to other fields. I crashed the gears and clung desperately to the wheel while Sonnie pointed out the site of one of the plague pits of London, or admired the façade of a Regency terrace.

'Ooh!' I'd shriek. 'There's a man on a bicycle in the way. The one with the funny hat.'

'That funny hat,' said Sonnie, 'is a Balaclava helmet. Now do you know why it is called a Balaclava helmet?'

I didn't need to reply for I knew that Sonnie would tell me.

'During the Crimean War there was a battle at Balaclava. You've heard of the Charge of the Light Brigade, haven't you?'

I was very impressed by the stream of knowledge that poured unchecked from Sonnie's lips. His command of English fascinated me. Any subject, any question and Sonnie had an answer. He was an introvert with an extrovert inside clamouring to get out. I listened spellbound, my eyes shining with admiration, and nothing could have pleased Sonnie more. He had been to a Catholic Public School, Beaumont College, and although he was a lapsed Catholic, he had within him the strong ties of his childhood faith. He was devoted to his family and charmed me with tales of his father, his Irish mother, and his brilliant sister, Binnie.

Sonnie would forget where we were going, and I didn't know how to get there anyway, so we ended up in some queer places. I turned off the Finchley Road, drove down through Swiss Cottage, turned right again and drove us into the middle of a churchyard. We sat among the tombstones and roared with laughter. My life had suddenly become sunny again, all my tensions and personal problems dissolved in laughter.

When I told Sonnie about my first love affair, he even turned that into a joke. 'So his name was Jorge. Tell me about Jorge.'

'He was my great love,' I declared soulfully.

Sonnie put his trilby hat on sideways, affected a terrible South American accent and proceeded to take the mickey out of Jorge. I had to laugh even though I felt slightly disloyal to Jorge. But Sonnie was such fun to be with. Our evening performances together were a riot. It was only when the curtain came down and I'd get into my little car to drive home that I'd remind myself that Sonnie had a wife he was going home to.

I suppose everyone in the theatre could see what was happening to us. But for some strange reason Sonnie and I didn't recognise the reason we found such joy in being together. Until one evening. The curtain rose as usual on a beautiful scene. The set showed the whitewashed walls of a country cottage. Wistaria climbed up the walls. Through the wide open windows could be glimpsed the interior with pictures on the wall. I sat on the window ledge, the full skirts of my rose-patterned ninon dress arranged to drape over the edge, Sonnie sat on the window seat a little below me. We held hands. The epitome of two young establishment lovers. The orchestra played, the music swelled and I sang:

'A room with a view and you, and no one to worry us, no
    one to hurry us,
  Through this dream we've found. We'll gaze at the sky
    and try

98

To guess what it's all about, then we will figure out,
Why the world is round.
We'll be so happy and contented as birds upon a tree,
  high above the mountains and sea,
We'll bill and we'll coo, ooh ooh, and sorrow will
  never come,
Oh, will it ever come true, a room with a view.'

We sang it together and on this special night every word
we sang had a meaning for us. At the end of our song, Sonnie
whispered, 'Let's make it come true.'

I caught my breath. We looked into each other's eyes, and
we were lost.

Who was to blame? Is there ever any blame in these things?
Could we blame Noël Coward for writing his sweet song that
we had made our own? For I defy any young couple to sing
that song together every night without a strong bond growing
between them.

But now we knew what had happened to us and, after the
first rapture of knowledge, to go any further would be to court
disaster. Sonnie was married, and it wasn't just an ordinary
marriage. It was blessed by two theatrical families and applauded by hosts of adoring fans. Evelyn was loved as few
actresses are loved. To even think of harming such a marriage
was impossible.

Sonnie made me agree to have lunch with him next day.
We must talk it out, he said. We went to the Moulin d'Or, a
restaurant always filled with people from the theatre. We sat
at a corner table and Sonnie, as had become his habit, did all
the talking. I had to marvel at the change that had come over
this once shy young man. I was his sounding board, his shadow,
his Galatea, and he couldn't let me go.

I tried half-heartedly to change the subject, I said how
delicious the lemon soufflé was that we were eating.

'Can you cook?'

'Not very well,' I answered.

'I'll teach you.'

I knew this was the time to say No! We must stop now
before we hurt anyone. 'No, Sonnie, it's no good.'

'Yes, it is.' He grabbed the edge of the table and clung to it
as if it were a life-raft. 'It could be wonderful, a new life

together.' Suddenly and for the very first time, he began to talk about his marriage, a marriage where he came second. It wasn't Evelyn's fault and perhaps it wasn't his. But he was young, just twenty-seven. Was it so wrong to want an ordinary life with a wife and children and a house . . . 'In the country, Jessie. . . . I'll teach you all about the country.'

'No, Sonnie.' My eyes were filled with tears.

'I'll move into my club. I'll tell Evelyn this evening.'

'No, Sonnie, no.' Oh, how I wanted to say yes. I wanted to snatch this happiness and let my love for this man grow. And Sonnie was a man, one of the first I'd met who really deserved the title, but I'd endured the misery of a marriage with an unfaithful husband, how could I wish this unhappiness on another woman? How could I break up another woman's marriage?

We sat and looked at each other. I know we both wanted to cry. But grown-up people don't cry because they have fallen in love and must part. The soufflé remained uneaten, the coffee grew cold and we decided bleakly that from now on we must be strangers to each other. We would act together, sing together, dance together but when we walked off the stage we would not speak another word to each other.

We kept our word. We were both completely miserable, we did our jobs as well as we could, and every night I walked off the stage, sat in my dressing-room and listened to his voice through the thin dressing-room wall. I knew everything he did, the times he played golf with Fred Groves, the restaurants where he would eat. Sometimes I wondered if his voice was deliberately loud so that I would hear. But he never mentioned my name.

The telephone rang at the Brayne's home. It was for me. I said 'Hello' and immediately felt icy tremors down my spine. It was Evelyn, Sonnie's wife.

'Is Sonnie there?' she asked abruptly, then without waiting for an answer, she said, 'Please ask him to come home.'

The shock of hearing Evelyn's voice, the realisation of what was behind her telephone call made me tremble. Although we had always been friendly and Evelyn's nature was sweet and kind, I hadn't spoken to her for a long time. 'Sonnie isn't here,' I told her as calmly as I could. 'Sonnie doesn't tell me what he's doing for we don't speak to each other.' There was silence for a moment. 'Evelyn,' I said, 'my dressing-room is next to his and I heard him tell Fred Groves about golf. Why don't you ring him at his club?'

An hour later Evelyn telephoned again. She was sorry she had bothered me. She had found Sonnie at his club.

As I walked off the stage that night after my first number with Sonnie, he caught my arm roughly. 'We're not children,' he said angrily. 'I've had enough of this. Evelyn told me that she telephoned you. For God's sake let's at least talk to each other.'

The fact that Evelyn knew made it worse. We felt that everyone was watching us, perhaps laying bets on how it would all come out. The next few months were a torment of trying to break off our association, failing, and then renewing promises to end it. To dance with a man who whispers, 'Please see me tomorrow', who sings his songs of love with such intensity that they must be believed. The temptation to pull off my mask of control, to savour these love scenes, to enjoy for a short time what couldn't be, was overwhelming.

Cochran was a good friend of Evelyn Laye's. He'd worked with her father, known her since she was a child, but man of the world that he was, he kept his opinions to himself, and went ahead with plans for the next Cochran show.

After the huge success of *This Year of Grace*, Sonnie and I were to be given even more work together in the new show *Wake Up and Dream*. Cochran asked us to go with him to visit the composer of the music. Cole Porter had come over from America and was living at the Savoy Hotel. I saw a dark, nervous little man who looked at me with large doleful protruding eyes.

'I don't know whether you'll like what I've written,' he said and rubbed his small sensitive hands together nervously.

It was an unforgettable experience to hear him play and sing *What is This Thing Called Love?* a number he had written for the show, but what stands out in my memory was the humility and nervousness of this American genius. I don't think any girl has ever been so well served by gifted composers as I was with my first three Cochran shows. Rodgers and Hart for *One Damn Thing*, Noël Coward for *This Year of Grace*, and now Cole Porter. Their wonderful music is as lyrical and lively today as it was all those years ago, and I know they were great stepping stones in my career.

The strain and exhaustion of rehearsing *Wake Up and Dream* by day and performing in *This Year of Grace* by night made us all edgy, and Sonnie and I, emotionally involved as we were, were nearly at the end of our tether. He had tried a trial separation from Evelyn, now they were back together again for an uneasy truce, now he wanted to leave again.

'We can't go on like this, Sonnie,' I told him. 'It's unfair to all of us. I shall tell Cochran that he must find someone else for this show. I can't cope with my life or my career any more. We must say goodbye Sonnie.'

That night, in an attempt to seal my decision, I went out for the first time for supper at the Kit Kat nightclub after the show. Mr and Mrs Brayne and a friend of theirs came with me. Sonnie must have followed our taxi, for when we took our seats at our table, there was Sonnie sitting above us in the balcony. He sat alone and with baleful eyes watched our every move. He even leant over the balcony in an effort to hear what we said. No midnight supper has ever been shrouded in such gloom and tension.

At 3 am when the Brayne household had turned out the lights and gone to bed, the telephone shrilled on the upstairs landing. Sonnie announced, in a composed matter-of-fact voice, that he had decided to kill himself. He sounded quite sober, Sonnie rarely drank. At first I laughed nervously and told him not to be a fool, but his calm voice repeated his decision. A fear began to grow that Sonnie meant just what he said.

'Don't do anything,' I begged. 'We'll talk in the morning.'

'If we talk it must be now,' he said. 'Tomorrow will be too late.'

In the end I agreed to see him. At that time he was living in a flat in Notting Hill Gate; he said he'd wait for me at Queensway tube station. I dressed, found a taxi and sat on the edge of the seat in an agony of doubt as the cab sped through the empty streets.

Sonnie was leaning dejectedly against the clock outside Queensway tube station. He came over, got in, and the taxi driver, no doubt thinking I had come to collect an erring husband, did a U-turn and started back towards Marble Arch. Sonnie began to talk in a flat monotone. He repeated that he would rather be dead than go on like this.

Keeping my voice down, hoping the taxi driver couldn't hear, I tried to make him change his mind. I echoed the arguments we were always repeating, we couldn't hurt Evelyn, we couldn't face the terrible scandal, we must say goodbye. Back and forth the conversation moved. We opened old wounds, we dragged out tattered philosophies, I even brought in his religion.

We were back in St John's Wood, a street light shone on Sonnie's tormented face. He banged on the dividing glass and told the taxi-man to keep driving. Exhaustion made my voice unsteady. 'Go home, Sonnie,' I pleaded. 'Get some sleep, tomorrow will be different.'

Suddenly Sonnie buried his face in his hands. 'Oh God, I feel so ill.'

For the first time, I realised that Sonnie, abstemious Sonnie who never drank more than two beers and a glass of sherry, was drunk, extremely drunk. The taxi trundled on through the darkness. Where were we? I pulled down a window and heard the shriek of a peacock. We must be in Regent's Park. I asked the long-suffering driver to stop.

Thank goodness the canal was near and Sonnie reached it in time. He was quickly and violently ill in the murky canal waters. Then he sank down panting on the wet grass. I knelt beside him and cleaned him up as best I could, dabbing eau-de-Cologne from a little handbag bottle onto his forehead. He was weeping now. Whether they were tears of woe or tears of alcohol, I didn't know, but my heart was torn to see his distress.

My arms went round him, he wept on my shoulder. To see Sonnie, whom I admired so much, break down like this touched me as nothing else could. All my good resolutions ebbed away, all my defences crumbled. On that damp canal bank we were close then as we had never been before. I told him that I would never leave him, we made sad tearful promises to each other, and I knew that whatever came next, whatever misery would follow, there was no turning back.

Chapter Eleven

From the Daily Mail, London, 22 November 1929:

> 'Miss Jessie Matthews' divorce suit.
> Discretion in her favour.
> Sonnie Hale named.'

The Daily Mail recorded that in the Divorce Division I was granted a divorce from Mr Lord Alva Lytton on the grounds of his adultery.

This was the first divorce. A second, more sensational, the Evelyn Laye versus Sonnie Hale petition was to follow.

The hunt was on, the hounds were after me, and the whole British public was going to be in at the kill. 'I wonder,' wrote one gossip columnist, mentioning no names of course, 'what makes a man leave a classical blonde beauty for a dark-eyed dancer?' The dark-eyed dancer had her own ideas on the subject but she wasn't telling. All the newspapers were read, all the sympathies decided, and very few were for Jessie Matthews. A scandal like this helped people forget there was a depression round the corner, and if someone got hurt, well it sold newspapers.

Even in New York, where I went with *Wake Up and Dream* there were banner headlines:

TWO WIVES ON BROADWAY
Two British actresses, Evelyn Laye and Jessie Matthews, whose domestic affairs have clashed in a drama of the divorce courts have now made Broadway, New York,

where they are playing to different audiences in rival revues, a stage on which they are unconsciously taking the leading roles in a drama of popularity with all intrigued America as an audience.

Evelyn was having a great success in *Bitter Sweet*. I don't know how she liked the publicity but I hated it, and I wondered just how much more I could take until the petition came up the following summer.

Even Cochran was beginning to worry about the adverse publicity. When the time came for *Wake Up and Dream* to go on an American tour, he took me aside. 'I want you to go to America without Sonnie.' He saw my look of dismay. 'It's better this way, darling, keep your names out of the newspapers for a few months.'

Sonnie and I were bitterly disappointed. We loved the show and Cole Porter's music was magic. *Let's do it* was our great favourite. 'Six months, how can I bear it?' I wept.

'Well, it will confirm that we're meant for each other *if* we can stand six months apart,' said Sonnie reasonably.

His words crept into my mind. If . . . if . . . if? How could he question our love? Didn't he mind our parting, as I did? Every time I felt low, his words dripped their unreasoning poison into my thoughts. Did he intend to desert me just as my first lover had done?

Jack Buchanan took on Sonnie's role but, talented as he was, the material of *Wake Up and Dream* had been tailormade for Sonnie and Jack's personality was very different. Sonnie was a hard one to follow. Noël Coward had discovered that when he went to New York with *This Year of Grace*. He wrote in his autobiography that he realised he wasn't half as effective as Sonnie had been.

From the very beginning I knew that these six months were going to drag, and I could never hope to recapture the same quality of the London show. The first night in New York I blotted my copybook in the most terrible way.

Lizzie Brayne had come over to New York with me. She was thrilled and excited and utterly at sea with life backstage, but she was determined to learn and help me all she could. In London a call boy always alerts a performer when an entrance is near but in New York there was no such warning. Lizzie, full of enthusiasm, said she'd act as my call boy. My first call was as soon as the overture started playing when I had to get into a trap under the stage to emerge through an opening made in a prop box.

Nervous and tense as always on opening nights, I had hardly listened when Cochran came round to my dressing-room and said how pleased he was with me, how hard I'd worked and what a great success I was going to be. After he'd gone, I sat there clutching my arms and waiting for Lizzie to burst in with the call. From far off I heard the thin strains of music. My God! Was that the overture? Where was Lizzie? I flung open the door and realised the overture was nearly over. Like a wild creature I flew down the stairs, found the trap empty, the stage hands had already sent it up to the stage. There was nothing to do but climb up the rigging to the stage. Sweating, dirty and dishevelled, I clambered through the prop box. The orchestra leader's face was a sight to behold. Down came his baton again and my song started. The audience reaction was decidedly cool. But that was nothing to what Cochran yelled at me when I came off stage.

'I take back everything,' he screamed, his face purple with rage. 'You've ruined the show. I take back every bloody word I said to you.'

My mouth opened, a long piercing wail came out.

Cochran, always the Showman first, controlled himself. 'That's all right, baby. Everyone makes mistakes. Just make sure the rest of the show is great.'

It was. The press gave us wonderful notices. Lizzie abdicated from her job as call boy. She said her nerves would never stand stage life. But she was always a wonderful friend and companion and helped the long six months pass more easily.

In an odd way, the emotional vacuum I was in helped to give my understudy her first big break. One day, after rehearsal, I saw Marjorie Robertson sitting by herself looking very miserable. 'What's wrong, love?'

To my surprise tears came to her eyes for Marjorie had always impressed me as a girl with great control. 'I'm so depressed,' she said unhappily. 'I try. I try. I work so hard and it gets me nowhere. I'm going to give up the stage. When I go home to England I'm going to take another kind of job, anywhere, typist, salesgirl, anything. I haven't the heart to go on any longer.'

I sat down beside her on the stage. 'Oh, don't give up, Marjorie. You've got so much talent. It would be a terrible pity.'

She dabbed her eyes with a hankie. 'I'll be old and grey before anyone notices me.'

'How old are you?'

'Twenty-four.'

'Give it another year. Iᵢ you haven't had a break by the time you're twenty-five, all right, give up the stage.'

We talked it over solemnly. Marjorie would try for another year. Neither of us knew that the big break was waiting just round the corner, and the one who would enable it to happen was sitting right beside her.

Jack Buchanan and I had our differences. In my eyes no one came near to Sonnie as a dancing partner and no doubt I didn't try to hide the fact too hard. We accepted an offer to do a suppertime cabaret act together. Every night we sang *Fancy our Meeting* with sweetness in our voices and something like murder in our hearts. The evening came when Jack saw a friend at a nearby table and sauntered off to have a word—in the middle of our act.

Jack could find someone else to sing for his supper with, I stormed. Marjorie was asked to do the cabaret act in my place. From then on she never looked back. She changed her name to Anna Neagle, she appeared in *Stand Up and Sing* with Jack Buchanan and soon she was the great star she deserved to be. There is no nicer person in the profession than Anna Neagle, no one who is more loved by all her fellow actors and actresses.

In this year of grace, 1974, not an eyebrow would be raised at the Evelyn Laye–Sonnie Hale divorce case. But in 1930, it hit all the headlines. It was one of the first show business marriages to end in a show business type divorce. Even the Judge showed what a bit of drama can do for the Law Courts. He spared neither Sonnie or myself. We were the villains of the piece.

'Jessie Matthews collapses and is assisted from the court,' blazoned the newspapers. Had we been criminals I don't think the Judge could have done a better job. And we were just two young people who had fallen in love.

That day in court marked me. It was an emotional blow

from which it was hard to recover. Why, I asked myself, can't both sides of the case be told? What have I done that makes a man say such hateful things? For days I sat at home and wept, quite sure that I was the most hated woman in England. I had done the unforgivable, taken the husband of the golden girl of song.

For a long time the newspapers dramatised the so-called feud between Evelyn Laye and myself. It wasn't like that. There was no feud. Although I must admit that our first face-to-face confrontation might have been dreamt up by a film script writer.

It happened some time later when I was making headway in films. Victor Saville had taken my career under his wing and I had the lead part, Susie Dean, in *The Good Companions*. Gaumont British asked me how I'd feel if Evelyn Laye made a film on the same studio floor. I didn't mind, although I didn't find it very amusing when some joker put Evelyn's dressing-room next to mine.

I knew perfectly well that this was the hot item of news in the studio. However, I was too worried about my own work to bother overmuch. John Gielgud was playing opposite me and I had to work very hard to make an impact against such a consummate artist.

Late one evening we filmed a very dramatic fire and riot scene when Edmund Gwenn, as Jess Oakroyd, was about to be burned to death. The strong emotional scene and dialogue had to be filmed next morning and fitted against this background. I'd sweated over that scene in rehearsal. I knew it had to be good, and I prayed I could deliver some good acting.

I came to the studio early next morning and rehearsed my lines, geared myself into the right emotional mood and at 9 am stepped out of my dressing-room to face the cameras. As soon as I opened the door I realised that something very strange was about to happen. Groups of extras were lurking around, the camera crew stood in one corner. The atmosphere was heavy with anticipation, and every eye was turned my way.

There outside my door, just a few paces away, stood Evelyn.

Who would speak first? Or would either of them speak at all? The deathly quiet, unusual in any film studio, and the still watchfulness of the people around us, were horrible. I was thrown into a turmoil of nerves and I'm sure Evelyn was too.

We both knew that every look, gesture and syllable would be chewed over by the onlookers.

Evelyn broke the silence. 'Hello, Jessie,' she said sweetly. 'Lovely to see you.'

We stood and chatted for a few minutes. I can't for the life of me remember a word we said but our performances were immaculate.

Victor Saville had no difficulty with his dramatic scene that morning. Pent-up emotions that had been repressed for years poured out. The trauma of meeting Evelyn for the first time since those unhappy days unlocked emotional powers that surprised even Victor. The scene I played before the cameras was valid in every way, the key to the emotional storm that ripped through me had unwittingly been handed to me by Evelyn.

Evelyn had found married happiness too. In March 1931, soon after Sonnie and I married, a newspaper printed a rumour that Evelyn Laye was engaged to Frank Lawton, the young actor who had scored such a hit in *Young Woodley* in 1928. This was hurriedly denied by Evelyn's mother, but they did marry later and Evelyn has stated that Frank was her first real love and that theirs was the happiest of marriages.

So the Laye–Hale divorce had all been a storm in a teacup. And yet the scars remain to this day.

Cochran had a new show lined up, the fourth in my contract with him. I was ready to begin work. Sonnie was ready to begin work. Only one thing was in our way—the climate of public opinion. Adverse publicity was making Cochran have second thoughts.

In his book, *The Cochran Story*, Charles Graves wrote: 'For the part of the leading lady, Cochran chose Jessie Matthews. This was a very bold move. Evelyn Laye had just divorced Sonnie Hale, citing Jessie Matthews. And the judge had been by no means friendly in his comments on Miss Matthews. All of which duly appeared in print. Evelyn Laye was much more popular with the groundlings than Jessie Matthews, and there was a considerable amount of feeling at the opening night.'

There was more to it than that. 'The bold move' Cochran made required more than a little pressure from me.

Cochran invited Sonnie and I down to his country house to hear the music of the proposed new show *Ever Green*. He had commissioned Richard Rodgers and Lorenz Hart to write the music and lyrics. Cochran was like that. He wanted the best musicians in the world and the most beautiful songs ever written.

As soon as we crossed the threshold and I saw the other weekend guest, and watched the fuss being made over her, my female hackles rose. Our fellow guest was Ada May, blonde, vivacious and American, who had appeared with Leslie Henson in *Follow Through*. This weekend, I told myself, was going to be interesting.

After lunch on Sunday, Cochran suggested that he show me his roses. I admired the rambling Dorothy Perkins and the garlands of Albertine, I sniffed the sweet fragrance of a damask rose, then Cochran led me purposefully to a secluded garden seat.

'It's all this unpleasant publicity, baby. Don't you think it might be better if Sonnie did the show without you?'

'*Without me*!' My voice rose and the petals from a hybrid tea sailed gracefully through the air.

Cochran attempted to soften the blow. 'Oh . . . I see . . . I suppose we could do it without Sonnie.'

'Darling! What are you trying to do? Separate us?' It was really an unnecessary question. He wanted me out of the show and Ada May in.

Cochran hedged. 'It's your career, darling. Just give the dust time to settle.'

'Sonnie and I have been through hell together.' I laid my hand on his arm. 'Please don't part us now. I wouldn't do the show without Sonnie and I'm pretty sure he feels the same way.'

The arguments went on all weekend. Sonnie agreed with me, we were a team and we stayed that way. Cochran knew perfectly well that I had a contract for four shows. He could get out of it, it's true, but not if I could help it. I loved the music, I wanted to do the show. This time I was going to fight like a tigress. Miss Jessie Matthews wasn't going to collapse again and be assisted out of the ring. I'd been knocked off my feet in the first round, but no more. Over my dead body was another actress going to play my part, no matter if she was the prettiest, winsomest blondest doll ever to cross the Atlantic.

Ever Green had a plot, a storyline. It wasn't revue and that meant I had to learn to act. Frank Collins, who had directed all my Cochran shows, was easy to work with, I could always please him. But the others, Richard Rodgers who wrote the music and Benn Levy who wrote the book, were very different. And Cochran still had his sights fixed on Ada May. He even brought her to rehearsals, which I found rather off-putting. What did they hope? That I'd fall down and break a leg?

Benn Levy and Richard Rodgers had their own ideas of how every line I said should be delivered.

'Remember this is a play, Jessie,' Benn Levy would call.

'I don't like what you're doing with your hands.' This time it was Richard Rodgers.

'A little more feeling, Jessie.' Frank Collins had his say.

And Cochran smiled benignly. He knew I didn't like the way things were going one little bit. Where had the old days gone when he let me create my own characters?

Dancing on the Ceiling was the big song and dance number and the way those men mauled it about. 'She's too coy,' Levy. 'She isn't coy enough,' Rodgers. 'Sweet and light, that's the theme,' Collins. And Cochran said, 'I don't like it.'

'Let's have it once more,' called Frank Collins.

I looked down at these four men so busy manipulating me. I felt like a puppet with tangled strings. Some demon took hold of me. What was I to them? Nothing but some image they had in their minds, an object, a bloody blueprint to scrawl their ideas on. I was sick and tired of letting four old men mess me about. What the hell did they know about love? How did they know how a girl in love feels? I'd damn well show them.

'I'm ready,' I called.

Script: In a pool of limelight she dances, so lightly, like a butterfly.

Music: Start of vocal refrain.

> 'He dances overhead, on the ceiling near my bed,
> In my sight, through the night.
> I try to hide in vain, underneath my counterpane,
> There's my love, up above . . .'

This was where I was going to show them.

> 'I whisper, go away my lover, it's not fair,
> But I'm so grateful to discover, he's still there,
> I love my ceiling more, since it is a dancing floor,
> Just for my love . . .'

I was really into it now, enjoying myself, singing the song as I thought it should be sung, not like a stupid little ninny bleating to her lover in the room overhead.

The four men were on their feet all screaming at me:

Benn Levy: 'What in God's name are you up to?'

Richard Rodgers: 'Gee, honey, that's not the way.'

Frank Collins: 'Jessie, for God's sake.'

Cochran: 'What the hell do you think you're doing?'

I was delighted to see that Cochran had lost his hat and his cigar had gone out. 'Okay!' I shouted back. 'For once in my life I wanted to do it my way.'

Of course I knew I must do as they said in the end. They were right anyway. *Ever Green* was their creation and even if I thought the storyline was corny and the character a mess, I was paid to play it. It was an odd story of a girl who pretends to be her mother, and in my role of the older woman I had to wear a platinum blonde wig. In spite of lashings of vaseline, the blonde hairs had a distracting way of sticking out, and I sometimes looked more like one of The Three Stooges than a glamorous grandmother.

Noël Coward came to the dress rehearsal. 'Noël, darling,' I called to him when the performance was over. 'If there's any advice you have, I'd be so grateful.'

The clear clipped tones of the Master sailed up to the stage. 'That wig, darling! Must you? It's hardly soignée, dear, hardly soignée at all.'

The press and the public loved the show. 'The most lavish and sumptuous production Cochran ever put on the British stage.'

'Theatrical history was made last night,' said another.

The advance bookings pleased Cochran, and Ada May left town. Perhaps she went back to America.

After the show opened there were two weddings in the company. The first was the marriage of Joyce Barbour to Richard Bird. Joyce was the actress who came out to America to take over my part in a Charlot revue. The second wedding very nearly didn't take place.

When you've been through the divorce courts, the blinding ecstasy that drove you to these courts sometimes dims with the passage of time. Sonnie and I were still in love but the first fine rapture had lessened. Very often I wanted to ask: 'Do you still feel the same way about me?' But I was afraid what the reply might be.

The newspaper men were outside Hampstead Town Hall en masse that cold January day in 1931 when Cochran and I alighted from his limousine.

'Hello, Jessie! Some coat you've got there. Did Sonnie buy it for you?'

'No, boys, I bought it myself.'

I could afford my own fur coat. I was earning £200 a week, which in present-day standards might be about £1,000 a week. That mink coat became an old and trusted friend. I think it finished up as a fur collar for Lena.

'Where's the happy bridegroom? Hasn't changed his mind, has he?'

Cochran's hand tightened on my arm. So Sonnie wasn't here. Where the devil had he got to? My face paled beneath my apple green cloche. Oh God, I thought, Rosie told me green was unlucky for a wedding.

Cochran beamed at the newsmen. 'He'll be along.'

Inside the Town Hall we sat down to wait. The minutes creaked by. We conversed in whispers, well aware of the presence of the Registrar who kept glancing at his watch in a worried way.

'Darling,' whispered Cochran, 'I don't think this marriage is going to work. Why don't you call it off?'

I didn't answer. I was too busy ordering myself not to panic. How could Sonnie do this to me? If he didn't want to marry me, he shouldn't do it in this cruel way. Had he only asked me to marry him to make amends for the terrible divorce?

'Darling,' Cochran's whisper came again, 'if you want to walk out, I'm ready.'

Walk out! Be mobbed by that crowd of newsmen. What a field day they'd have. 'Chorus girl jilted at the altar!' I'd always be 'a chorus girl' to them, I thought bitterly. I looked at my watch, 'We'll give him another two minutes.'

Sonnie breezed in. 'Hello, old girl. Sorry I'm late. Hadn't got a clean shirt. Had to send my best man out to buy one.'

The marriage ceremony was conducted in an icy atmosphere. But by the time the newsmen came in for the pictures, the icicles were melting. As the cameras clicked, Sonnie and I made it up.

Few marriages can have started quite so coolly yet it was a marriage that worked. Abnormal our lives might be—a smile for the cameras when you're kicking each other under the table—but we loved each other. There was a bond between us, a look or the right word and that bond sealed again. I felt safe, this was how marriage should be.

Some time in the night I would say a prayer, 'Thank you, God.' All we needed now was the child we had promised each other.

Chapter Twelve

The scene was the star's dressing-room. The mirror and make-up table were draped in pale chiffon and the star herself was clad in the filmiest of negligees.

'You're not wearing very much, are you, Miss?' said her dresser severely.

The star turned round to face the audience, her large eyes rimmed with black, her outrageous toothy smile engineered with cardboard teeth. 'Ah!' she cried, 'but I'm wearing more than my sister-in-law did on the opening night of *Ever Green*.'

The audience roared with laughter. It was such a clever impersonation, the prominent teeth, the dainty mannerisms, the trilling voice. Binnie Hale was taking off the girl her brother had just married—Jessie Matthews.

She was very funny. I sat in my seat at the Hippodrome matinee of Binnie's new revue and had to admit she was a scream. Perhaps having the hide of an elephant and no tender spots can help you laugh when you see yourself being cruelly caricatured, but I was very young, as touchy as hell and hurt by the slightest criticism. I never felt quite the same about Binnie again. I don't know how she felt about me, we never became intimate enough to find out.

The sketch was derived from my number *Dancing on the Ceiling*. Under my filmy chiffon pyjamas I wore, for decency's sake, a flesh-coloured jersey silk leotard—a close-fitting costume rather like a bathing dress. On opening night when the battery of lights suddenly blazed on the darkened bedroom scene, the audience gasped. 'They like me,' I thought happily. I didn't

know that the lights had cut straight through my leotard
and it appeared that I wore nothing underneath. Before the
next performance a non-see-through lining had been sewn in,
but I was upset about the incident and blamed the direction
for not rehearsing the lights properly. For my part, the sooner
it was all forgotten the better. To have it aired, twice nightly
at the London Hippodrome, did not help me love my new
sister-in-law more.

Sonnie's other sister, Georgie, and his brother, Bogie, were
very kind and welcomed me into the family. We became great
friends. Robert Hale, Sonnie's father, who was a Scot and
whose real name was Munro, was the dearest of men. 'I'm on
your side, Jessie,' he'd say to me. 'Just be patient, give Belle
time.'

Belle was Sonnie's mother. She was Irish and a devout
Catholic, and she wanted none of me. She refused to meet me
until I was pregnant and carrying Sonnie's child. I'll never
forget the first time I went to Raylands, their large rambling
house in Maidenhead. Everywhere, I saw pictures of Evelyn
Laye, in each nook and cranny was a photo of Sonnie's ex-
wife. Belle, who was a warm friendly woman to everyone but her
new daughter-in-law, watched my startled face with cold eyes.

On another occasion, in my own home, Binnie sat down at
the piano to entertain us. The Hale family, when they liked
you, could be the gayest, most boisterous of families. She
showed she could be just as clever at impersonating Evelyn
Laye as she could me. I laughed until I cried, finishing up with
a mild bout of hysterics. Binnie said wonderingly, 'We do seem
to have a funny effect on you.'

I wanted desperately to be liked and accepted by the Hales
but the atmosphere of disapprobation was always there.
Belle had decided that I was to blame for breaking up Sonnie's
marriage and nothing would convince her otherwise. No one
could tell her that it takes two people to make a marriage
work.

I tried, but it was a losing battle. Once I asked Belle if she
would like a picture of myself and our adored new daughter.
Next time we called, there on the piano in a new frame was
Catharine our daughter, but I had been carefully cut out of
the picture.

We had bought a house near the river. Sonnie loved the

Thames and he'd spent his youth near its banks. One afternoon, driving through Hampton, we'd seen a long low sprawling farmhouse fallen into decay. The walls were covered with ivy and the two acre garden was a jungle, but that didn't stop us falling in love with the house.

No young couple, whether in a suburban-semi or a stately home, had more fun than we did putting that house in order. Psmith, the dalmatian dog that had been presented to us by one of the chorus girls in *Ever Green*, went berserk when he saw that he had green fields instead of pavements to frolic in. Sonnie scythed his way through the nettles and I slapped paint on the kitchen walls. All my life I've loved painting walls. As I mixed the paint I daydreamed. How would it be if I gave up the stage and became a housewife? Sonnie's expression when I told him assured me that it must stay a daydream.

Sonnie was becoming very interested in films. 'They're going to empty the theatres,' he declared, 'our future's in the film industry.' Finally he persuaded me to make a talkie while *Ever Green* was still running. It was a disaster. *Out of the Blue* was adapted from a stage musical and it should never have left the boards. I hated getting up at six in order to be made-up and ready in the studio by nine. I hated the restriction of keeping to lines chalked on the studio floor after the freedom of the stage, but most of all I hated the contemptuous way the film people treated anyone who wasn't in the film business.

My face, they told me, was a mess. 'There's a gap between your front teeth. And that turned-up nose! Those eyebrows! Have them off.' The make-up man took out his razor and they've never grown again. He placed daubs of black under my nose to straighten it, streaked white on my face to fatten it, and then he said I wasn't photogenic. I wasn't. I looked like Frankenstein's little sister.

What relief when that film was over, and then *Ever Green* finally ended and my four production contract with Cochran was over. Sonnie, rightly I suppose, wanted us to try something new. We were a team, that was true, but he'd always had an urge for slapstick comedy.

Stanley Lupino was one of England's greatest comic actors. He came from a long line of comedians, and what wasn't bred in the bone had been created by his understanding of the fundamental things that make everybody laugh.

OMS—E   *117*

Hold My Hand was the show we did together. Stanley insisted that I should have my share of the comedy. I said I couldn't do comedy, he said I could, he would teach me, and he wrote in a scene where I wore a baby's rompers and fell all over the stage with him. The first time I heard the audience laugh I was amazed. 'They're laughing at me, Stanley,' I whispered. 'Whoopee!' After that there was no holding me back.

It was a lovely show and we had the man I thought was the best dance director in the world to help us. Buddy Bradley had been brought over from America by Cochran. He liked England and he's stayed here ever since. No praise is too great for Buddy, he's a genius of the dance. He taught Fred Astaire and Eleanor Powell, and when he opened his dance studio, I was his regular pupil.

In my new home I experimented with gracious living. Naturally my first guests were my own family. Sonnie and my family got on fairly well but there were reservations on both sides. Unexpectedly, however, my father found an ally. Not in Sonnie, there was no meeting of minds there, but with Robert Hale, my new father-in-law. They got on like a house on fire. They laughed at each other's jokes. 'He's a real character, your father,' said Robert, and 'He's a real gent,' said Dad.

Lena, my sister, came to stay. One morning we walked into Hampton village with Psmith, the dog. We watched his nose wrinkle with ecstasy when we passed the fish and chip shop.

'Chips!' I reminisced. 'Remember William and Mary and the shop on the corner. Salt and pepper and a squirt of vinegar.'

We looked at each other and five minutes later we were walking back along the country lane holding greasy newspapers in our hands and stuffing hot delicious chips into our mouths.

'Isn't that Sonnie coming towards us?' said Lena.

Without stopping to think, automatically, I had to get rid of my lowly newspaper bundle. I buried it in a ditch.

'Why d'you do that?' asked Lena, dropping another chip into her mouth. 'Are you afraid of him, or something?'

I suppose I was. Afraid that Sonnie would not approve of a wife who ate chips out of a newspaper, or afraid of tarnishing my carefully tended image. Perhaps I was trying to forget who Jessie Matthews really was and I was busy pasting on layer upon layer of the kind of personality I thought she should have.

*   *   *

My mother didn't come over to see us at the Old House in Hampton very often, she was too busy looking after her family. I talked it over with Sonnie and suggested a way that might make her life easier. We agreed that we would take one of my young brothers to live with us and educate him.

I had two younger brothers, Eddie, aged fourteen and about to leave school and Harry, three years younger. In my family the characters of the four boys were divided. Georgie, the eldest, was the gentlest of men; Billy was the fighter, with some of my father's fire and fury; then Eddie was like Georgie, and Harry, the baby, was like Billy.

Much as I loved all my brothers I thought I could manage Eddie without too many problems while Harry's personality might be too strong for me. Of course there remained the worry that the one who was left out might feel hurt.

Eddie, a tall handsome boy, came to live with us. He and Sonnie took to each other at once. Sonnie taught Eddie how to play cricket and I'd see Eddie swaggering round the garden, hands behind his back, unconsciously imitating Sonnie's walk. Eddie, however, sounded exactly as I used to when I played in William and Mary years ago.

He dashed in from the garden. 'Smiff's cu' 'is tile onna pile!'

'What?' cried Sonnie.

I translated quickly, 'Psmith's cut his tail on the pail.'

Unless Eddie could speak a recognisable version of the King's English we couldn't send him to the school Sonnie had in mind and his council school education wasn't up to much either. Sonnie decided to engage a tutor to bring Eddie up to Common Entrance standards.

While we waited for Eddie's education to begin, I started him on the same painful path I had trodden with Rosie. Psmith gambolled on the lawn while over the shrubbery floated Eddie's cockney vowels and my hard-won rounded ones.

'How now brown cow! Oh, that's much better, Eddie. Now try this: "Oh, why do you look so sad?" Make your mouth all round . . .'

He was a very good-tempered boy, he was eager to learn and did his very best. At the end of a long elocution lesson Sonnie's voice could be heard in the distance: 'Who wants to play cricket?'

Eddie's large brown eyes looked up at me appealingly, 'Oh, Jessie, issa toime forra goime?'

A young man telephoned from Hampton Station. His name, he said, was Elwyn Jones. He was the new tutor. Sonnie drove over to pick him up and came back with a tall, broad-shouldered young Welshman. He had just left Cambridge where he was reading for the Bar, and wanted a source of employment, some job that would enable him to live near London for the reading he had to do.

Recently I met Elwyn again and asked if he remembered that summer day when he first came to the Old House.

'Very well indeed,' he told me. 'I remember you coming in with Eddie, who looked as if he'd just been given the death sentence, and how I couldn't understand a word he said. But what really bowled me over was discovering that Mr and Mrs Hale-Munro, my new employers, were the stage stars, Sonnie Hale and Jessie Matthews.'

If Elwyn was impressed with our household, that was little in comparison to how impressive Elwyn's future career was to be. I couldn't guess then that this dark-haired young man with the musical voice would one day be Baron Elwyn Jones, Lord Chancellor of Great Britain.

Elwyn soon became immersed in life at the Old House. He and Eddie worked every day in the library; slowly they became friends and gradually Elwyn won Eddie's confidence. But it wasn't easy. After a month or so Elwyn said to me, 'I'm afraid I'm not really getting through to Eddie. I wonder whether we should go on?'

I didn't know what to say. How could I tell this well-educated young man that Eddie had been thrown head-first into another world? A world he knew nothing about, where people took for granted things like soup spoons and butter knives and side plates. Where every time he opened his mouth the wrong sounds came out. Where an ordinary conversation took on the dimensions of an examination, and ever present was the constant fear of ridicule. I knew exactly how Eddie felt for I had been through it all myself.

I tried to explain: 'There is an improvement, really there is.' I told him about our elocution lessons in the garden. 'Just give him a little more time.'

Elwyn understood, 'If you can do it, then so can I. No girl's going to beat me.' Then his smile broadened. 'But I'm glad you told me about those elocution lessons. You've solved a mystery for me, Jessie, bach . . . every time Eddie opens his mouth nowadays your voice comes out. Now I know the reason why.'

The musical comedy *Hold my Hand* at the Gaiety was responsible for both Sonnie and me going into films. It was a shop window for film directors looking for talent.

One night after the show my dresser handed me a card left by a Mr Albert de Courville, a film director from Gaumont British.

A dark dapper man of about forty came into my dressing room. 'I would like you to make a film test at Shepherd's Bush studios for the leading part in my film *There Goes the Bride*.'

'No thank you,' I said firmly, remembering my awful experience with the first film.

'But you are what I want. You are a natural comic, and a pretty one. An unusual combination.'

I shook my head.

Albert de Courville shrugged. He didn't seem at all put out. His rather strange penetrating eyes continued to assess me as if he were setting up a camera shot. 'I shall come back. You will change your mind,' he said confidently.

The next film offer was for Sonnie. Erich Pommer, the famous German film director, wanted Sonnie for the English versions of successful Berlin comedies. German films were booming, *Sunshine Susie* with the irresistible Renate Muller and Jack Hulbert was a great hit in England. Sonnie would play the part made famous by Pommer's star Willy Forst.

Sonnie couldn't resist the idea. 'But you'll be in Germany and I'll be stuck in London,' I cried.

'There are aeroplanes,' said Sonnie blithely.

But travel in 1932 was a slow business. No one drove out to Heathrow or Gatwick and boarded a plane. I did fly over to see him once and Sonnie flew to see me once, but both times we were working and they were wasted journeys.

Albert de Courville was quite right, I did change my mind. Partly because Sonnie was leaving and partly because I didn't like failure any more than the next actress. I might have looked like a gargoyle in *Out of the Blue*, but I'd try again. Work on *Here Comes the Bride* started while *Hold my Hand* was still running at the Gaiety. It was an exhausting business for Albert de

Courville wanted the film on the studio floor at once. Made-up and on the set at 9 am, a long day at the studios, then an evening performance at the Gaiety. I never got to bed until 1 am. and four and a half hours' sleep was the most I ever got. By the time the stage show was over and the film was in the can, I felt a mental and physical wreck. I had lost a stone in weight and I had lost the ability to go to bed at night and sleep.

'It's not worth it,' I told Sonnie. 'Why should I kill myself for money?'

Michael Balcon of Gaumont British had seen the rushes and offered me a two year contract. £7,000 for the first year and £9,000 for the second year.

There were reasons why I should accept. The higher the rate you live the more money you need, and The Old House was fairly eating money. Our plans to modernise were costing much more than we imagined, and now I worked all the time we needed a staff to run the place. I signed the contract.

I wasn't happy about it. I felt I was giving up the warmth and friendship of life in the theatre for the strange new world of film-making. And Albert de Courville was beginning to frighten me. He wanted to take control of me completely, to remould my personality to the fantasy film heroine he had in his head. He wanted to be Svengali to my Trilby. This did happen in the cinema, I knew. There was Greta Garbo and Maurice Stiller, Dietrich and Von Sternberg, but the idea frightened me. And I hadn't the physical stamina to keep up with his inexhaustible energy. When he suggested we start the next film, I said, 'I'm tired, I must have a holiday.'

'Holiday!' All the contempt in the world was in his voice. 'Who do you think you are? A film star? Your first film hasn't been shown yet. I started you in pictures and I can finish you in pictures.'

I wished Sonnie was at home. I needed the comfort of his presence. I could talk it over with him and he'd reassure me, tell me that de Courville wasn't the ogre I was building in my mind. De Courville agreed to give me a break over Easter and because we were alone, I asked Harry, my youngest brother, to come over and keep Eddie company.

I had been told by the studio to stay at home near the telephone in case there was an urgent call to report for work, and I hoped a few days' rest would pull me together. Any fool could have told me that two high-spirited young boys about the place would give no one any rest. A crash from the living room and Harry and Eddie doing handstands had brought down china plaques from the wall. A scream from the cook: they'd barged into her carrying a chocolate cake.

Each new day brought new catastrophes. Eddie became just as wild as Harry, they egged each other on. They played Tarzan through the trees, and I could see all the efforts of myself and Elwyn being undermined. After a week of sound and fury, my aching nerves could stand no more. 'Harry,' I screamed over the din, 'It's time you went home.'

The two boys unlocked themselves from a life and death struggle on the hall carpet, it was raining and they couldn't go out. They came towards me unusually silent. Harry's young face looked shocked. I packed Harry's suitcase, rang for a hired car; I wrote a note to my mother and pressed a £5 note into Harry's hand.

Eddie watched unbelievingly as the hired car drew up outside. 'Why, Jessie?' he asked. 'Why?'

Why? I hardly knew myself. Was it because every time the boys yelled it seemed to spin me round, leaving a roaring sound in my ears? Because my nerves were stretched and taught? Because I wasn't sleeping? I missed Sonnie, and all I wanted to do was sit in a corner and cry. We all cried. Harry sitting stiffly in his corner of the hired car, brushing away a tear angrily with the back of his hand, refusing to say goodbye, and leaving me with a feeling that he would never forgive me. Eddie, alone and bereft of his best pal, looking at me with his miserable brown eyes. And me? I was bitterly ashamed that I couldn't cope with two children. What had I done? Sending my own brother away? But I was so tired with all the worries of the studio.

That afternoon Eddie and I went out into the garden. A plane flew overhead and buzzed us. I knew who was the pilot. He was a young man who had appeared in *Hold my Hand* and ever since I had become a grass widow had pursued me relentlessly. I didn't want him or his attentions and I'd told him so. I wondered why he had come back?

As he roared overhead he leant out of the bucket seat and a shower of small objects floated to the ground. Eddie raced after them. He came back carrying a cluster of matchboxes. Inside each one was a small red fruit. A raspberry! This was the young man's final goodbye. He'd delivered exactly the right sour note to end my unhappy holiday.

Chapter Thirteen

His face came nearer, he was bellowing like a bull. 'Temperament, temperament!' I thrust out my hand to keep his angry blast of words away from me. He caught my wrist. I wrenched it away and shouted at the top of my voice, 'You killed two men . . . all right . . . but you're not going to kill me.'

I pushed at him. I pushed at everyone who was in my way on my flight to the stairs. 'Temperament!' his voice yelled after me. 'Just bloody temperament and I won't have it.' I could hardly see the stairs I was crying so hard. Another face loomed in front of me, someone else trying to stop me. I pushed at the man with all my force.

'Jessie!' Oh, God! It was Michael Balcon, the head of production. Had I hurt him? I didn't stop to find out. I ran down the stairs into my dressing-room and slammed the door. I turned the key in the lock.

Someone hammered on the door. 'Let me in.'

'Go away,' I yelled. 'Go away. I'm never coming out.'

I sank down on the floor, shaking all over, wracked with sobs that seemed to tear my chest apart. 'Who was making that awful noise?' a reasonable voice inside me asked. 'It's you. Shut up. Stop crying.' But I couldn't stop and suddenly the whole world seemed to be slipping out of control.

I don't know how long I stayed like that. The banging on the door stopped, the voices went away. 'Jessie.' This was a new voice, soft and kind. 'Can I come in, please? I'm a doctor. I'm quite alone.'

I stretched up my arm and wearily turned the key. A pair of strong arms lifted me up and laid me on the couch. A cool hand brushed the tousled hair back from my swollen eyes and a man looked at me with clear compassionate eyes. 'Let's have a cup of tea, shall we? Then you tell me all about it.'

'He told me that I hadn't any guts . . . that he'd made a film with some flyers and two men were killed . . . but they didn't stop filming . . . so why was I making such a fuss?'

'Why did you make a fuss?'

'I was so hungry.'

The doctor smiled. 'Tea's on the way and a sandwich. When did you eat last?'

'This morning. He wouldn't stop for lunch . . . or tea.'

I drank the tea when it came, it was warm and comforting.

'Was that all it was?' asked the doctor. He was a nice looking man with fair brushed hair and blue eyes, and he was very gentle. 'Just because you were hungry.'

I pushed the hair out of my eyes. 'No, it's much more than that. I know it sounds silly, but he's trying to change me, crush me to pieces, so that I'll be obedient and do whatever he says.'

A wary look came into the doctor's eyes.

'Please try and understand,' I begged, 'I'm not crazy. But it's hard for me to find the right words. Every day he reduces me, makes me feel more inferior.' It was hard to explain to this doctor how the film director was becoming so obsessed with his fantasy dream of me that he forgot that I was a vulnerable human being. How I had to be at his side every day whether I was wanted on the set or not. How I was not allowed to speak to anyone, and any actor who spoke or joked with me might find his close-up lying on the cutting-room floor.

'You mean he's in love with you?' asked the doctor quietly.

'Oh no.' It wasn't love, it was something else, something I couldn't understand. He wanted to possess my mind. A sudden thought struck me. 'Am I going mad?' I asked.

'No, of course not. You're exhausted, your nerves gave way and you had a fit of hysteria. You need a rest.' He got up and opened the door. I saw the director standing outside. 'Is she ready to come back?'

'I'm taking her home to bed.'

'Tomorrow? Will she be back tomorrow?'

'Not if you want her to finish the picture.'

The young doctor took me out to his little two-seater car. A Great Dane dog was sitting in the front seat, there was hardly room for the three of us. He drove me home and I was given a week's rest. But I gained much more than a respite from the picture, I gained a real friend in Dr Henry Rowan. He was employed as studio doctor and the big brass could easily have sacked him for standing up to them as he did.

Albert Pierre de Courville was a brilliant director. He was born in London of French parents, he'd been a journalist, a director of revues and finally he was directing films for Gaumont-British. He had a strong personality, there was in him some of the stuff that makes dictators for at work he was utterly ruthless.

A film director who has to hold all the threads of the story together, who determines the daily life of the vulnerable and sometimes childish actors around him, does often come to regard himself as a ruler or even a creator. I think Albert de Courville thought he had created me, taken a stage actress and turned her into a film actress. 'Don't get any ideas,' he'd say to me, 'I'm the only director who can get a performance out of you. Without me, you don't function.'

I was never quite sure whether to believe him or not. All I knew was that I thrived on praise and now all the confidence was being squeezed from me. He'd take my face in his hands, twist it from side to side, 'The nose is wrong, the chin's wrong. Put wax between her teeth . . .'

Film making in 1932 needed enormous physical stamina. Long hours under hot arc lights, no stand-ins, uncertain sound equipment which meant take after take. Without unions to protect their rights, the crew and the cast were kept working as long as the director could stay on his feet.

The Front Office were very pleased with my first two films and other directors showed interest in me. One of them was Victor Saville who was casting for a new film called *The Good Companions*.

'You're going to do *The Midshipmaid* with me,' de Courville told me. 'I made you and I'm keeping you.' I'd signed the contract for two years, there was nothing I could do. A huge set depicting a battleship was built on the studio floor, and the long exhausting process of making another film began.

One night we worked until 1 am. De Courville said he

needed one more shot of a close-up. I wasn't needed, I was just the voice off, so when I'd informed the actor, Basil Sydney, I told my little dark-haired dresser called Kitty that I was leaving. De Courville watched me. 'And where do you think you're going?' he demanded.

'Home! You don't need me any more.'

'Listen to her conceit,' he roared. 'A couple of pictures and she thinks she's the big star. She thinks she runs the bloody studio. You're staying, do you hear, until I say you can go.'

I began to cry. I was always crying nowadays.

'Get her a glass of water,' he shouted to Kitty.

Kitty, frightened and as tired as the rest of us, hurried over to the lift to get some water from my dressing-room. The next thing we heard was an awful scream and Kitty was lying on the floor. Her arm was thrown out at a strange angle. Poor Kitty, in her haste, had seen the lift going up past her, thrust her arm through the bars to catch the handle, missed and by some ghastly mischance the edge of the lift had broken her arm.

What happened afterwards was even more horrible. Voices rose, tempers snapped. I comforted the moaning Kitty, someone rang for an ambulance and someone produced a flask of whisky and made her sip a little.

I turned round and saw de Courville behind us. My anger blazed. 'It's all your fault,' I shouted. 'You're insane! Mad as a hatter! Just because you're inhuman, you think you can treat us like dirt!'

'Mad!' de Courville yelled back. 'I'm not mad and I've got a certificate to prove it.' He pulled his wallet from a back pocket, tore at the papers inside. Banknotes and bills fluttered out. He grabbed at a piece of paper. 'It's here in black and white. I'm sane, d'you hear. I'm sane.'

Suddenly everyone was quiet. I felt sick and horrified. Not at what de Courville had done, but at what my words had done to him. I couldn't bear to look at his face. I was filled with pity.

Sitting in the ambulance with Kitty I made a firm resolve. I would never make another picture with de Courville. I knew he had chosen me to make into a film star. I was grateful that he believed I had talent. Without him I might never have gone into films. But flesh and blood can only stand so much.

* * *

Sonnie came home from Germany. 'God!' he said when he saw me. 'What's happened. You're as thin as a rake.'

'I missed you,' I said simply, and in a way that was the reason why I looked so haggard. In those days one couldn't pick up a phone and put a call through to Berlin, New York, Australia, the telephone hadn't become the universal comforter that it is today. We'd written to each other regularly, but how many times had I wanted to rush home and pour out my troubles to my husband. How often had I come home to an empty house. Even Eddie was now at school, and Elwyn had been called to the Bar. The months without Sonnie had been dreadful.

Sonnie's loud and lively voice now filled the house. As always he was bubbling over with new ideas, new plans. Films, it was all films.

'I hate films, Sonnie,' I told him. 'I want to be happy again, go back to the theatre and work for live audiences.'

'But there's this marvellous chance, coming up. They want you to test for *The Good Companions*!'

About five years before, a Yorkshireman called J. B. Priestley had written a novel about a concert party touring the English provinces. *The Good Companions* had been a runaway best-seller and a great success when it was dramatised. John Gielgud, a young actor with a great future, had played the hero Inigo Jollifant on the stage, and now Gaumont-British who had bought the film rights, had asked him to again play the ex-schoolteacher who became pianist to the company. Victor Saville, the director, had tested hundreds of girls for the female lead of Susie Dean and now he wanted me for the part.

Sonnie, who could talk the hindleg off a donkey, started a new campaign. It was a great book, it was a glorious chance for me. Acting? I'd be acting with a wonderful actor. Why, half the actresses in London would fight for the chance.

Sonnie was cooking the supper that evening as that was the cook's day off. In spite of his claims to be the great gourmet cook, fry-ups were his speciality, mushrooms and bacon, sausages and fried eggs. I cleaned up the mess he'd made slicing the tomatoes. 'How would it be,' I said carefully, 'if I gave it all up for a while? If I stayed home . . . perhaps had a baby?'

The egg Sonnie was about to drop into the frying-pan missed and splashed onto the kitchen floor.

'Sonnie, I'm frightened,' I said desperately. 'I haven't got the kind of strength that films need. I'm afraid I might crack up.'

Sonnie turned round, he walked over to me, he pulled out a chair, he sat me down. 'You're tired,' he said. 'You've been working too hard, but we'll fix it. When the time comes for a new contract we'll get special privileges written in. Time off, so many hours to work. Holidays. We'll have a country cottage. How would you like a cottage in Cornwall?'

'You want it?' I asked.

He nodded. 'We haven't got much time,' he said. 'In this business you have to snatch at your chances. I think films are the thing of the future, and you've got to have that certain something that comes across on the screen. You have it,' he looked straight at me, 'and I haven't.'

'Oh, Sonnie, you have.' But I realised what he meant. Sonnie wasn't built in the mould of the film heroes of the thirties. His face, though so pleasant and good-natured, wasn't that of a matinee idol. He was a wonderful dancer, a great comedian—all this came over on the stage—but films hadn't got round to his kind of talent yet.

'I'm going to direct films. I'm going to direct you. That's why I want you to stay in films.'

The bacon burned, the sausages burst wide open. I was going back to work tomorrow on a film I hated, but Sonnie was home and he was going to look after me.

I met Victor Saville. He wore a sober business suit and round glasses, and he radiated confidence. He said, 'I want to make a test, not to satisfy me because I know you're the girl I want for the part, but to show you how you'll look when you're properly photographed.'

'But my face is awful. I must tell you, I don't want to do this film. I want to go back to the theatre.'

'Make a picture with me and then decide. All you've made so far are disasters.'

His confidence, the warmth of his personality began to make its impact on me. He was honest. Here was an honest man working in the most screwy, fraudulent, false-faced industry. I knew I was going to like him.

'But I've still got a film to finish and the director is going to drag it out, re-take by re-take.'

'I've got a plan in my mind which I'll tell you about later. By the way, I should warn you, I'm the only one who wants you for the part. Get ready for some opposition.'

The opposition showed itself when I was summoned to Michael Balcon's office some time later. Michael Balcon had been chief of production for Gaumont-British for over ten years and he was responsible for many of the pictures that had put British films on the map. Victor Saville was already there, I caught his eye, and he gave me the briefest of winks. But he knew, just as I knew, that Michael Balcon had the final word on the casting.

'I think this is the position,' Michael began. 'We didn't buy this book as a vehicle for anybody. It's a rich, colourful, very English story, and we're more interested in getting the right people for the parts than anything else.' He gave me a regretful smile, as if to soften the blow that was coming.

'But the actress who plays Susie Dean must have a star personality,' insisted Victor. 'Not only has she to act well but she must be a damned good singer and dancer. And Jessie's all that.'

The arguments went back and forth until Michael Balcon played his trump card. 'The author, J. B. Priestley, doesn't think she's right for the part.'

Victor's smile vanished. The arguments grew fiercer.

Michael Balcon finally threw down his ace. 'We have to get the film on the floor at once. We have no time to waste. And Jessie isn't free. She hasn't finished her last film.'

Victor gave me a quick sidelong glance. 'Jessie is quite agreeable to work in the two films at the same time. She'll finish *The Midshipmaid* in the mornings and work on *The Good Companions* in the afternoon.' He gave me one of his beaming smiles, sweeping me along on his wave of enthusiasm. 'That's so, isn't it, Jessie?'

What could I say to such a man?

The first afternoon's work on *The Good Companions* was a scene between Inigo Jollifant, the ex-schoolmaster, played by John Geilgud and Susie Dean, played by Jessie Matthews.

It was John's first film. He has admitted in print several times that he only did it for the money. But superb artist that he is, every scene in which he played was worth watching, and his beautiful voice was something to listen to with joy. He was one of the nicest and easiest of leading men, no tantrums, no side, always co-operative and gentle and helpful, and I loved playing my scenes with him because he made it all seem so easy. He had one disarming caprice. Every time a scene was shot he would disappear.

'Where the hell's John?' Victor would demand.

I was the one who always went to find him. There he'd be hidden behind a piece of scenery, his nose deep in a book.

In our first scene together, Inigo was seated at the piano onstage of an empty provincial theatre rehearsing a song with Susie. The dialogue of the thirties went like this:

Inigo: I say, these numbers of yours—you know, they're pretty feeble.

Susie: You think so?

Inigo: Good Lord, I could turn out half a dozen better than this in a morning. Oh, I don't say mine wouldn't be tripe too, but after all there is tripe and tripe, isn't there? Absolutely?

Susie: You've got a damn nerve.

Inigo: What?

Susie: You've been in the show five minutes—never seen an audience in your life and you start telling me my songs are all rot.

Inigo: Here, I didn't mean . . .

Susie: I suppose you think I'm in your infant's class. Oh yerse, there's traipe and traipe, isn't there. Oh, absolutely!

Inigo: I'm sorry, Susie.

Susie: Miss Dean to you, and if you wrote the best soubrette songs here and now, I wouldn't sing 'em if you paid me.

Susie Dean marches off in a huff.

I was happy about that first afternoon. I felt I was right in the part of Susie. I could understand her spirited personality.

Next morning I reported for work on the set of *The Midshipmaid*, the film that was intended to be a gay rollicking comedy against the background of the grey papier-maché battleship. There was a funeral-like atmosphere here. All the studio knew about the feud between the director and his leading lady, and how the director had said she would never make *The Good Companions*, if he had anything to do with it.

132

'I hear poor old Henry Ainley's got shingles,' he announced with some satisfaction, 'that's going to put your picture back a bit. Isn't he the actor you made your test with? Hope it's not catching.'

I didn't give a damn whether shingles was catching or not, but Henry Ainley out of the film was a blow. He was a great actor and his divine voice had held me spellbound when we made the test. Joss Ackroyd was a big part and it needed a big actor.

As usual everything I did was wrong, even the way I looked. 'Change her make-up,' he ordered, 'make her face fatter.' To me, he said, 'you're too thin. Thin and ugly.'

Re-take followed re-take. When we broke for lunch he handed me an envelope. 'Here's a message for you from Victor. He's got problems with his film, and I know what one of them is. I always told Front Office you were hard to handle.'

On my way down the stairs to my dressing-room I opened the envelope. Victor asked me to go along and see yesterday's rushes with him before we started work that afternoon. I was determined not to let de Courville's words rattle me, but I was worried stiff. If Victor was disappointed with my work, that was it, I would be out of a job and I could kiss my film career goodbye.

Chapter Fourteen

The operator switched off his noisy machine. Someone switched on the lights and Victor swivelled round in his seat to look at me. 'Tell me, Jessie,' he said. 'Why do you look at the camera as if it's going to bite you?'

This is it, I told myself, the polite brush-off. Now he'll tell me that he's very sorry but I'm not quite right for the part. Oh well, I decided, what have I got to lose? I may as well tell him the truth. At least he's not the kind of man who'll start abusing me.

'The camera scares me stiff,' I said slowly. 'It tells the truth about me. It shows just what an ugly little bitch I am.'

Victor Saville shook his head, 'What an inferiority complex you've got there, kid. Come on'—he caught my arm—'we'd better work this one out.'

In my dressing-room he sat me down in front of the mirror and told me to wipe the heavy make-up off my face. 'Now brush your hair back.'

'Oh no, I mustn't do that. My face is too thin and it makes my nose look funny.'

'Do as I say, kid.'

I liked the way he called me kid, it reminded me of Georgie. Victor came from Birmingham and he had a nice voice, with enough of his home-town left in it to make it comfortable.

He leant over and studied my face earnestly. 'Put on some powder, lipstick and a touch of mascara.'

I put on the minimum of make-up, the kind I used for the street.

'Right,' said Victor, 'that's it. We're going to shoot you just like that.' He stood behind me, staring at my face in the mirror. 'It's a damn good face, Jessie. Look at those eyes, wide spaced, enquiring. I want to get that look when you open them wide. And that nose! It's cute.'

I felt a glow of pleasure suffusing my face with pink.

'Now when you get out onto the set you're going to hold up your head, you're going to stare straight at that camera and say to it, "I'm beautiful. I'm beautiful." And by God you will be beautiful.'

The rushes next day showed a completely different girl. The anxious frightened look had gone, and a new confident personality was coming over. And that was the day when for the first time I knew that making films could be fun. There was such a difference working for a man like Victor. Here was a man who would guide, not command, a man who would teach me, not lecture remorselessly. Oh, Victor Saville was a lovely man.

I didn't even mind having to work on two films at the same time. Edmund Gwenn, my old friend from Charlot's revue days, took over the part of Joss Ackroyd and later he went on to Hollywood and even more fame. Working in *The Good Companions* was rather like being back in the theatre. We developed the same team spirit. We knew the film would be good. It had to be for we loved our parts.

I only regretted that I didn't play opposite John Gielgud again. Our paths didn't cross until much much later, in Venice, in high summer when the canals have their own special odour. He was there standing on the Rialto Bridge. I rushed up to him and we embraced. 'Darling,' he cried, throwing his arms wide, 'isn't it divine here? Absolutely divine!'

'But the smells, John, the smells.'

'You must rise above it, my darling, rise above it!'

The Good Companions was the first 'talkie' to be shown publicly to the King and Queen of England. The Royal Standard flew over the New Victoria Cinema for the first Royal Command Performance, an occasion that was to follow year after year.

Unlike the present day, it was a matinée performance and King George V, a strict disciplinarian about meals, wanted to be home again in Buckingham Palace in time for tea. The film went on rather longer than was expected and when the cast

135

was presented the King wanted to hear the details from Victor Saville about the fire, the climax of the film.

I was not presented to the King and Queen. I was a divorced woman, and in those days divorcées were not considered fit people to meet their sovereigns. Naturally I was intensely disappointed. The lady in waiting to Queen Mary knew about this and sympathised. As the royal party got up to leave the royal box, the lady in waiting whispered to the Queen. I was standing by my aisle seat in the stalls. Queen Mary looked down and saw me. She gave me the sweetest of smiles and called the attention of the King. He came back down the stairs, stood at the edge of the box and acknowledged me. My curtsey in return was one of complete allegiance to the Crown. I was their good and faithful subject for ever. I hope they weren't too late for tea.

Sonnie and I had a holiday in Cadaqués, a fishing village on the Costa Brava. It was a paradise of peace and quiet—forty years ago. One evening out for a walk we peered through a window of what we thought was a deserted cottage and saw a young artist hard at work by lamplight. He turned, saw us and asked us in. His name was Salvador Dali.

Both of us came back to work on a film called *Friday the 13th* then on to another film *Waltzes in Vienna*. Alfred Hitchcock directed this one. Our life had become one of rising early, the studio, home late, no social life, no parties and Sunday spent getting over the week's work. I'd made three films in a year and every film had started before the last one was finished.

There were always lines to be learnt. Trying to concentrate on my work between takes, with electricians rushing about, carpenters hammering, prop men, assistant directors, make-up men fiddling with my face, journalists coming up and asking for an interview, and all the time I had to hold on to the character I was playing, trying not to break the continuity. The memory of the days with Albert de Courville, when we had take after take, were always with me. I never wanted that to happen again. I demanded of myself that I get it right first time. 'First-take Jessie,' they called me nowadays, and it was like getting a medal.

Victor Saville, although he was never hard on me, was a

great man for perfection. He took me over a new set, walking backwards and forwards, listening. 'There's a squeak here,' he called to Chippy the carpenter.

'But, Mr Saville . . .' Chippy protested.

'And one here. And another there.'

'But, Mr Saville . . .'

'Get them all out!'

'But, Mr Saville, this isn't your set. That's your new set over there.'

One more film to go and then I'd worked my contract. 'You'll get a big contract offered you next time,' Victor predicted. 'This film's going to show the Front Office that you've got real star quality.'

Ever Green was to be the next film. Gaumont-British had bought the film rights from Cochran. Victor didn't like the story very much, it was written by Rodgers and Hart, and although we had done well with it in London, it had never appeared on Broadway. Rather like Cole Porter's *Nymph Errant* that did well in London but didn't get to Broadway.

Sonnie had great ideas about changing the story and Emlyn Williams, under contract to the studios, was doing the script. Fred Astaire was playing at the Palace in *The Gay Divorce*, he had made a film called *Flying Down to Rio*, and Victor thought he would be perfect as the male lead in *Evergreen*. He went along to see him with the script and Fred Astaire was keen to play the part. He'd work at the Palace in the evening and do the film in the daytime. I was delighted, who wouldn't be at the prospect of dancing with Fred Astaire?

All our spare time was now filled with discussions about the script, the new music that must be composed, the dances and the inevitable disappointments. The first was a refusal from Fred Astaire's Hollywood studio, he must not play in the British film. Victor had to find another leading man. 'Sonnie,' I suggested, 'what about Sonnie?' 'He's not the romantic type,' said Victor. 'He can have the comedy lead, but we'll have to find another leading man.'

We went to the studio to have our routine medical examinations so that insurance could be taken out to cover the film. I remember how tired I felt that morning as we drove over from Hampton, tired and anxious. I'd developed a strange habit of biting my nails.

'You've got nothing to worry about,' said Sonnie, 'you're as fit as a fiddle.'

The doctor examined me, passed me as okay. We all talked for a moment then off he went. I felt hot, a strange warmth all over me.

'Good God,' said Sonnie. He was staring at me, his mouth open. Victor was staring at me too. 'What'll we do?' he said. 'What'll we do?'

'What's the matter with me? What are you talking about?' I jumped up and rushed to a mirror. My face was covered with large white wheals, red-rimmed. They seemed everywhere, on my neck, on my hands. They started to itch, oh, how they itched. I wanted to tear my face to pieces.

'Keep her hands down,' yelled Victor. 'I'll get some cold cloths. And keep the door closed until I get back.'

I was having an attack of urticaria, a nervous rash. The wheals subsided on my face and neck but under the hot lights of the studio my hands still irritated. I took an hour off one afternoon and drove into London to see Henry Rowan. He was no longer our studio doctor, he had started his own practice in a quiet London street.

'Yes, it's urticaria all right. I'll give you a soothing cream. Keep your hands out of water, if you can.'

'It's a stupid thing to happen, just after the insurance doctor had passed me as fit.'

He stood up, came round to the other side of his desk and studied my face. 'Are you worried about this new film?'

I shrugged. 'I always panic over anything new.'

He picked up one of my hands and touched an angry red patch. 'We've some new theories in the medical world, some illnesses are caused by worry.'

'All right, Henry, so I'm worried sick, whether the studio give me another contract after this film, whether Sonnie will get a chance to direct, whether . . . oh dear . . . where's your medicine for worry?'

'Stop working, that's your medicine.'

'And who'll pay the bills?'

'You get indigestion, you can't eat, you don't sleep. How much longer can you go on, Jessie, one day . . .' He stopped abruptly. 'I'm wasting my breath.'

I smiled at him, he was a doctor in a million. Ever since that

138

first day on the set when I poured out my trouble to him, Henry had been trying to make me stop working. 'As soon as *Evergreen* is in the can, Sonnie and I are going on holiday. Spain! Blue skies, red geraniums, lots and lots of sun.'

I didn't go to Spain. I had a nervous breakdown instead. Just a little one, hardly worth mentioning, I was only away from the studios for a week or two. I fainted when I was having a costume fitting for *Evergreen*. When I came round I was taken to a nursing home but I couldn't eat and I couldn't sleep. Sonnie asked me what was wrong and all I could say was, 'I'm so unhappy.' He told me afterwards that when he left the nursing home he went into a church and prayed. He said nothing in his life had been so awful as seeing the one he loved crouched in a corner of her bed, looking very frightened and starting to weep.

It was nervous collapse, they said. Psychiatry wasn't taken too seriously then, in fact the only drug or attention I was given was a tablet of phenobarbitone to put me to sleep. When I woke up a brisk matter-of-fact sister said, 'Come along now, dear. Pull yourself together.'

That was the last thing I could do. I couldn't have pulled my socks up, never mind my aching nerve ends. I must say, I couldn't have had my breakdown at a worst time. Medical men in the thirties were not ready to cope with healing the mind as well as the body. Fortunately I was rich and could break down in luxury, but if you were hard up there was a very good chance that you'd be locked away.

The publicity over my breakdown was handled carefully. I was overtired and having a rest, they informed the press, but Miss Matthews would be back on the set any day now.

'Shall I?' I asked Sonnie when the grey depression lifted.

'It's up to you, darling. But they've promised to have a nurse on the set and a doctor on call. You'll be taken great care of, a sofa to rest on. Home every night by six.'

Henry Rowan shook his head when I told him, 'You haven't had a bad cold or the flu, you know. You've had a breakdown, and you run the risk of another collapse if you're not careful.'

'I'll make you a promise,' I said to him. 'After *Evergreen* I'll take a year off.' I smiled, it was nice to feel like smiling again, 'I might even have a baby.'

I couldn't let everybody down, there were so many people

whose jobs depended on me making the picture. Gaumont-British had made me, I hadn't done it on my own, they had poured their resources into my screen image. This was the first film set up as a vehicle for Jessie Matthews. They hoped to get American distribution—a breakthrough for British films. And I'd always been so proud of being British. I was raised on loyal parades and Union Jacks flapping in the wind.

My family were disturbed over my illness. It was something they didn't understand, and when they came to see me they didn't want to talk about it, thinking perhaps, if it wasn't mentioned it would go away. I wanted to forget it too, but buried insecurely at the back of my mind, to be disinterred and examined in the middle of a long night when sleep wouldn't come, was a tiny stinging fear. Why had this happened to me? What was wrong with me? Would it ever happen again?

Kitty, wreathed in smiles, was waiting for me in my dressing-room. The hairdresser washed and set my hair into a high pompadour. The make-up man gently patted in the powder and said, 'You're looking lovely, Jessie. The rest has done you good.' Kitty hooked me into my costume, a tight, silk, off-the-shoulder evening dress with a long feathered train, and I walked onto the set. The crew shouted their cheery, 'Welcome back, Jessie.' The other actors and actresses greeted me with hugs and kisses. There is nothing quite like the warmth and affection one gets from people in show business. To outsiders it may sometimes look false, as if the acting is still going on when the performance is over, but show peoples' emotions are so near the surface that they brim over easily.

The first scene to be shot was in the set depicting the stage of the Tivoli Music Hall. I was a belle of 1909 on stage, surrounded by baskets of flowers, saying goodbye to my adoring public. We rehearsed the scene thoroughly, all went well and Victor moved in for the first take. The sound was checked, the lights were checked, the camera moved towards me, the assistant director shouted, 'Quiet please.' The sound man called, 'We're rolling.' Victor pointed his finger at me.

I opened my mouth and then the floor began to quiver under my feet. The wooden planks of the stage felt soft as if I was sinking through them. My clothes felt as though they were weighted with lead. I was being drawn down through the wooden stage. My scream of terror rang out, cutting the still atmosphere like a knife.

All hell broke loose, everyone talked at once. The actors, completely unnerved, crowded round me, and suddenly the floor was firm under my feet again. I raised my hand and wiped my forehead, 'I'm so sorry,' I apologised. 'I felt dizzy for a moment. I'm all right now.'

The wardrobe lady hurried to adjust my shoulder line, the make-up man powdered my damp face. Everyone talking, everyone being kind. And then we tried the take again.

The gay atmosphere was built up, the extras applauded, another basket of flowers was handed up to me. I smiled and started my speech of thanks. 'Thank you,' I began, 'thank you . . .' Then with a terrible sense of panic I realised that I hadn't the faintest idea what I was supposed to say. The words had gone.

I saw the look of anguish cross Victor's face. I felt the awful tenseness in the air. The crew on the gantry waited, poised and silent. Hundreds of eyes stared at the mute and helpless creature on the stage. The creature who was the reason for their jobs, their livelihood.

'Cut!' shouted Victor. 'What the hell's happened to "one-take Jessie"?'

There was nothing he could have said that eased the tension so suddenly. Everybody laughed, we tried it again and the scene was shot. That was Victor's attitude all through the making of *Evergreen*. He knew perfectly well that he had a sick girl on his hands, but instinctively he had the right touch.

He was right all through that film, he even hit on the right kind of song for one particular scene. He was working out in his mind how to engineer the dénouement that the heroine was not an elderly woman but a young and attractive girl.

'Take your clothes off, that's it, Jessie. Pull off those old-fashioned things, toss them over your shoulder. Over your shoulder goes that one . . .'

Harry Woods, who was writing additional songs for the film, liked the idea. And that's how the hit song *Over my Shoulder* was born, out of the action of the film. He wrote another one for us that still lives today, called *When you've got a little Springtime in your heart*. Rodgers and Hart's music and lyrics were still in but the musical play had been improved immensely. In fact when *Evergreen* was shown, Victor had a wire from Rodgers and Hart saying, 'Wish we'd thought up this story.' Barry MacKay was the new leading man. He was tall, dark, very good-looking and he could also sing and dance.

Of course I was sorry not to be dancing with Fred Astaire. Radio Pictures were now making *The Gay Divorce* with Ginger Rogers as his partner. 'The story's corny, but the dancing will be great and Astaire's got all the charm,' Victor told me. 'But you should be his partner, the others can't hold a candle to you as a performer.' I was grateful for his praise, grateful for the way he pulled me through *Evergreen*. I'd rehearsed the intricate dance number for *Dancing on the Ceiling* with Buddy Bradley one morning, and Victor had shot it the same afternoon. When I was going well, he didn't waste a moment.

Suddenly it was all happening. *Evergreen* was going to be a smash hit. The new contract was drawn up. '£50,000!' Even Sonnie was startled. And then Metro-Goldwyn-Mayer wanted me to go to Hollywood. They made wonderful musicals and they had plans to turn me into an international star.

Gaumont-British wouldn't let me go.

'Oh well,' I said to Sonnie, 'That's fate for you. I'm going to ask them to give me a year off.'

'What!' screamed the film moguls. 'Take a year off? Impossible! You'll be forgotten in a year!'

Chapter Fifteen

In Madeira it was carnival time. Gay lanterns swung in the hotel gardens; there was laughter and music and dancing. And when we came home it was still like a holiday, for the daffodils were blooming on the lawn and there was time to admire them. There was time to do everything I wanted.

Gaumont-British had reluctantly given me time off. After all, if I was having a baby, that was an act of God. 'Just a public appearance now and then,' they urged, and they offered to buy me a new wardrobe filled with star-quality clothes to show me off properly. Between three and four thousand pounds would be spent on me.

'My wife,' said Sonnie tersely, 'dresses to please me.' He turned the offer down flat. Afterwards he told me, 'I'm not having them dress you.' I was rather sorry. No woman likes to turn down a new wardrobe especially when the dresses are by Dior and Molyneux.

Sonnie was like that, very conservative. He would have liked to run our home on the lines of an English country house. Breakfast at eight sharp, silver entrée dishes on the sideboard filled with bacon and eggs and sausages and kidneys. Even when we had to leave the house at six to go to the studios, Sonnie always sat down and ate breakfast in style. I tried to please him when we weren't working, and nibbled a piece of toast and drank a cup of coffee, but when I was working nothing on earth would make me eat.

It was so nice to be rich and have time to spend some money: to go to Wartski's the jewellers, have diamonds laid on a blue velvet cushion and design my own necklace; to order hand-made chiffon undies and lace negligées, which I didn't wear and gave away to my sisters. Playing the hot-house orchid wasn't really my scene. The best times were spent with Sonnie digging in the garden of the Old House at Hampton. I still called the asparagus bed the aspidistra patch and some of the shrubs I planted folded and died as soon as I turned my back, but I was learning to tend a garden and starting what was to become a life-long joy.

One weekend we drove down to Cornwall in search of our country cottage. The estate agent in Truro sent us on a fifteen-mile journey to see a cottage that could only be reached by walking half a mile across a field. It had no gas, no electricity, and the water was drawn up by a pump.

The cottage, built of stone and timber, stood on the slope of a hill overlooking a small tributary that ran down into the estuary of the River Fal. It was small and primitive, two rooms and a kitchen, but from the parlour window was a view that took one's breath away. We'd found our 'room with a view'.

We spent the following weeks searching for furniture in the shops of Falmouth. Everything had to come across on the ferry and then be transported by hand across the fields. I shall never forget the sight of Sonnie trudging home with a roll of linoleum on his back. He dropped it and it rolled all the way down the hill towards the river with Sonnie chasing after it. Just like a scene from a Mack Sennett comedy.

We fried eggs on an oil stove, built log fires in the hearth, and at night we slept in a strange silence broken only by the cry of a cormorant. When the tide was out we had to wear gum boots in the mud at the bottom of our garden, and when the tide was in we rowed our new dinghy down to the village to buy the stores. For a long time I was petrified by the animals that strayed from the nearby farm until I learned to distinguish cows from bulls and found out that pigs do not bite.

During the school holidays Eddie came down with us. He was very good at helping with the chores; he always made the early morning cuppa. One morning we heard him using the pump in the garden, and then he started to sing, a rich tenor voice. 'Good God,' said Sonnie, 'another Matthews stealing the limelight.' Before he returned to school I took him to my singing teacher, Rudolfo Melé, and he said that Eddie's voice should be trained for Grand Opera.

The waiting time was nearly over and I was sublimely happy. If he was a boy, I decided, we'd call him Robert after Sonnie and his father. If she was a girl, we'd call her Catharine after Henry Rowan's wife. I made the kind of plans that every pregnant woman makes. I painted nursery frescoes on the walls of our new extension.

In December my child was born. The nurse showed me Robert in his little quilt of cottonwool. 'His eyes,' she said, when I insisted on knowing, 'are . . .' she hesitated, 'were blue.' Robert had lived for four brief hours.

I lay staring at the ceiling. I could find no tears to soothe the pain. There are not enough words to explain how a woman feels at a time like this. Bereft. Rejected. Abandoned. Then I sat up in bed. I shouted, 'Why? Why? Why does this happen to me?'

Henry rubbed a piece of damp cottonwool against my arm. 'Stop fighting,' he said. His eyes were full of pity and concern as he gave me an injection. I lay back exhausted. What could I do? Life was a dirty fighter. She played too many tricks.

In the days that followed Henry tried to pull me out of my apathy. 'These changes occur with childbirth,' he tried to explain, 'complex emotional changes. You'll soon feel better.' I believe they give women electric shock nowadays to jolt them out of their despair. In those days Henry Rowan did his best with words. 'There could be another baby quite soon. You need not wait for two years.'

A shaft of impossible hope pierced my heart. 'How?'

'You could adopt a child, choose a baby of your own.'

'No! No! No!'

But we did.

She was a very small baby even for only three weeks old. A bare head, creased little face, very underweight. I remember thinking, 'Poor little plain baby. You're so thin. My heart goes out to you. You're so ugly, you need love so badly.'

Catharine grew plumper and prettier every week. 'Look at her hands,' cried Sonnie. 'Have you ever seen such beautiful hands?' For one terrible moment I felt despair that they were not my own baby's hands that Sonnie called so beautiful. But then the feeling went, and it never came back. Catharine was my beloved daughter.

Lena, my sister, came to live with us to look after Catharine while I worked. In a strange way I was reminded that this was my mother's life all over again, bringing in a sister to mind the baby. I didn't want to go back to work. I wanted to stay at home and play with my child and be a housekeeper and a wife. Lena understood this, but she was the only one. Everyone else, including Sonnie, thought there was nothing more exciting than taking up the life again of Jessie Matthews, film star.

The studio spoiled me now. If I wanted a cup of tea, there was one at my elbow. There was always someone around to zip me up, arrange my hair, powder the shine from my nose, run my errands. I knew it wasn't because of my fatal charm, it was to take good care of the company's asset. I was to be kept happy, kept well and kept working. I was getting very well paid but I earned my money. My private life was non-existent. I had two stand-ins now, three hundred fan letters a week and a secretary to answer them, but I was never home early enough to see my daughter in her bath. The films rolled on. *First a Girl*, and then a very happy film called *It's Love Again* with Cyril Wells who was to become one of my great friends. Victor said it was the best picture I had ever made.

During these pictures Victor took Sonnie through the business of directing a film, step by step, showing him what he was doing with the script and all the mechanics of picture making. We knew it was in readiness for the day when Sonnie would direct a film on his own. I wasn't at all prepared when Victor said, 'I can trust you to him rather than anyone else.'

'What do you mean, Victor?'

'I have to move on, kid. I can't go on making the same kind of pictures, I shall lose all my enthusiasm for my professional life. I shall get stale. I'm going to make a picture with Vivien Leigh and Rex Harrison.'

'You're dropping me.'

'Of course not. It's for no other reason than that I want to make a different kind of picture.'

I didn't want Victor Saville to change studios, but he was absolutely right. He went on to make *The Citadel* with Robert Donat and Rosalind Russell, and *Goodbye Mr Chips*.

I then made a picture called *Head over Heels* with my husband as my director. This had always been Sonnie's ambition. He had spent years watching directors at work, asking questions, learning. As Michael Balcon said, he knew the technical side of films thoroughly, he knew production backwards, and of course he knew the personality of his star intimately. But I still wondered, should a husband direct his wife?

Sonnie was a man of many talents. But I'm not sure if film directing was one of them. He was too volatile. Now that he was to direct my new picture it was like starting up a dynamo. He never stopped talking. 'Jessie, what do you think of this? Jessie, say these lines. Let me hear them.' It was a fatal mistake to bring his work home from the studios, it meant that we never had any respite from the picture. 'The Picture' took on enormous, gigantic proportions in Sonnie's life. The film had to succeed, he was going to make it succeed—and I was the core of the film.

Sometimes I wanted to shout, 'For God's sake stop talking, Sonnie. Let's be quiet.' Even driving to the studios at six in the morning, I had to rehearse my lines, listen to my director telling me how I should play the first scene. Of course, I wanted him to make a wonderful film, it was my career too—and there lay the rub. It is a thousand times harder to keep a star on the heights than to get her there. If *Head over Heels* flopped, all the tremendous effort that had made me a star would be wasted. I felt torn so many ways, by my husband, by my director, and by my fear that Sonnie was no Victor Saville.

I knew that Victor had given me this screen personality that went down so well with the public. 'Our Jessie,' the little girl from Soho, the waif with the great big eyes, who had become a sex symbol, the 'pin-up' with the legs, who adorned the bedroom walls of so many young men. He'd handled this image so well, with enough discretion never to make it vulgar. Instinctively, I realised that the time had come for me to move on as well as Victor. I wasn't a little girl any more. I was in my late twenties, I should expand my personality, but Sonnie was sure that 'Our Jessie' was good for a lot more films.

Naturally enough, *Head over Heels* was not an easy film to make. And something else was happening, it was more than a worry, it was an ache, a dread that was with me every day. My mother was ill. She had been suffering from heart trouble for some time, and now the doctor had told her that she must stay permanently in bed. I tried to get over to see her as much as possible. Sometimes Sonnie, under duress, would drive me over to St John's Wood when the work in the studio was over. There was no ill feeling between my husband and my family, but early on Sonnie had decided that my family's way of life and his did not mix.

He parked the car some way from their house this evening, and told me he'd wait for me. Dad opened the door. I noticed that although his hair was greying, his moustache was blacker than ever. I had a strong suspicion that he'd been at the dye bottle. Growing old was something else Dad was going to fight.

My mother was sitting up in bed. Her lovely hair was in two plaits and she wore a green bedjacket that matched the ribbon in her hair. She looked like a little girl who was wearing her mother's pearl earrings. But I noticed that her ears were tinged with blue and she seemed more breathless than ever.

'Where's Sonnie?' she asked.

I wasn't going to say a word that would ripple her happiness at seeing me. 'Hard at work at the studios, darling. He sends his love.'

The bedroom door burst open and Eve, my pretty young sister, rushed in. She was in outdoor clothes and was back from a vaudeville tour. 'I saw Sonnie sitting in the car,' she said. 'I waved, but I'm not sure if he saw me.'

My mother looked at me. 'Why did you lie?' she asked quietly.

She would forgive me I knew, she would understand, but as we drove home tears filled my eyes. Although Sonnie wasn't to blame, I blamed him for my mother's hurt.

The film was nearly over, only nine more days and I should be free. And the rushes were good, Michael Balcon was very pleased. On that particular morning things were going well. The last dance number was nearly over and that meant all the dance sequences would be filmed and in the can. Dressed in a short frilly black dress, I was doing a complicated routine in my role as a French cabaret artiste. It was a good day for me, the adrenalin was running through my blood-stream, my heart was beating faster, and I had the right upsurge of emotional excitement that communicated straight to the camera. Victor

IE HALE   JESSIE MATTHEWS

Jessie played in *This Year of Grace* with her second husband, Sonnie Hale.
Photo: Mitchenson and Mander.

Jessie relaxes with Sonnie from *There Goes the Bride.*

Her first diamond necklace—a g. occasion.

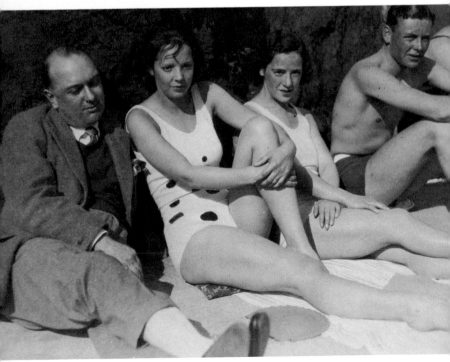

Holidaying in Madeira; sister Lena on her right.

...ie and Lena, two bathing beauties in Madeira.

Off again: Sonnie, Jessie and Lena.

...essie is interviewed and has her hair dressed on the set of *It's Love Again*. Her father-in-law, Robert Hale, is second from right.

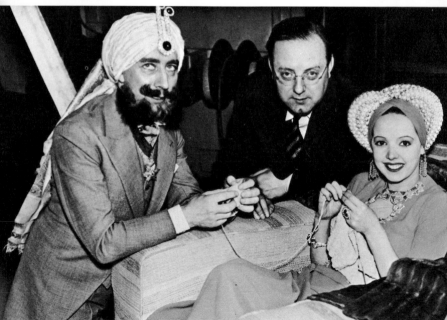

Sonnie, Robert Hale and Jessie relax from *It's Love Again*.
Top: Anton Dolin and Jessie rehearse for the Royal Command Performance 1935.
Right: Exotic costuming for *It's Love Again*.

First a Girl 1935.

Fan picture of the thirties.

Cyril Wells and Jessie in action.
Previous page: Jessie with Cyril Wells, her dancing partner in *It's Love Again*.

had taught me how to sustain this feeling, and when it came, we had always known that the thing to do was to get it on film and keep going.

A scene rarely runs for more than four or five minutes but Sonnie was lagging. To my annoyance he kept stopping the action with instructions to the extras, commands to the prop men.

'Oh, Sonnie, please,' I begged, 'let's get this sequence finished.'

We started again, it was running well, and then 'Cut' once more. Sonnie signalled to the assistant director. 'Lunch, everybody,' called the assistant. 'Back on the set in one hour's time.'

I couldn't believe my ears. How could Sonnie do such a thing? It would only require a few more takes to have the sequence wrapped up. And now I had to stop. Wait for an hour and then get the machine steamed up again. I rushed over to him, blind with anger. 'Don't I matter?' I shouted. 'Couldn't you, at least, have asked me first? Victor would never have done such a thing.'

Sonnie looked up from the running order he was studying. His eyes were cold. 'Shut up,' he said. 'Don't tell me what Victor would do. I'm in charge here.'

'Shut up!' I exploded. 'How dare you! I won't shut up . . . I won't . . .'

Sonnie caught me by the shoulders. He pushed me into a chair. 'Shut up, I say. Calm down.' His voice was filled with contempt. 'You know what will happen if you shout like this. You'll be ill again. You'll cost us all a lot of money.'

I did fall ill again: this time with appendicitis. In the course of the operation the surgeon discovered a piece of twisted gut that had to be removed. Afterwards, I developed a thrombosis in my left leg and immediately began to worry about what would happen. The pain was excruciating. Every now and then I would peep down under the bedclothes to make sure my legs were still there. More than anything I feared to lose my legs.

Another operation followed and then, after weeks in a nursing home, I was allowed home, taking along my Irish nurse, since I couldn't walk and had to be confined to bed. Still, no one would tell me how my legs would turn out.

But one day, Henry my doctor came to see me.

He asked, 'Jessie, would you mind if you had to give up the sort of dancing you do with Buddy Bradley?'

'But that's the easiest sort,' I protested. 'It's my ballet that's really hard.'

Then I realised what he was trying to tell me.

'If I don't dance, I don't live,' I shouted.

Henry left me in the care of my nurse, Harpie as I nicknamed her, because she wore round, pebble glasses, had false teeth and would primp herself in front of the mirror for ages.

In the long hours while I lay in bed a voice would keep going through my head, like a snatch of song you can't forget. It said 'Tell Harpie that you're going to get up, walk round the bed to the door and back again.' I couldn't forget it and one day I startled Harpie as I said 'God says you are to help me up from the bed and let me walk across the room.' I had to mention God: I couldn't think of any other way to explain this voice.

She retorted, 'Tell God from me, he's asking the impossible.'

'Don't argue with God,' I said.

She started to leave the room.

'If you go I will get up on my own. If I do I will hurt myself and you will be responsible.'

She came rushing back, helped me, lifted me to my feet.

'Don't touch me anymore.'

But she hovered near and as I took the first tentative steps I glimpsed her reflection in the mirror. She was holding up the hem of my long white night gown, afraid that I would trip on it. I reached the door and performed a half-pirouette. It had worked!

On my way back to bed I stopped at the window and looked out. The crocuses were in bloom; there was a breath of spring in the air. I felt all the excitement and thrill of life going through me. Lying back against the pillows I experienced the most wonderful, glowing feeling I had ever had. Harpie rushed off to phone Henry. When he came he was livid with anger. What had I been doing, he asked. Did I know I had undone months of work? And, anyway, what was this nonsense? Walking was just impossible.

But I knew it had happened. As he tried to examine me I lay there giggling. 'There's nothing wrong any more,' I insisted.

Henry could find nothing and was very puzzled. But next day he allowed me up for the first time and from then on I mended rapidly. It was a hard struggle. Henry had told me that with my will power I was sure to dance again but it would be agony. And it was. I practised over and over again, fighting against the pain. In the end I won. I could dance again. I had achieved my goal.

Some time after that, I was in a show in Brighton and Henry came to see me with his family. With the show over, Henry came backstage and greeted me with tears in his eyes.

'I watched the miracle leg,' he said.

The day I went back to the studios we had a party on the set. Everyone was very kind. The newspapers printed a picture of a frail looking actress, 'Jessie Matthews, victim of stardom, goes back to work' was the headline, and in the next column Sir Alexander Korda was quoted on how great are the pressures on a star.

It was all over and I was well again. When the picture was finished Sonnie and I went to South America for our holiday, all the bad days forgotten and the same warm feeling between us once more. On the ship sailing back from Rio de Janeiro we made our plans for the next film. Suntanned, delighted to be home again, we came down the gangway at Southampton. Photographers and reporters jostled for a place.

'What are your plans, Miss Matthews?' someone shouts.

'Our next film . . .' I start to say.

'What next film?' a reporter calls. 'There aren't going to be any films. Haven't you heard? They've gone broke.'

Sonnie drops his briefcase. I clutch his arm. The cameras click and our astonished faces go down on print for posterity.

'Production's stopped at Gaumont-British. They're finished.'

What had happened while we were sunbathing in the sun? We didn't stop to answer any more questions. We went straight from the ship to a meeting of Gaumont-British directors at their offices in Wardour Street. It was true. Gaumont-British were in deep trouble. The Ostrer Brothers, Isadore, Mark and Maurice were going to concentrate on showing films in their chain of cinemas, instead of making them. And I had a contract to make three more films!

Lena was waiting for us at Hampton holding little

Catharine's hand. Eddie was grinning in the background. We'd been away for just six weeks and even at home things had changed. Lena was engaged to be married to her Leslie and was leaving us. And then there was Eddie's news. 'I've got a job as a chorus boy,' he told us. He was going into a Cochran show.

We sat at home and tried not to watch the telephone. Sonnie dug the garden and I practised in my dance studio that had been converted from an old barn. The bills came through the letter box for this part of the house we'd had converted, for that new extension. For the past few years we'd been spending money as if it grew on trees. Suddenly it looked as if it was all over.

And then the summons came from Wardour Street. I was still a good money-maker. *Head over Heels* was making money in the circuit, we had the go-ahead to make our next film *Gangway*. It wasn't quite the same. Shepherd's Bush studios were closed down, and we worked in rented studios in Pinewood. People talked about budgets now and costing, and we were asked to make public appearances to open new cinemas where they were showing American films.

But we were working and making money. After the next film in my contract *Sailing Along*, we took Catharine for a holiday to Switzerland. She was three now but I still refused to let newspapers take pictures of her. I wanted no one to accuse me of using my child for publicity, and when I spoke of her I always said, 'Catharine, my adopted daughter.' I wanted Catharine to grow up with nothing to hide.

The show business label that Sonnie and I had one of the happiest of marriages was peeling a little at one corner. Sonnie wandered now and then. But never too far and never enough to really hurt. When he brought me a lovely gift or a new piece of jewellery, I guessed that Sonnie and some lady in the film business might be holding hands. But he was always discreet, and it never lasted very long. I knew the dangers we had around us, we were young and well-off, but most of the time we worked too hard to have time to play.

It was during this time that we lost the heart of our family. All Berwick Market came to my mother's funeral. 'To the lady of the market' was written on so many wreaths and a hundred cars were in her farewell procession. I don't think she would have wanted so much pomp and ceremony. But for us who were left behind and for whom life would never be quite the same again, we were glad to know that she was so well loved.

I was sad that she would never live in the little house I had bought for her and my father in Ruislip, Middlesex; that she would never see the green fields and the pretty valleys. Dad, in his long overcoat, looked old and bowed after the funeral. All the fight went out of him when mother died, and Rosie and her husband agreed to live with him in the new house.

'Our next film,' said Sonnie, who was now confident of his powers of direction, 'will be a big one. A musical extravaganza. We'll put British films back on the map.'

The Ostrer brothers agreed. Sonnie and Lesser Samuels sat down to write the script: I rehearsed the dances with Buddy Bradley, the music was composed, the recordings made and the production was ready to go on the floor. 'Wait!' commanded Front Office. We waited. 'Go ahead!' ordered the big brass, and then had a re-think, 'no, wait another week.' The setting up of a film before it goes on the floor is always an uncertain business. A great deal of money is involved, and the company was having its troubles. 'Scrap it!' Sonnie's big musical was axed. 'Turn the script into something cheaper to make.'

Sonnie was angry. Weeks of frustrating delay before they made up their minds and worse still, during this time his contract had lapsed and now they decided not to renew it.

'Who do they think I am?' he raged. 'An office boy? I've slaved my guts out on this script and now they say they don't want me.'

'If they haven't the money, there's not much they can do.'

'Fine words,' retorted Sonnie. 'Your contract's still got months to run. Tell them you won't do it,' he ordered. 'Tell them, no!'

Then we'd both be out of a job, I thought. We'd make enemies at the studio and when the industry recovered where should we be. 'There are other films for you, Sonnie.'

'Never.' He was adamant. 'I'll never make another film.' He did, of course, he took a part in the Edgar Wallace film, *The Ringer*, but he was very angry and resentful. And a lot of his spleen was vented on me. I shall always remember those days, for Sonnie's ill humour made me glad to go off to the studios every day. Then as the film progressed I was anxious to get to the studios but for a very different reason.

Maurice Ostrer gave me director approval. I went along to the projection room with him to watch three reels taken from films by three directors to decide which man I should prefer. Of the three Ostrer brothers Maurice was the one who decided about the pictures; Isadore, reputed to be the real brains of the company, was the big financial man at the back, and Mark was the brother who looked after the distribution of the pictures.

I chose the reel from the film I liked best. Maurice looked surprised. 'He's one of our contract directors. Rather young, and he's never done a musical.'

'But this isn't going to be a musical.'

The young director, I learned afterwards, was just as surprised as Maurice. He was also slightly embarrassed because Sonnie had been taken off the picture and he wasn't sure if he could succeed with a musical star like Jessie Matthews. 'I don't know anything about music,' he told Maurice.

'Don't worry,' said Maurice. 'We're just doing the book.'

'But how can you make a film of a musical comedy book without the music? The situation won't be strong enough to hold on its own.'

I went along to meet the young director knowing nothing of this. Not realising that *Climbing High*, as the film was to be called, was considered to be a risky subject and was going to be pared to the bone. He was a very large young man, unusually tall and broad shouldered, nice looking with strong features. But a completely new breed of director to me. All the other directors I'd known looked as if they'd been born in the business. There was no slickness about this young man. He was calm and gentle, and his name was Carol Reed.

I left that meeting aware of two things, and both of them made me feel awkward. First, my loyalty to Sonnie, my husband, whose script was going to be drastically changed, and second, this was my last film on contract and Carol Reed didn't like what was happening any more than I did.

Four weeks later we were on the floor shooting the film. I met my leading man and five minutes later I found myself lying on the studio floor making love to a handsome young man who was billed as, 'The Wonder Boy of Modern Filmland'.

'Oh God,' the young man, whose name was Michael Redgrave, removed himself from our tight embrace and sat up. 'Must I say these dreadful lines?' he asked in a pained Royal Academy of Dramatic Art voice. 'Such ghastly musical comedy dialogue.'

I surveyed the wonder boy. He'd made three films in rapid succession and behaved as if he'd invented the medium. 'My husband wrote that ghastly dialogue.' You could have scraped the ice off my voice.

'Sorry, darling,' said Michael, 'but one must admit . . . mustn't one?' Carol Reed looked down at us, there was a twinkle in his eye.

When I got home that night I exploded to Sonnie. 'Those two young know-alls. They're still wet behind the ears and yet they act as if they'd just made *The Birth of a Nation*.'

Sonnie was delighted. For all the wrong reasons he crowed with laughter. 'I told you how it would be without me.'

Chapter Sixteen

I walked onto the set. Regal. Shoulders back, head held high. Yards of pink chiffon designed by Norman Hartnell swirled around my ankles. On my head rested a turban to match. I loved the way I looked. I loved the whistles I was getting from the boys up on the gantry.

Carol Reed regarded me carefully. He examined the exquisite Hartnell gown and the chic turban. 'Matthews,' he said gently, 'when you take off that "I'm so beautiful" look we might start shooting.'

It was as if he'd poured a bucket of water over me. Every vestige of my self-confidence vanished. Then it came back, like a tornado. 'How dare you?' I cried. 'It took Victor Saville five years to get that look on my face. I used to sidle on to the set looking like a half-drowned cat until I learned not to be frightened of people like you. That look, as you call it, is on! And it bloody well stays on!'

The silence on the set was absolute. At last the young director and the star had clashed. And then Carol Reed laughed, a deep infectious laugh. 'Keep it,' he laughed, 'keep it, but not the hat. Not the hat, please. You don't need all these trimmings. You've got enough without them.'

The tension vanished. He was right, I knew. My gorgeous gowns were wrong for the cheap budget film *Climbing High* must become. In fact to make this film succeed would take a minor miracle. That wasn't going to stop us trying, of course. Carol told me, 'I have to be in love with my picture to make it work.' I understood exactly how he felt. Whatever the material you must have faith in it, believe in it, or it wouldn't come across. We needed a lot of faith for this film.

Carol Reed was an unusual man to work with. There was none of the brisk camaraderie that would be gone just as soon as the last shot was in the can. He lived with the picture. He had a habit of walking up and down, his head bent, worrying, working out the next scene. 'I'm not critical of what you're doing,' he said to me. 'I'm just thinking. I admire those directors who can sit around and have cups of tea and laugh and joke and tell stories, but I cannot.'

He worried that the film was wasting my talent as a dancer and singer, worried that this was the first film with a 'personality' that he'd tried. 'I'm feeling a little ashamed, Matthews,' he said. 'You deserve more than you're getting this time.'

He need not have been. We were both the same age, getting on for thirty, but I'd been in films ever since the old silent days, while his ideas were new and interesting. And he passed them on to me, showed me another dimension of the movie business. 'The whole point is,' he told me, 'that you put the damn thing into a can and send it off all over the world. There's a tremendous international market. I'm going to travel, Matthews, and find out what these audiences want.'

And I could pass on my years of experience to him. He listened attentively when we discussed camera shots. Arguments between us were over after the sparks of the first three days. We discussed the problems of scaling down the sets designed for a musical extravanganza. There was no point any more in having a great baronial staircase and a ballroom designed for a thousand extras. The art director was outraged by the new simplicity and departed in a huff. A new art director was engaged.

Michael Redgrave and I still had our differences. Sometimes he acted as if he knew every angle of the film business. I longed to tell him to stop teaching Granny to suck eggs. One day I was able to. There was a short dance sequence left in the film. Surely to God, I thought, Michael won't turn out to be a second Nijinski? He came over to me and said 'Now this is where you can teach me to dance.' I replied, 'Michael, I can teach you *nothing*.'

An awkward situation developed rapidly. Carol Reed

walked over to me, he led me out of earshot. 'Matthews,' he said severely, 'you're a bad girl. Apologise. At once!'

After my apology Michael and I became friends. I even let him into one of my little secrets: putting a tiny piece of embalming wax between the space in my two upper teeth. Michael had the same problem with a gap in his lower teeth. 'But keep away from tomato sauce,' I told him, 'it stains, and you'll look like Dracula.'

Climbing High had its share of slapstick. There was one ridiculous scene where I had a tin of paint poured over me and then received a custard pie slap in the face. On the day of the shooting I begged Carol to get it over with early so that I could have my hair washed and set to go to the ballet at Covent Garden. He promised that he'd try. For some reason or other shooting was delayed and by late afternoon I knew that my evening at the ballet was off. The studio wind machine whirred, the pies flew, two of them scored a bull's eye, and with custard pie dripping all over me the scene was shot.

Later when I returned to the set in slacks and sweater with a towel around my head, there was Carol engrossed in the script, seated in his chair at the edge of the set. Nearby was a prop cake rake with one unused custard pie on top. It was too good an opportunity to pass by. I'd missed the ballet after all. I picked up the pie, tiptoed up behind him. Wallop! The stunned expression on his face as he pushed away the oozing mess was too much for the crew on the gantry. They hooted with laughter, and I was laughing so hard that I forgot to run for shelter.

Carol was up and after me. I climbed towards the gantry with him in pursuit. The crew and the electricians tried to trip him up, but at last he caught up with me.

'Matthews,' he cried, 'now you're for it.' Bits of pie showered from his head as he whirled me round. He may have given me a whack, I don't know, but in that second, we both knew that the reason for the chase was as old as Adam and Eve. He might be the most promising young director, I might be the most modern of actresses, but our instincts were suddenly as old-fashioned as a Victorian Valentine.

One afternoon we finished early at the studios and Carol drove me home to Hampton. I couldn't resist asking him in and showing him over the Old House.

He came slowly down the wide staircase, and he had enough of the actor in him to make it look impressive. I watched him pause and admire the oil paintings, run his hand over the gleaming mahogany of the balustrade. With pride surging inside me, I asked him how he liked the home that had taken me so much time and money to perfect. It was as important that he should admire the Old House as I did.

'It's too much, Matthews,' he said, 'it's all too much.'

My face fell. And yet I should have known. He'd told me often enough that possessions bored him. He didn't want to be tied to any place, any town, or, I thought sadly, any woman. He didn't want marriage.

He stood on the bottom step looking down at me. 'It's a very grand house,' he said gently, 'too grand for me.'

After he'd seen all there was to be seen, we went for a walk in the park. My housekeeper came too, for in 1938 it was not admissable that we walk alone. When she ran on with the dogs, Carol and I held hands and talked about a solution—that was growing more and more obscure.

Sonnie didn't know that his wife had fallen in love with her director. We were working in different studios, on different films and we saw little of each other nowadays. I felt that Sonnie's character had changed. He seemed single-minded, ruthless in his efforts to get back on top. He still felt keenly the disappointment over the cancelled musical and his lapsed contract. I had forgotten that Sonnie had always been fired with ambition. Perhaps I was now comparing him to another man who did not value the material things of life as he did.

Carol's ideas were bohemian for those days. He didn't want a large home with servants. A hotel room or a rented flat while the film was shooting was enough. Then on to the next film. He showed me a new kind of freedom, and I was very tempted.

When the film was over we arranged to meet in Madame Tussauds' of all places, and afterwards we went for a drive round Regent's Park. He stopped his little car outside one of the beautiful Regency houses of Cumberland Terrace. The sun shone on the magnificently windowed façade. We sat and admired it. 'I'll buy you a house like this, one day,' he said.

I shook my head. 'Far too many windows to clean.'

We were saying goodbye. I couldn't go with him because I was a puritan at heart and thought that love must lead to marriage. I couldn't go with him because I would lose my daughter Catharine and I couldn't bear to inflict such a hurt on her.

'I wish I could have done more for you, Matthews,' he said softly. 'I wish the picture could have been better.'

'It doesn't matter. I met you. That's enough.'

For years afterwards every time I heard his name mentioned and they talked of the new girl he had on his arm, I felt I had suffered a loss. Would I have been happier had I gone with him? I don't know. But it is always the chances you turn down that are the chances you regret most.

The rift between Sonnie and myself took time to heal. Sonnie had always been the leader in our partnership; the intellect, as he often told me, was all on his side. When he told me that he had decided we should return to the stage and do a musical play, he took it for granted that I would raise no objection. As a team I knew we were tops, a return to the theatre would be lovely, but for some strange reason I felt we might be doing the wrong thing.

The arguments ended in the usual way. Sonnie won. But one afternoon I leant out of the window and called to Sonnie, 'September 3rd,' I announced dramatically. I don't know why I said it, it just popped out of my head.

Sonnie looked up at me. 'You silly cow,' he said amiably, 'it's gone.'

'You silly sod,' I retorted, 'it's coming. That's the danger for our show.' I felt quite proud of my premonition, although I hadn't a clue what it meant.

But there were real, down to earth reasons why I was unsure about our new venture. Putting on a big musical play is enormously expensive, and we should be footing the bills. Hale Productions, as Sonnie called our company, would be in clover if the show succeeded, but if it failed all our savings would go straight down the drain.

My farewell film *Climbing High*, in spite of Carol Reed's faultless direction, had just missed the carefree touch so necessary for the type of light comedy done so well in Hollywood. But if the film was a failure, the new musical show *I Can Take It* was going to be a smash hit. Every town we visited on our provincial tour had 'Sold Out' boards on the theatre doors. Sir

Oswald Stoll came down and saw us at Southsea and our London opening was assured. We should play at the London Coliseum and he hoped we'd score as big a hit as *The White Horse Inn*.

The show was a family affair. Robert Hale, Sonnie's father, had a part, and so had Eddie, my brother. Then every time we played a seaside town, Catharine and her Nanny came down to stay with us. Since Lena had left us, finding the right nanny had been difficult, but Beth, a Norland House nanny, had joined us. A couple of years younger than I was, pretty in a fair English way, Beth was absolutely trustworthy and responsible, and Catharine soon grew to love her.

'See how wrong you were,' Sonnie reminded me. 'Isn't it great to be back in the theatre, playing to full houses and with a success on our hands.'

Only one dark cloud marred out tour. My father was dying. Towards the end of the tour I was going back and forth to Ruislip by train two or three times a week. On our last day at the King's Theatre, Southsea, I phoned Ruislip for news and decided I would return, but an hour before I left a telegram came from home: 'Stay with the show Love Dad.' He died that night, only sixty-three years old. Not a great age, but perhaps when you've done a man's job from the age of ten and raised a large family of children, he felt it was time enough.

My love–hate relationship with my father always worried me. Rosie and Lena have told me that he was very proud of me, that I always misunderstood him. Perhaps I did. Now I can remember him with love. Whatever he was, I am a part of it.

The tour of *I Can Take It* began in Sheffield at Christmas 1938 and ended in July 1939 in Blackpool. Our next hurdle was the London opening on September 12th. The original date was September 13th, but because of my premonition about dates, we thought the 13th might be unlucky and chose the 12th.

History changed all the dates. But no one could believe that Hitler would really march into Poland, that we would go to war. We spent £3,000 improving and enlarging the sets for the Coliseum and at 10.45 am. on Sunday September 3rd, 1939, two large vans containing the scenery for our show rolled up the ramp to the back of the Coliseum theatre. Sonnie and I had driven down and were waiting in our car. Beth and Catharine sat in the back seat—they had come for the outing.

I saw a man coming towards us. He was weeping. Every few paces he stopped and wiped the tears from his dark cheeks. It was Buddy Bradley. I threw open the door and raced towards him.

'What is it, Buddy? What is it?'

At first he couldn't speak, his distress was too great. Then he wept, 'It's all over. Everything's finished. We're at war.'

When we got back to the car Sonnie announced in a lost voice, 'I've just been told. There's going to be an immediate blackout. All cinemas and theatres will be closed down. We're done for.'

Inside the theatre the rest of the company waited for us. Sonnie mounted a wooden box. 'You'll all be paid,' he shouted. 'Don't worry, kids. We'll wind up the show, and you'll all get what's coming to you.'

The chorus girls, twelve of them, were the first to answer. 'We're all in the same boat, Mr Hale,' shouted one. 'Don't lose heart,' called another. 'We can wait.' It was heart-warming to hear them and their courage and goodwill helped, but the bleak realisation that we'd lost every penny we had was hard to bear.

To add to our misery, the air sirens sounded and we all crawled under the ancient stage of the Coliseum waiting for the first bombs to fall. It was a false alarm. The all-clear sounded, we said our goodbyes and drove with Sonnie's father down to Maidenhead. As we turned into the drive of Raylands, I began to cry. 'It's happened,' I sobbed. 'Just like I said it would on September 3rd.'

'Christ!' said Sonnie. 'That's all I need, a bloody soothsayer.'

Belle, my mother-in-law, opened the door. Belle didn't believe in letting 'nervy people' collapse. She caught me by the shoulders and gave me a good shake. I cried even harder. 'Give her some whisky,' Belle cried. 'Where's the whisky?'

'I need it more than she does,' declared Sonnie, and then he took charge. Give Sonnie an emergency and he was wonderful. 'Get back in the car,' he ordered. An hour later, God knows how, our suitcases were put back and the four of us were driving down to the cottage in Cornwall.

We drove non-stop all through the night while Sonnie settled the war, what regiment he'd join, what work I'd do, where Catharine would be evacuated. He was still talking when we arrived at the cottage. I made us all a cup of tea, and then in the middle of a sentence, Sonnie stopped, laid down his cup and saucer, and started to laugh. 'But, of course,' he crowed, 'of course.' He marched off to the spare room, locked himself in, and began to write.

Sonnie sat down with a pencil and a pad of paper and started to turn the musical play *I Can Take It* into a small intimate revue. I thought he'd gone off his head but it was probably his therapy to ease the strains and stresses of the past few weeks. And he was right. A couple of weeks after war was declared theatres were allowed to open again, but by then the £15,000 advance booking fees for the Coliseum Show had all gone back into the public's pockets and audiences in London were thin on the ground. But the London suburbs and provinces still needed entertainment and an economical revue could and did survive.

Come Out to Play was the lifeline we clung to until London audiences showed signs of revival. The scenery and props and the company from the big show were pared down, and it worked. We toured the suburbs and provinces and in March 1940 we opened at the Phoenix Theatre in Charing Cross Road. The autumn of 1940 marked the onset of the long grim struggle against Hitler. We were frightened. Who isn't frightened of a bomb that might blast you to hell? But we decided that if we were going to die, then let it be in London and let it be together. Catharine and Beth came back from their unwelcome evacuation in Cornwall, we moved our beds down to the ground floor of the Old House, and in the end we slept through the bombings.

Our problems grew. The domestic staff, except for Mr and Mrs Gatfield, had left us. Sonnie did as much gardening as he had time for, and we ate his vegetables. I cleaned before we left for the theatre and Beth took over the jobs I had no time to do. I was always afraid she might be called up and then who would look after Catharine? 'Don't worry, Mrs Hale,' she told me. 'You're my war work.' And she did become part of our family.

Before *Come Out to Play* ended I had an offer from John Gielgud to appear in *French Without Tears*. I was overjoyed, a great opportunity, I could move into stage comedy, but Sonnie had other ideas. He wanted to play Dame in the pantomime *Aladdin* in Birmingham, and the proviso was that I play principal boy.

Sonnie had always wanted to be a Dame in pantomime and he was determined not to lose this opportunity. 'What happens if you're taken ill when touring with Gielgud?'

'Why on earth should I be taken ill?'

'I'm not saying you *will* be taken ill. I'm saying, *suppose* you're taken ill.'

I went to Birmingham. The script for the pantomime had been pulled straight out of mothballs. It reeked with age. And the times of the performances made my blood run cold. First performance eleven in the morning, second, two in the afternoon. There were compensations. Good friends, the Prices, with a house in Solihull invited us to stay with them, and Beth and Catharine came too. Sonnie and I used to look out of our bedroom window at night and see the evil glow of fires raging in Birmingham after the savage bombings, and hear the nightmare waves of Nazi bombers devastating Coventry. In the morning we would drive into Birmingham and feel physically ill when we saw the rows of trim houses with their walls ripped off, and factories razed to the ground, burying hundreds of night workers.

The doors of the Alexandra Theatre opened at 10.30 am. and our audiences poured in. Bless their hearts, they laughed at our antics and for a short time forgot the horror outside. Sid Fields, the most talented comedian I have ever had the good fortune to work with, was in *Aladdin*. His great bleary face, his beautiful eyes, and the effeminate voice he affected played on the audience till they rolled in the aisles. He'd fold his cloth cap very carefully and dab it at his stooge. His material was so polished, so great. I'm sure some of the later comics, Tony Hancock and Frankie Howerd, were influenced by him. Off stage he was just as funny, we all loved him. Dear Sid, it was a great tragedy that he died just when he was at the height of his great success.

After a three-month run we returned unscathed to Hampton. As a matter of fact a bomb did sail right through the theatre roof during the 'dead week' before the next show came on, but obviously it was not meant for us.

Sonnie answered the phone the day after we arrived back.

He came out to the kitchen where I was washing up. 'It's an offer for you,' he said. 'A musical show called *The Lady Comes Across.*'

I turned, delighted at the news. 'That's great.'

'I'm not so sure you'll think it's great when you know where you have to go.'

At that moment Beth came in from the garden where she'd been hanging out the washing. She stood in the doorway pushing back the pale strands of hair that had blown across her face. Sonnie's eyes rested on her and I caught the fleeting expression that came over his face. Sudden swift joy. A split second and it vanished.

Sonnie turned his head and looked at me. 'The show will open in New York. You'll have to go to America. Why do you look so shocked? It's good news.'

I felt shocked, but it wasn't about going to America, it was the sudden knowledge of what had happened to Sonnie that shook me.

Chapter Seventeen

'You can't come running back here with your tail between your legs,' shouted Sonnie over the telephone, as if a continent already separated us instead of barely one hundred miles—the distance from Hampton to this bleak airfield outside Bristol. 'Catch that plane. You must go.'

From the second I fastened my seat belt on that small noisy plane there was no going back. How many times afterwards did I wish I had walked out of that wooden hut on the airfield, halted a car, walked, hitch-hiked, anything rather than have set off on that journey. But it was too late when we got to Ireland, too late in Lisbon, and in New York, with a million lights piercing the peaceful American skies, it was much too late.

Yesterday hadn't been easy. The three of them, Sonnie, Catharine and Beth, stood by the gate waving goodbye. I clung to my view of them from the taxi window. I was still waving when the car turned the corner, but they had already gone and I was waving to an empty space. Not for the first time I wondered if I was making a monumental mistake. An urgent call at the airfield, from the agency who had booked me for the American show, made me turn back as I was about to mount the steps to the plane. 'There's a hold-up in New York. The show won't be ready to start rehearsals for a month at least. Delay your departure.'

It seemed reasonable to telephone Sonnie and say I was coming home. But Sonnie told me to board the plane and go. So used to obeying him, I went.

The thought of going to America alone had filled me with dread from the onset. As soon as I took down my suitcase and started packing I was scared. The truth is that my work has always scared me, and I start fretting the moment I know it is settled and I must go.

In 1941 I was more scared than usual. It was wartime and I didn't want to leave my loved ones. Of course Sonnie and I bickered now and then, but ours was a marriage with the cracks cemented by years of working together and our understanding that performers are hell to live with. Tempers could rocket and blaze but tensions would evaporate when we told each other to stop acting our heads off.

God knows every marriage has its rough patches, especially in show business where the temptations lie thick on the ground. Sonnie's eyes might wander, a man with gentle ways might woo me, but we always came back together. It wasn't a 'slippers by the fire, cocoa in the kitchen sort of marriage'. It was a relationship tangled up with love and hate, but it was the only marriage I wanted. Why did we have to separate now, I asked him?

'*I Can Take It* nearly wiped us out. Think of the money you'll earn. American dollars for Britain, and a balance in the bank again.'

'But I'll be alone. What about if I'm ill?' I reminded him how he'd persuaded me to turn down the Gielgud play.

Sonnie could win any argument. He brushed aside my doubts. 'You'll soon be alone, anyway. I'm going to be called up.' He had volunteered for war service but they'd always turned him down because of his poor eyesight. Now the authorities weren't so particular. 'Anyway,' he insisted, 'you won't be away long, your visa is only for six months, and as soon as you get to New York send for Catharine and give the kid a real holiday.'

It wasn't easy to say goodbye to Catharine. She had grown into the prettiest little girl, a shy little mite with a sweet nature who could twist me round her little finger.

'If you go away, Mummy, can I have a pony?'

'We'll see, darling.'

Her face suddenly crumpled with apprehension. She threw her arms around my waist. 'I don't want a pony, Mummy, I want you to stay. Please don't go.'

I held her tight. 'If I go, you shall come over to New York. I promise.'

* * *

167

The promise I had made to my daughter was with me as the Imperial Airways plane rose in the sky leaving the chequered fields of England behind. We flew across the Irish Sea to Dublin and the strange neutrality of Ireland. We were a mixed bag of travellers. Apart from a few tight-lipped diplomatic types, there were two young American brothers called Heil who said, most unconvincingly, that they had been on a fishing trip. I noticed that the elder, Henry, had a white exhausted look on his face, the kind of look I had seen on my own face after six weeks of gruelling rehearsals. To my amazement he told me that he'd seen me in pantomime in Birmingham that winter.

'Whatever were you doing in Birmingham?' I asked.

'Fishing,' he said laconically.

In Dublin we all piled into a bus and were driven across to Shannon on the west coast. Next to me on the bus sat a Spaniard who whispered that he was Franco's special envoy and gave me his leather briefcase filled with top secret documents to use as a head rest.

I spent a night in Lisbon then boarded a Pan American Clipper en route to the Azores. As I took my seat next to an elegant American lady, in the row opposite I caught a glimpse of a head of shining black hair. 'Bebe!' I cried. There sat Bebe Daniels, looking as young and lovely as when she was leading lady to Douglas Fairbanks in those early movies. Next to her sat Ben Lyon, her husband, and the kindest and nicest of men.

Bebe and Ben were going home to America to see their two children, Barbara and Richard, and have a break from the tough months spent entertaining the bombed-out British. Bebe introduced me to the charming American lady who sat in the seat next to mine. She was Mrs Rose Kennedy, the wife of Joseph Kennedy who had been American Ambassador in London, and whose extraordinary family had a tragic destiny awaiting them.

Mrs Kennedy was a very pleasant companion and we talked about our children. 'How old is your little daughter?' she asked.

'Just six.'

'You're going to miss her.' I explained that I had been told to apply for permission to bring her over as soon as I got to New York.

Mrs Kennedy looked at me curiously, 'That isn't possible. I'm afraid whoever told you that told you a lie. You should have arranged all that in London. I doubt very much if you'll be able to bring her over now.'

I couldn't believe what she said, but as she answered my questions I had to accept that the wife of an American diplomat could not be wrong. Who had made the mistake then? Sonnie? At length Mrs Kennedy murmured something about taking a nap and suggested we close our eyes.

My mind was in a ferment. Didn't Sonnie want Catharine to follow me? Had he known that I could do nothing once I left England? Two small pictures clicked in and out of my mind. Beth's face as she came in from the garden. Sonnie's when he'd looked at her. I told myself that I was insanely jealous to imagine such things. But the misgivings already with me burst out of their hiding place. Words screeched around my mind. 'You've lost your husband. Lost your home. Lost your child. You're alone. Rejected!'

I told myself not to be a fool, not to cry. But the tears rolled down my cheeks remorselessly. Nothing would stay them. I felt that I would cry for ever.

'Hi, kid,' a low voice said in my ear, 'what's wrong?'

'Help me,' I managed to say, 'please help me, Ben.'

Within seconds Bebe was at my side. She took my seat while Ben guided me across the aisle to take her's. Shielding me with his back from the rest of the passengers, he talked to me.

'Keep talking, Ben, anything,' I pleaded. He told me about his home in America, his children. 'D'you know what Barbara did then . . .?' He cracked jokes, tossed in the corniest gags, he put on a great display of non-stop patter—and he saved me. My tears dried, my mind slowed down and I could smile. Gratitude is a small word for what I owed to Ben and Bebe. All through the long exhausting flight I knew they were there if I needed them. By the time we arrived in New York and came down the steps to face a battery of cameras and newsmen, I had on my public face and was ready.

'Lift your skirt another inch, will you, Jessie.'

'Great big smile now, baby.'

Surrounded by newsmen firing questions, flashing pictures, I knew I had entered a world where privations and rationing were unheard of. Big, noisy, booming America.

Broadway, here I come. And God help me, I prayed.

It was the smell of New York that I remember most, the over-powering stink of petrol fumes. No matter on what street or avenue I had lived in that city the tall buildings seemed to trap the pungent odour of petrol fumes. When I'd first gone there as a sixteen year old, New York had reminded me of a gigantic circus, somehow transitory, as if all the rainbow lights and sky-high façades might be taken down when the audience went home. In 1930, when I came again, the buildings had multi-plied, steadied themselves, and looked more permanent. Now, eleven years later, New York was a wonderful place all right. It seemed like one huge dazzling shop window filled with all the luxuries we'd forgotten about in England. And the food . . . oh dear, what food they had in New York.

The theatre management met me and escorted me to a delightful apartment hotel called the Windsor. I'd hardly had time to smell the bouquets of flowers or admire the magnificent bowls of fruit when the phone rang. A well remembered voice said, 'Hi, Mugsy!'

I was so happy to hear a known voice, so delighted that I wasn't completely alone in this great overpowering city, that I forgot the owner of this voice had always brought disastrous complications into my life.

Johnny Nathan, a young Jewish lawyer, had elbowed his way into my life eleven years ago when I went to New York with *Wake Up and Dream*—at Cochran's suggestion that I keep out of the way until Sonnie's divorce. Johnny, in spite of his brash ways, had been fun, and although he knew I was marry-ing Sonnie, he escorted Lizzie Brayne and myself to all the night spots.

He was a real whizz kid, the kind that Jewish New York seems to breed. His personality crackled, he knew everyone, everyone liked him, and his outrageousness bowled Lizzie and I over. His tough, wise-cracking conversation enchanted us, he was right out of the new gangster movies.

'My brain's as quick as lightning and just as crooked,' he'd joke. But there was more than a vestige of truth in that, for he wasn't fussy about the kind of case he took on.

Johnny was the perfect companion until he decided to embark on a violent courtship. 'Come on, come on,' he said one day. 'You don't want to marry that goddamn Limey. Marry me.' Lizzie and I fell about laughing, especially when he swore he'd kill himself if I didn't agree. At 3 am. next morning the phone started ringing. The desk clerk in the lobby begged me to come down as Mr Nathan had had an accident. I refused. The phone rang again. 'Mr Nathan had shot himself and was dying.' This time the horrified voice at the other end convinced me. I rushed into Lizzie Brayne's room. Lizzie, usually calm and collected, went berserk. 'Oh God,' she groaned, 'there'll be newsmen, police, bad publicity. Just what we mustn't have. I'll go down, but you stay here. Don't move!'

Almost beside myself with worry I waited for her to return. Eventually I heard a commotion outside the door. I jerked it open. Beside Lizzie swayed an extremely drunk man. Johnny, his hat on the back of his head, a cigar between his fingers, roared with laughter.

The cruelty of his joke appalled me. That, as far as I was concerned, was the last I wanted to see of Johnny Nathan. But later he persisted, once more bouncing through the door, good looking, debonair, full of plans to help me, entertain me, be my business manager—and afterwards I fell for it all over again.

I'd barely settled down when Victor Saville telephoned from Hollywood and asked me to do three days' shooting on a charity film that the British community were making in appreciation of Roosevelt's help to Britain. With the musical's rehearsals still undecided, I accepted happily. Technically, I was still a free agent as I hadn't signed the theatrical contract, and the management agreed that I should go.

Just as I was about to board the plane I was called back to reception. There in a frenzy of excitement was Johnny Nathan. In his hand was the contract. 'Come on, come on, sign it, sign it, before you leave,' he pressurised. I signed.

If New York had seemed a haven of plenty, Hollywood was paradise. From the heights of Beverley Hills where I stayed with Victor and Phoebe Saville, the lights of Los Angeles sparkled like a diamond treasure trove against a black velvet sky. For two weeks I was fêted and spoiled and I loved every moment. My part in the film *Forever and a Day* with Ian Hunter and Buster Keaton was soon over, and then I was invited to the kind of Hollywood parties I'd read about in fan magazines. So many of my old friends were in Hollywood: Anna Neagle, Gladys Cooper, Cedric Hardwicke, Charles Laughton. . . . Of all the famous faces I saw at these parties, one stands out in my memory: Merle Oberon, veiled in black, a purple orchid in her hair, looking the most exotic blossom this side of Samarkand.

For two weeks I'd been too busy and excited to stop and think about the problems I had left in England. I didn't want to go back to New York to a lonely apartment and my lonely thoughts. Then it happened. I was asked to make a film. Shooting was scheduled to start at once and the film would be finished in four weeks. Even more exciting, my co-star would be Fred Astaire. I was being given back a dream.

'Remember, way back in the thirties, when you were offered a contract to dance with me,' Fred said when he met me. 'Why didn't you come? Wasn't I good enough for you?'

We laughed together, and I thanked him again for the telegram he'd sent me all those years ago urging me to accept. I hadn't been able to accept, my British studio wouldn't let me go. Now I was free to do what I wanted. I remembered the theatre contract and brushed it aside. Of course they wouldn't mind. Why, the script of the musical play wasn't even finished, and there was no date fixed for rehearsals.

'Even if rehearsals don't begin for months, you have signed a contract with us.' The crisp voice over the telephone from New York refused to listen to my pleas. 'Just four weeks,' I begged. The management were obdurate. No film company was going to use me. It was one of the hardest blows I have ever received.

Oh, Johnny, why didn't your car break down on the way to the airport!

I returned to New York and the long wait. The management paid my hotel bills but nothing else. Wartime exchange control had allowed me to bring little money with me, and it wasn't much fun to be surrounded by shops crammed with beautiful things if you had only a dollar in your purse. I longed for rehearsals to begin, work to start and to have something other than what was happening at the Old House to brood about.

Everyone was very kind. Anton Dolin also lived in the Windsor Hotel and often came to see me. Henry Heil, the young man I'd met on the plane, sometimes took me dancing and dining. He was a great dancer. And then there was my self-appointed business manager, Johnny Nathan. After a lot of argument he managed to get a script of the show for me to read, and then he took me to see my old friend, Gertie Lawrence, in her Broadway hit *Lady in the Dark*.

'You get it?' said Johnny.

I got it all right. *Lady in the Dark* and my proposed show *The Lady Comes Across* were very much alike in content. How could two shows on Broadway compete if they had almost identical stories?

Most musicals have to be beaten into shape. *The Lady Comes Across* was very nearly battered to death. The script had to be changed and they'd left it a little late. Rehearsals had started. In the original script I was cast as an English girl who gets mixed up in a spy ring. Each morning new pages of dialogue were handed to the cast, and we looked to see who was left in and who'd been cut out. Spies came and spies went, actors were sacked and scenes were deleted. This does work in film-land, but in the theatre constant changing spells disaster. I was still a spy-catcher, I still had to master the odd sentence in French, German and Swedish, but I hadn't a clue whom I was supposed to catch.

Organisation was non-existent. The book of the play was hacked to pieces and none of the joins met. We got through three directors and two producers before the show limped off to Boston for its try-out.

Each new director had changed the sets, and this changed the movement on and off stage; to an actor who must have everything solid and complete in his mind it meant constant confusion. After Cochran and Charlot who left nothing to chance, who worked out every detail and tucked away every loose end, it was unbelievable chaos. New dialogue and new lyrics for the songs arrived monotonously every morning, I used to pin the lyrics to my muff, my handbag, anywhere for quick study, for there was no longer time to learn them.

We were all having a very rough ride.

Exhausted because we had worked non-stop, depressed because that grey Boston December seemed to colour the gloominess of our hopes, we came back to New York. We'd been so busy trying to keep our ailing show alive that the big news of Pearl Harbour had almost passed us by. In New York it hit us hard. Uniforms on the street, flashing slogans in Times

Square, an atmosphere of urgency, for America was in the War. Even the Windsor Hotel had changed. The old staff had gone. Unknown faces eyed me as I walked into the lobby.

'What's happened?' I asked. 'Where's everybody?'

'Drafted,' said the sombre hall porter. He watched me while I leafed through my mail. Each envelope had been opened and re-sealed with official tape. 'Foreign mail's censored,' he announced in a loud voice so that everyone in the lobby could hear. 'Gotta be careful. Spies!'

Spies! I'd been living with spies for weeks. Every battered scene in *The Lady Comes Across* reeked with spies. And now here they were in the lobby of the Windsor.

I let myself wearily into my hotel apartment. A cup of tea would help. I lifted down my china tea cup with the roses round the rim and the little teapot to match. I always needed small treasures around to comfort me. As I sipped my tea I felt so tired that I wanted to curl up and sleep for ever. I looked at my letters spread out on the table. Someone had read them all, knew every word they contained. Someone knew all about me.

That was when it all started. Slowly, imperceptibly, as if the solid ground under my feet shifted like sand, every normal happening became tinged with the abnormal and the next days slowly shredded into nightmare.

To me it was all real—it still is real—to me.

'Hear it was kinda tough in Boston, Mugsy.' Johnny Nathan came round to see me at the theatre. 'Take it easy, babe, you look kinda peaky.'

Rehearsals for the opening started, along with interviews with the press, photographs, radio shows; all the high-pressure build-up for the Broadway opening. Anton Dolin came to one rehearsal. I was having trouble. I kept getting the wrong cues. I raised my arm and the seams of my newly fitted costume split from wrist to armpit. 'Oh, God,' I yelled, and in a torment of frustration ripped it out at the shoulder.

'Stop acting like a temperamental bitch, Jessie, and get on with it,' a loud voice shouted from the stalls.

Shocked into silence, the company stood still. The piano player stubbed out his cigarette. I stared into the stalls. Anton was standing up, shouting, raving at me like a lunatic, telling me to get on with it. How could he do this to me? He must understand the strain, the tight fear that this show could be an appalling mess. And I was carrying the show. If it flopped, my name too would end up in the mire.

I found myself running. I was off the stage, going down into the stalls. My anger blazed like a torch. I raised my hand. I slapped his face hard. Then I fled back to the stage, buried my face against the dusty curtains in the wings and sobbed. One of the girls, a little fair-haired dancer, took me in her arms and soothed me. She was used to it. Someone cried every day.

Henry Heil, the young American I had met on the plane, was a doctor. He knew I was having a rough time with the show and he gave me a repeat prescription for the mild nembutal tablets that sent me to sleep when I was over-tired. On the Sunday before the show opened, he made me go out to Scarsdale with him to meet his parents and relax.

The Heils were a charming couple, and I enjoyed my restful day. Only one incident disturbed me. Ernst Heil, Henry's father, sold photographic equipment in Japan. He showed me some of his pictures. 'Henry took this,' he said. 'It's of Birmingham, England.'

I gazed at an aerial picture of a large mass of buildings. Henry looked over my shoulder. 'Why did you take such a picture?' I asked.

He laughed. 'I'm a spy, didn't you know?'

Spies, I'm getting spies on the brain, I told myself. But it was odd that Henry should have been in Birmingham so recently especially since America wasn't in the war then. And he'd never tell me why.

Next morning he came round to the theatre unexpectedly. He brought a friend with him, a shortish man with a broad bald head and rather thick lips. His name was Doctor Koch, and in spite of his unprepossessing appearance, he seemed nice enough and I couldn't refuse when Henry asked if they could stay and watch the afternoon rehearsal.

We had trouble again that afternoon. Mischa Auer, the tall, doleful Russian comedian, found his entrance had been switched from Scene One to Scene Three. Dressed as a countess in flowing black gown (he was a spy, of course) he scuttled back and forth, trying to get his lines in at the right place.

Doctor Koch was waiting for me when I came out of the

stage door that evening. Henry had left, but he asked if I'd do him the honour of having dinner with him. I was tired, I would much rather have gone home, but he was Henry's friend and Henry was always so kind.

We went to a quiet restaurant and while Doctor Koch was ordering the meal, he urged me to open the bundle of mail I had with me. I'd picked it up at the hotel desk that morning but hadn't found time to open it. I'm a great letter writer and letters from home are wonderful when you're on tour. The first letter I opened was from my agent, I could tell that by the embossed address on the envelope, but inside was a letter from my brother Eddie in the Air Force. In Eddie's envelope was the letter from my agent. I looked up wonderingly, could the censor have put them back in the wrong envelopes?

Doctor Koch was watching me. 'Do you often have trouble with your mail?' he asked. 'Open that big one, see what's in that?'

Sonnie's writing was on the envelope and inside were photographs taken at our cottage in Cornwall. 'May I see them?' the doctor enquired. The answer was No: some instinct warned me.

We ate the huge steaks he had ordered. Mine was very good, but I was too tired to eat more than a small piece of it. He watched my look of dismay when the waiter took away my plate. 'Are you afraid it's poisoned?'

'Poisoned?' What a queer thing to say.

'Well, you looked very disturbed.'

'That's because I hate waste. It's awful to think that huge steak will be tossed into the ashcan.'

'Do you hate many things about New York?'

'Doctor Koch,' I pleaded, 'I love New York, don't take everything I say so seriously.'

His smile was meant to humour me, but the questions kept on. Why was I so tired? Had I a worry? Was someone persecuting me?

Suddenly aware, I asked. 'Are you a psychiatrist? Are you trying to assess me or something? If so, please don't. The last thing I need at this moment is a psychiatrist. All I need is the strength to get through to opening night.'

His face stiffened. 'I only wish to help, but tell me . . .' the man couldn't stop his relentless questions, 'how did you find time to learn all the languages you speak in the show?'

176

'I'm like a parrot. I repeat what the director says. I can't speak a word of any language but my own.'

He was still examining me as if I was a specimen under a microscope, as if he didn't believe a word I said.

'Oh please,' I said impatiently, 'I'm an actress.'

'You dramatise,' said Doctor Koch severely. 'You keep inventing. That is why it is so difficult.'

He paid the bill and walked me back to my hotel. I couldn't think why he'd taken me to dinner, why we'd spent such an uncomfortable evening together, but as we entered the lobby, he said something that jerked me wide awake. 'There's someone in your apartment. Henry thinks you should have a companion. A nurse.'

'I'm not ill,' I exclaimed angrily.

'Not that kind of nurse,' he assured me. 'Just someone to do your chores until the show opens. She's Swedish. You'll like her.'

I protested that I didn't want her, couldn't afford her, but he was placating. 'The management will pay. I'll just ring her from this booth and let her know you're coming up.'

As I waited for him, everything began to fall into place with a terrible finality. That was why he'd taken me to dinner, so that Henry could install some spy in my apartment. What right had Henry Heil to interfere. And this man Koch? They had German names! Fear, like a soft grey net, tightened round me. The hall porter watched me from behind his desk. The lift attendant stared at me from his stool next to the lift. I had no one to turn to. I was trapped.

And then I was in the lift, the doors closed firmly. 'Help me,' I implored the lift attendant. 'I'm in danger. German spies. Please take me up to Mr Dolin's flat.'

His face was impassive. 'I've been told to take you straight to your apartment.'

I caught his arm. 'Please, help me. Have you got a gun?'

The lift stopped, the doors opened. A huge Brunhilde of a woman with golden plaits wound around her head stood there. She opened her arms wide. 'Komme, mein kinde.'

All I could think as she grasped me and led me inside was, 'That's German she's talking. She's not Swedish.'

'Ach, you are sie schön, so pretty. And what you have in all those letters. From home, ya? From England, ya?'

177

So that was it, I thought, they're after my letters, my letters from Eddie and Billy, both in the Services, the pictures from Sonnie and the childish scribble and kisses from Catharine. I clutched my bundle tightly, she'd never get them.

I hated having a strange woman snoring in the bed next to mine. I insisted on leaving a side-lamp on, I tucked my letters under my pillow and then I got out of bed to drape the light with a scarf. Brunhilde was out of bed like a rocket. So she was just as afraid of me as I was of her.

Next morning I was as cunning as a fox. I strolled into the living room with Brunhilde puffing behind me, then, in a flash, I darted back into the bedroom and locked the communicating door. I dialled Johnny Nathan. 'It's life or death,' I panted, explaining what had happened. 'Don't open the goddam door until you hear my voice, Mugsy,' he ordered.

With my precious bundle of letters I locked myself in the bathroom. I had to destroy each and every one of them, they must contain vital information. I meticulously ripped them into tiny pieces and flushed them down the lavatory. Sonnie's photographs were hard work. Could they be what the spies were after? There were radar installations tucked in those innocent Cornish meadows.

Brunhilde found the porter and soon they had opened the communicating door and were pounding on my frail partition. Johnny's voice at last. I flung open my door. The room was filled with people: waiters, maids, strangers. Johnny shouted, 'Get the hell outta here,' to the curious mob, and ordered Brunhilde 'to pack her bags and scram'.

I told my strange story to Johnny and his uncle, a doctor, who was with him. They fed me tea, toast and sympathy in the little kitchenette. 'Henry Heil's behind it,' I insisted. 'He's a German spy.'

Johnny, with his hat still on the back of his head, and a cigar between his teeth had other ideas. 'That guy Heil's a brain surgeon. I read about him in *Time* magazine. He's been in Britain operating on kids with brain damage after the bombings.'

'Then why didn't he tell me?' I was utterly confused now. And Johnny was acting so strangely. He was marching round the kitchenette opening packets of food, smelling, tasting. 'Don't eat a goddam thing in this apartment. That dame may

178

have poisoned something.' He was overdoing his gangster dialogue, I thought, and yet Johnny must know, he was a criminal lawyer. 'Even the toothpaste might be drugged.'

'The toothpaste!' I echoed weakly.

Johnny suddenly brandished a card. On it was inscribed, 'Naval Intelligence'. He nodded sagely. 'Top secret. Keep it to yourself, Mugsy.'

'Johnny,' said his uncle quietly, 'you're frightening the girl.'

I stared from one to the other of them. 'What shall I do?'

'Get to the theatre, real fast, Mugsy. It's not safe around here. They'll shoot you on sight.'

At the theatre, a young journalist was waiting for me. He was to take me to lunch and interview me. He was very pleasant and earnest looking and his name was Elmer. I've often wondered what that young man thought of that interview. Elmer took me to a very select restaurant. We'd hardly sat down when he said it was the best German restaurant in town.

German! All my new-found confidence drained away. One of the waiters, a huge blonde man who could have been Brunhilde's twin brother, stared at me as he served the food. It was just an ordinary interview about my career, but every time I looked up there was the waiter.

'Elmer,' I said desperately, 'I'm in a show about spies, but there's a real life drama going on around me.' I told him what had happened. 'Even the toothpaste might be poisoned.'

'Toothpaste!' Elmer's eyes bulged. 'Don't touch the food. Well, eat the roll, that can't be poisoned.' He grew more distraught. 'Let's get out of here.' He threw some bills on the table and caught my hand. We hurried through the lounge to collect our coats and there stood the waiter, looking like a gangster in overcoat and pulled-down hat as if he was waiting for us. I grabbed my coat but Elmer didn't have time to get his. Hand in hand we ran with the waiter in pursuit. Into the first open door we saw. It turned out to be a department store. Up the stairs we dashed, through the toy department, down another flight to the china. Out of breath, we staggered through a back entrance. The waiter had been foiled.

Where to go now? My apartment was out of the question. We jumped into a passing cab and I remembered a rather eccentric French painter called Moise Kisling, who lived not far away at the top of Madison Avenue. He'd given me painting lessons when I was waiting for rehearsals to start.

Moise was in and he welcomed us. In his paint-stained shirt and trousers with his large head of shaggy black hair and his almost non-existent English, he somehow emanated the warmth I needed so desperately. I sat in his studio that smelled of turpentine with canvases piled around the walls and ate an apple and drank a glass of milk. Then he lifted my feet up onto the sofa, told me to rest, and I fell into a deep sleep.

When I awoke Moise's studio was filled with people. Johnny was there, a man from the theatre management, a strange woman who smelled of antiseptic and wore a hard felt hat, and Elmer.

Moise was shouting, 'Führer win, I die.'

The woman leaned over me and muttered, 'Hallucinations.'

Johnny shouted, 'But I saw the goddamn phoney Swede myself. She even spoke to me, thanking us for letting her go.'

Elmer saw I was awake and nudged Johnny.

'We're taking you somewhere safe, Mugsy. Where they can't get at you.' He patted my hand comfortingly. I closed my eyes and went back to my quiet dreamless sleep.

I was in a dark room. Someone had dressed me in a rough shift that scrubbed against my skin. I was on a bed and the covers seemed to tie me down. I couldn't move my hands, they felt manacled. Had the Germans caught me? What had they done to me? I heard someone screaming. My throat hurt and my mouth was open and dry. And then I knew that the woman who screamed was myself.

new wing is built on to the Old House at Hampton where Jessie and Sonnie moved in
1930.

The completed Old House; Jessie lived here for fifteen years.

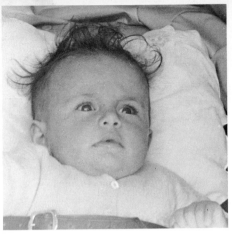

Jessie's adopted daughter, Catharine, at six months.

Catharine aged five.

With Jenny (right) at Frinton-on-sea.

Catharine and Lena.

Wendy Lewis, mother of Brian Jessie's third husband.

Jessie as she is today. *Photo: Angus McBean.*

Lieutenant Lewis, as he was when Je
first met him.

Brian and Jessie behind the bar of their pub, *The Alliance* in Farnham.
Previous page: Mr and Mrs Brian Lewis on their wedding day, August 1945.

Goodbye to the Dales—a final drink for the cast. *Photo: The Sun.*

ssie meets up with her past on *This is Your Life* and has her family beside her. From left
to right Billy, George, Eamonn Andrews, Rosie, Eve, Jessie, Eddie, Harry, Ray.
Photo: BBC.

Jessie shows her OBE to Rosie, next to her Catharine, Jessie's adopted daughter, a Eddie, her brother. *Photo: Westminster Press.*

A family reunion: Jessie seated left with brother George and adopted daughter Cathar behind. Next to her Eve, Lena and Rosie.

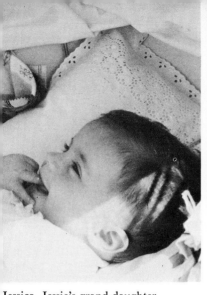

Jessica, Jessie's grand-daughter.

Jessica at four months.

e on board the *Queen Elizabeth* for a
trip to New York.

Catharine and Jessie's first grandson.

Next page: The latest Jessie—serene, calm and happy. *Photo: Simon Kossoff.*

Chapter Eighteen

She had a thin, drawn face with what looked like centuries of oppression etched around her sad Jewish eyes. Her name was Smithy and she was the night nurse. She lived in a place called Brooklyn Heights, and every night I longed for her frail, bird-like figure to walk through the door of the room I had grown to hate; her solid, rubber-soled white oxfords looking absurdly big at the end of her twig-thin legs.

'What kind of a day has it been, hon?'

'Pull back the covers!'

'Jeeze! They done it again.' She rapidly undid the restraining belts that tied me to the bed. 'What d'ya do this time, hon?'

'That bitch with the warts said I bit her. I wish to God I I had, but I didn't, Smithy. She kept wagging her finger in front of my face saying she was going to force me to eat, so I said, "Keep away from me or I'll take a lump out of you." Oh, Smithy, why do they do this to me? Only mad people bite, and I'm not mad, am I?'

She sat on the edge of the bed and put her arms around me. 'Sure you're not, honey. I've fixed a bowl of soup and some crackers for you. Get that down and you'll feel real good.'

'I can't, Smithy.' I began to weep. But because it was her, I tried and managed to eat them.

She stroked my hair and held my wasted body tight. She rocked me like a child in her arms, and I wasn't so mad that I didn't know that love was my cure, and here, in this small, Jewish woman, lay my salvation.

It was the never-ending questions that made me wonder if I was, after all, in a hospital, or if I were being tortured until I gave them the information they demanded. They weren't Germans, I knew that much, but they seemed to think I could be a foreign spy.

This morning, the two great strapping women who guarded me dragged me up in bed and tried to make me eat. Their daily interrogation went on: 'Now what's the name of that place you come from—Hampton Court?' The chief wardress, who had a face like a granite slab, winked at her partner. 'Classy, eh?'

I knew I must watch what I said. One slip and they might get what they wanted out of me. As I mustn't talk I quoted Shakespeare to confound them:

> '. . . it is twice blessed. It blesseth him that gives and him
>   that takes.
>   T'is mightiest in the mightiest; it becomes the throned
>   monarch better than his throne.'

'What's that you're spouting, kiddo?'

'The most beautiful language in the world. It's about mercy, a quality you've forgotten.'

There was a man in this chamber of horrors who said he was a doctor. He was gentle and I liked him until I discovered he was as bad as the rest of them. 'Put your arms in this,' he said one day. I obeyed because I trusted him. The slab-faced wardress nipped behind me and laced up the canvas jacket, then pushed me back on the bed.

'Why?' I asked him sadly. 'Just tell me why? You don't have to put me in a straight-jacket.'

'You've lost a lot of weight,' said the doctor, 'and we're going to feed you.' He was harping on the same old subject, food. I kept my lips tightly closed so that he couldn't shove his poison down my throat. But he stuck a tube in my nose and that forced its way down to my stomach. He poured pint after pint of liquid down it. I pleaded with my eyes but then I gave up. If they wanted to kill me there was nothing I could do.

The water treatment came next. I was immersed in a tub of boiling water, wrapped in rubber sheeting for protection. It was supposed to relax me. All it did was to make me perspire and lose more weight. Nothing made sense. I was according to them too thin from lack of food.

Some medieval monster may have played with the soothing power of water idea, but, as the victim, let me tell the whole of the medical profession that it was purgatory. They should have tried it out for themselves. From wet tub back to bed I went, with bouts of forcible feeding as the final torture. Once they forgot me and I was able to raise one leg and with my strong dancer's toes grasp the end of the tube and withdraw it. Coming back, the slab-faced wardress slapped my face, 'you shouldn't oughta done that, kiddo.'

One night I came to and found I was back in the first room. There was Smithy sitting next to my bed. I hadn't seen her for ages. She was staring at me and all the pain in the world seemed to be there in her dark eyes.

'Why, Smithy?' I whispered. It was the only word that made any sense to me. 'Why?'

'Because you won't eat.' She leant over and took one of my hands in hers. 'You gotta eat,' she said fiercely. 'You gotta eat and get the hell out of here.'

I tried to lift her hand, to pull it up. I wanted to tell her that I loved her, that I was grateful. It seemed that I was lifting a great weight, but eventually I was able to touch her hand with my lips. I laid my cheek against the cool skin, it was cool like ivory. 'Eat, and get the hell out of here,' Smithy said hoarsely. 'Please, hon.'

Food still revolted me but when Smithy brought it to me, I ate it.

My strength returned when I ate. They gave me a loom to work, bits of coloured wool that grew into a long mat. I didn't know how long I'd been in this awful place, the only friend I had was Smithy and I began to wonder why no one cared, why no one ever came to visit me.

Once when Smithy had her night off, the whole depressing nightmare exploded. The night nurse went out and locked the door behind her. To hear the key turn in the lock is one of the most dreadful, humiliating sounds—when you are the one locked in. I couldn't take it any longer. I didn't care if they killed me, I'd make one last effort to escape. I banged on the door, I yelled, I shouted. The door opened with a thud that knocked me backwards. A team of men, looking like all-in wrestlers in white coats, rushed in. I scrambled up, dodged, jumped, kicked out at them. One of them caught my arm and twisted it backwards. Another huge brute threw me on the bed, then all sixteen stone of him came down on top of me. 'Got ya, Jessie,' he cried triumphantly.

'Don't call me Jessie,' I yelled. 'My name is Mrs Hale-Munro. If my brothers were here, they'd kill you.'

Bruised and battered, I stared up at Smithy when she came on duty next night. 'Why d'ya do it?' she asked mournfully. 'They'll send you back to tubs.'

I turned my face to the wall. 'If I'm going to die I want it to be in an honourable way. I'm an Englishwoman.'

I heard Smithy's, 'Help us. Why do you fight us?'

I turned abruptly. 'I have to fight, Smithy. It's my way. I can't let them . . . extinguish me, like this.'

'Atta boy,' said Smithy with relish. 'That's the first time you've talked sense, hon.'

'If I could talk to someone,' I begged, 'someone from home.'

A man stood at the foot of my bed. He was middle-aged with thinning grey hair, and he brought with him a smell of tobacco and a breath of the outside world. When he smiled, as he did now, the wrinkled skin lay in folds around his eyes. 'It's raining,' he said, 'quite a downpour,' and his voice was like hearing the bells of a village church across a meadow. It was so very English.

He told me he was from the British Consul, and spoke gently to me. When he talked to me there was none of this, 'Quit horsing around, babe', or 'Can the society talk, kiddo', that I got every day. He treated me as if I was a rational human being who could understand what he said. In his hand he held the dog-eared script of *The Lady Comes Across*. As he talked to me he turned the leaves and I could see the underscoring, the inserts, the deletions. 'How did you ever manage to learn a part like this?' he asked. 'It's enough to drive anyone crazy.'

I gave him a wry smile. 'It did.'

'Did you know that Mitzi Gaynor took your part and the show folded after three performances?'

I shook my head. No one had told me anything, and now it was all too late. I didn't want to think about it, the memories were too bitter. But there was something I cared about very

184

deeply, 'I don't want to die in this terrible place.' I looked at him, half expecting the usual scornful reply.

He smiled again and quoted in his lovely voice: '. . . some corner of a foreign field that is for ever England . . .'. Then we'd better get you out of here, hadn't we?' From his briefcase he produced a pad of paper and a pencil and gave them to me. I held them almost reverently, I hadn't seen a letter or written a letter for so long. 'Write and tell your husband that you want to come home.'

I held the pencil in my hand but my brain couldn't form the letters on the page. 'You do it, please,' I said.

He wrote my letter for me as I dictated, 'Dearest Sonnie,' I began, 'It's been so long, so very long . . .' Foolish tears ran down my cheeks, but the words gushed out and the dam gates lifted.

I thought I was dying. That night I had a dream. I saw the most beautiful sunrise. It was in the shape of a fan, each ray of colour slowly becoming radiant with glorious light. I waited for the last ray to shine on me . . . but then I awoke, happy and refreshed, aware that the terror had gone and I wasn't frightened any more.

Anton Dolin came to see me. Over his arm, hanging in soft shining folds was a mink coat. Gertie Lawrence had sent it for me to wear when I took an airing in her car. 'Do you want to slap my face again?' asked Anton. He had a very Irish sense of humour.

Gracie Fields came in. She lent me fifty pounds so that I should have some money to travel home. Gertie arranged that I fly to Bermuda to convalesce with some friends of hers on the way home. The management sent a bunch of flowers. And there, to close the episode in his own sadistic way, was Johnny Nathan waiting at the airport to wish me goodbye.

'Daddy says that late mornings will start again now that you're home, Mummy.' Little Catharine, who was called Katie now, repeated everything to me that was said around the house verbatim.

'That's won't do, will it darling,' I answered. 'I'll have to get up early now that I'm to be a farmer's wife.'

Sonnie's schoolboy dream of farming was now being realised to a certain degree. His faulty eyesight had prevented his call-up, and he worked steadily in the theatre, but between dates he had made changes around the Old House. There was a landgirl planting vegetables. There were ducks on my lily pond outside the studio, turkeys and geese on the lawn, and two nanny goats which I hated from the moment I laid eyes on them.

My ship docked in Liverpool and Sonnie met my train at Euston Station. I longed for him to enfold me in his arms, to whisper, 'Thank God you're back safe and well.' I longed for a story-book reunion. In reality, Sonnie gave me a quick peck on the cheek and said, 'we must get a move on or we'll miss our connection and I've got some goats arriving today.' I hated those bloody goats even before I saw them, everyone seemed much more pleased to see them than me.

Katie was as sweet and loving as ever, but unconsciously she proved to me that every one of those eight months I'd been away had loosened the bonds that tied my family together. She turned to Beth now when she wanted anything. Beth wore slacks and a blue bow in her hair, the nurse's uniform had gone. 'You don't mind, do you?' she asked. I smiled, but of course I minded. I minded every time Katie turned to her, every time Sonnie said, 'Oh Beth knows about that.' Another woman had taken my place in my home, no matter how kindly or well meant, and I minded like hell.

'Jessie's back' said the newspapers. The headlines weren't quite so big, and the columns not quite so long, but they ran a photograph of me with a garden fork in my hand, the caption read: 'After her serious illness in America, the famous film star digs for victory.'

I didn't talk to Sonnie about what had happened in America for a long time: he didn't seem to want to know. Anyway I'd talked about it enough in Bermuda. Margaret Gosling, Gertie's friend, had been the perfect person to stay with, she'd given me the understanding and friendship I craved, and she'd listened patiently. I let the warm sunshine wash over me, the sun always healed me. The kindness and hospitality of the people I met in Bermuda was indescribable, but I longed to get home. There were no plane seats available so I took the first ship.

Sonnie and I were on our own one afternoon, walking down a country lane. For the first time I thought I could confide in him. 'I felt completely isolated,' I told him, 'as if I'd been sentenced to prison in a strange country for a crime I didn't commit.'

'You know what was wrong with you, don't you?' he asked.

'Yes, I had a nervous breakdown.'

'That's not quite right,' said Sonnie. He avoided my surprised gaze and stared straight ahead. 'The hospital reported that you were on the edge.'

'The edge of what, for goodness' sake?'

'Madness!' He spat the word out as if it was unclean.

I was shaken beyond belief by his attitude. 'You don't believe that, do you?' I could hear my voice trembling.

He didn't answer, he was busily slashing at nettles with his stick. 'Sonnie, please answer me.' I had to know how he felt. Sonnie was good with words, he would find the right ones.

At length, he said slowly, 'you've got to take things easily for a while. Beth and I can run the house. You must rest.'

'But I don't want to rest, Sonnie. I've been shut away long enough. I want to work.'

'Jessie'—Sonnie was looking at me at last—'every time you're ill, it costs a great deal of money.'

We walked on together in silence. So this was how my husband felt, he was unable to give me a word of comfort. Is my illness a sin, I thought desperately. Is it a sin for which I must be punished? So I am to move into the background of his life, be put out to pasture like those damned nanny goats. A slow burn of resentment began inside me. Who did he think I was? I'd be damned if I'd sit back like he suggested. I'd get back to work, prove that my star hadn't flickered out, and more important, prove to myself that I could still fill a theatre. Still hold that curtain up!

The first offer of work I received was from Firth Shepherd. Darling Firth Shepherd, I wonder if he realised that he was not only offering me the lead in a musical comedy but giving me a chance to live again. *Wild Rose*, which was to open at the Princes Theatre in Shaftesbury Avenue, was a new treatment of *Sally*, the original Gertie Miller hit of the twenties. Firth's idea was to take audiences away from the grey reality of wartime England to the glitter and gaiety that was New York at the turn of the century. The music was by Jerome Kern and Robert Helpmann would arrange the dances.

I started training in the lofty barn that was my studio. The floors were well sprung, there were limbering barres around the three walls, and a large mirror on the other. I hadn't been so happy for months. The ducks could quack their silly heads off on the lily pond outside, the nanny goats could butt their lord and master, and someone else could milk them for a change. I wasn't cut out to be a farmer's wife. I was going back to work. I was dancing again.

As soon as Sonnie started work on a revival of *The Maid of the Mountains* at the Coliseum, we left the Gatfields to run the Old House. I hoped that now we were both back in the profession, Sonnie would turn to me again and we could gossip and laugh and our marriage would become a real one again.

Wild Rose was a hard show to do physically. I had a lot of dancing to do, one Spanish dance was on full points, but I could cope. After America, nothing was hard any more. Danny O'Neill was stage manager and we had a management who cared for their employees' well-being. It was paradise after the rough ride in New York.

'Sonnie sprints from the Coliseum to get to Jessie's opening night before the curtain comes down . . .'

The newspaper article reminded the public of the happiest marriage in show business. Well we did go home together that night. But that was the last time. Sonnie's show closed fifteen minutes before mine, and he always made sure that he caught an early train. By the time I got home he had eaten his supper and was reading in another room. He made it very obvious that he didn't want my company.

I fought to stop my marriage disintegrating. It was like fighting a brick wall, but because I was only human I kept banging away. Discussions that started calmly would end in raging quarrels. And there are no quarrels quite so sordid as those between married people. I remember shouting at him, 'if you want dirty linen washed in public, by God, I'll bring some out.' In an agony of jealousy, I threatened and wept and prayed that one day Sonnie would love me again.

I was sitting on a stool in the bathroom wrapped in a large blue towel. Sonnie put his head round the door, he was going to Birmingham where he was booked to play the Dame in pantomime. 'I'm off now,' he said. I turned round, ready to wish him luck, tell him I'd phone. 'And I shan't be coming back.' The door closed and he was gone.

All that day I tried to tell myself that he didn't mean it, that he wouldn't end our thirteen years of marriage with six little words. I couldn't believe it was true until I had a letter from Sonnie asking me to divorce him for adultery.

The Christmas holidays were over, the tree was down, the decorations put away. Katie was starting school again. I went to the door with her and waved her goodbye. Then I stopped pretending. My husband had left me. He didn't want to live with me anymore. My show had closed and what did I do next? I told myself, 'keep going, you can't afford to be ill. You've got to earn a living and look after Katie.'

My family and friends bore with me patiently. I must have been a problem with my continual monologue about Sonnie. Bob Busby, my piano accompanist, and his wife Madge, who lived nearby, came in every day to try and cheer me up. 'Get away from this house for awhile,' Bob told me. 'Let's go away for a holiday.'

'Where?' I asked despondently. Where could we go with a war on? We went to the cottage in Cornwall. At least we could go for long walks and come back to a blazing log fire. If the house at Hampton had sad memories for me, Ker Vean in Cornwall was much worse. The view down to the river was my undoing. 'Our room with a view,' Sonnie had said. Years ago, the words of that song seemed to have been written for us. 'We'll bill and we'll coo, ooh, ooh, and sadness will never come . . .' I sat down on the window seat and stared out at the soft Cornish valley. I sat there all day, the black despair of my thoughts closing round me, cutting me off from the rest of the world.

Madge called me to supper. I looked at the delicious fresh plaice she had grilled. I forked up a morsel. The smell of putrefying fish was nauseating. Everything smelled the same to me. Rotten. Stinking. The water I tried to drink, the food I tried to eat. Jenny, my sister, who lived in a little house we had bought at Hampton, came hurrying down. She brought me a cup of tea. 'Drink it,' she ordered. Her black eyes flashed. She looked more than ever like Grandma from Poplar. 'For ten days you have had nothing to eat or drink. If you don't drink this you will die.'

I shook my head sadly. How stupid of Jenny not to understand her own words. Not to understand that was precisely why I must not drink. I got into an ambulance with her. She said, 'we're taking you home,' but after a long journey, we turned into a drive I did not know, up to a house that wasn't mine. There were bars on the windows and a white-capped nurse unlocked the door before we went into the room where I was to sleep. 'Jenny,' strength came back to my voice, 'where have you brought me?'

Jenny went on unpacking my suitcase. 'You won't eat, darling, and you've lost a lot of weight.' Out of a long tunnel, those very words, torn from my memory, came shrieking towards me. *'You've lost a lot of weight,'* said the American doctor. *'We're going to feed you. Put your arms in this . . .'*

'No, Jenny,' I cried, 'not that, please. I'll eat. Oh, God, I'll eat, but don't let them do that to me again.' They were going to lock me in, torture me. The thought was unbearable. 'Jenny, you're my sister. If you love me, don't leave me here.'

The two doctors stood over me, discussing me as if I wasn't there. 'Looks like the classical syndrome,' said the one with the funny foreign accent, 'probably drink and drugs, the usual thing.' I lay there with my eyes closed, recovering from their drug-induced sleep. How could they believe such things? I must tell them they are completely wrong. Gentlemen, I do not drink! I do not take drugs! Carefully I rehearsed in my mind what I would say: 'I do not drink. I have never touched alcohol. I saw what it did to my father, how it turned him into a fearsome bully. I don't even like the taste of alcohol . . .' No, perhaps I'd better not say that. I must pretend to like the taste of everything, if I'm to get out of this place.

'Drugs, gentlemen,' I allowed myself a smile. 'Henry would never prescribe drugs for me. Just the mildest nembutal sleeping pill, and only if I'm too exhausted to sleep. I'm afraid of drugs, they're dangerous.' No, here again, be careful Matthews, don't use the word 'afraid'. It's one of those words they latch onto and they'll spend hours asking you just what you're afraid of.

Had I got it straight? Yes, now I could tell them. I opened my eyes and saw the door close. The key turned in the lock and they'd gone.

*　　*　　*

Jenny came to see me after I'd been there for ten days. I was sitting up in a chair. I was eating everything they placed before me. After this experience I always forced myself to eat, even when I wasn't very hungry, and gave myself a lifelong weight problem.

I was doing everything I was told to, hating every moment, but enduring the humiliation of nurses and doctors who treated me as if I was a child.

Jenny sat opposite to me, trying to behave as if I was getting over influenza, instead of something which frightened the living daylights out of her. 'They think I drink, that I'm an alcoholic. You know that's a joke,' I told her. 'I heard them say that I take drugs. Have you ever heard anything so ridiculous? But they frighten me, Jenny, oh, the questions, the questions. . . . Please get me home. Ask Sonnie to help, after all, he's still my husband.'

'It was Sonnie who arranged to have you brought here,' said Jenny sombrely. She twisted her hands together, a sure sign that she was desperate. 'As a matter of fact he's been on to us, they want him to sign a paper, but he thinks it's up to us, your family.'

'For goodness' sake, Jenny, sign it. Anything to get me out of here. I know I was depressed, that I acted foolishly, but I'm well now. I want to get away from these locked doors, they terrify me.'

'Darling, the doctors here think you're still ill. They want you to stay.'

'Jenny . . . Jenny . . .' My voice grew hoarse and trembling. 'What are you saying? They want you to sign a paper to keep me here?'

'It's called a Reception Order. They want us to commit you legally to their care.'

Chapter Nineteen

Bob Busby's voice was loud and angry. I could hear him shouting in the corridor outside my room. 'I'm taking her home. Committal Order, what damned nonsense!'

I heard the sister in charge, just as indignant and just as angry. But Bob shouted her down. 'All right, and if you can't find petrol for a car, I'll just carry her myself. What kind of a place do you run? This girl's husband left her, so she got depressed and couldn't eat. She needs love and kindness and that's what we're going to give her.'

I thanked God for friends like Bob and Madge. Bob Busby, a man of gentle ways, a true musician, was outraged at my treatment. Dear Bob, he didn't have to carry me. I went home by car and my family found a sweet nurse, nicknamed Cloudy, to go with me. Cloudy, kind and sensitive, became one of my best friends and her wisdom and good nursing soon had me well again.

'Can't you find me a pill, Henry?' I asked when my friend and doctor came to call. 'Something to put me right if ever I get depressed again.'

'Not yet,' Henry answered, 'but one day I will. There are sulphanomides and new antibacterial drugs and it's only a matter of time before they come up with something for the nervous system.' Henry knew about the misery I'd endured behind locked doors. 'There's still so much ignorance about mental health. Can you believe it, until very recently students weren't even trained to understand psychiatric illness? Lock 'em away where no one can see them, that was the policy.'

The thought of what could have happened if my family had signed my rights away still made my blood run cold. Rightly or wrongly, I blamed Sonnie. I had started divorce proceedings at once. Our marriage was dead and done for—I understood now how he felt about me—and the sooner we were legally free of each other, the better.

I was thirty-six years old. I had been told by my trusted doctor that if I wanted to avoid illness I must not return to my profession. What was I supposed to do? Take out my knitting needles and knit my life away? True, I looked after Katie, but she went off to school every day in Hampton. 'The girls at school said you were famous once, Mummy. Why aren't you a film star any more?' she asked me once.

'I like staying at home with you, darling.'

I wasn't sure just how much longer we could afford to stay at the Old House. As it had been bought and maintained with my earnings, it was agreed that I should have it, and Sonnie should have the cottage in Cornwall. But the Old House needed a film star's salary to maintain it. I decided I must sell and went to London to place it on the books of an estate agency. Walking down Piccadilly, a smart young officer with a beautiful girl on his arm suddenly halted in front of me.

'Jessie,' he cried, 'where have you been?'

It was Tony Foreward and his wife, film star Glynis Johns. The last time we had met was backstage after a performance of *Wild Rose*. 'We were on our honeymoon,' said Glynis. 'You made me cry, you were wonderful.'

Such praise from a girl who was on her way to the top of our profession was sweet indeed, but I told them that I had retired from the stage. 'I can never face an audience again. It's all over.'

They seemed sad about my decision and Tony, who was with ENSA, begged me to consider giving concerts for the troops. I promised to telephone him, but in my heart I knew I would do no such thing. If returning to the stage meant the threat of another breakdown and submitting to another bout of barbarous torture, then I couldn't face it.

I started to pack up our belongings at the Old House. My garden studio looked so neglected as I sorted through the gramophone records. I put my hand on the practice barre and felt the smooth silk of the wood. No dancer can resist remembering the very first time. . . . 'Up,' cried Madame Clare, 'Jeté . . . jeté . . . like Spion Kop.' Spion Kop was a racehorse and we were supposed to jump like Spion Kop.

I could picture Madame Clare sitting in her high chair calling, 'Here, child.' All I dared to look at were her black-buttoned boots covered with spats. 'Head up! Shoulders back!' And then she drove her fist into my stomach. 'Muscles, strengthen them. Guts, guts, where are your guts?'

Automatically I pulled my stomach in, held my shoulders back and gave my reflection in the mirror a false smile. Like a brisk breeze that revives a limp summer day, I felt emotion run through me. 'You silly, stupid bitch,' a braver, younger me marched into my bloodstream. 'Primping in a glass, that's all you're good for. You're frightened to face an audience, are you? Of course you're frightened. The whole bloody world is frightened. Boys are dying every day in this beastly war, aren't they frightened? Where are your guts?'

I listened to this angry voice inside me. 'So you're throwing it all up. The work that others, not just you, have poured through your veins. The hours, the days, the months they have given to you . . . Madame Clare . . . Terry . . . Rosie . . . Charlot . . . Cochran . . .'

She had to give up, she couldn't think of any more names . . . although there were so many more. I was laughing. 'You're good,' I cried, 'you can still give a performance! Matthews,' I announced to the woman in the mirror, 'you may well have a future on the stage!'

'What's wrong?' I asked Bob Busby.

'What's right?' he answered gloomily.

'As bad as that?'

Bob pressed another ivory of the ancient piano and we heard a dull thunk. 'There are four, no perhaps five notes in tune here. You don't need me, darling, you need a piano tuner.'

We were in a large canvas tent in the middle of Salisbury plain, the rain was coming down, the wind howled through the canvas flaps, and my first ENSA concert was about to begin. Soldiers were making a lot of noise upturning wooden chairs, a white mongrel dog ran up and down the aisle looking for his master, and a good looking young subaltern, appointed stage manager, was getting under our feet.

'No more coffee,' I told him. I wished he'd get off the platform and leave me to rehearse with Bob. We had enough trouble what with the piano. 'It must be fun being on the stage,' said the young man. He had fair wavy hair and a great deal to learn about stage-management. 'I've often thought of it myself. I used to sing. . . .' Here we go again, I thought, another enthusiastic amateur. 'Ah,' he had an afterthought, 'if you don't want coffee, how about tea?'

'No, thank you. No tea, no coffee, just . . .' I had to say it, even if I hurt his feeiings, 'could you leave us alone for five minutes?'

He froze. Surprise, dismay, and then anger shone on his handsome face. 'That,' he announced to the white mongrel dog as he climbed down from the platform, 'was "La Matthews", that was.'

I had to be unkind. I had to protect myself. Even in a tent on Salisbury plain in the pouring rain, I had to give my best. I had to prove to myself that I was as good as I'd been before my last illness. Every time I gave a performance it was a 'return' and it had to be right.

Very few people ever understood this. When I appeared in the revue *Maid to Measure* much later, Harold Hobson brought up this very question when he wrote the following gratifying notice:

'Miss Jessie Matthews has transferred herself into the West End, which is magnificent. . . . Miss Matthews could always sing and dance and speak, in addition she used to add to the allure of a pretty and clever woman, a childlike innocence. I lay my hand on my heart and declare that for me at any rate she still has. Why then the atmosphere that surrounds this show of the 'return' of Miss Matthews to the stage, as if her past successes were incredibly remote? For the glory is not gone . . . it is here.'

I kept my secret. Very few people knew that every 'return' was a battle I must win, and every 'return' could be my last performance.

That troop concert may have been a struggle for both Bob Busby and myself, but my audience in uniform were wonderful. Afterwards Tony Foreward said to me, 'You've hurt the feelings of one of your most ardent admirers. He's a nice chap. Come and talk to him.'

I found the stage manager, Lieutenant Brian Lewis, still ruffled and decidedly arrogant, and I wished I hadn't bothered. However, we met again at another concert, and I found out that he wasn't so much arrogant as shy. He put himself out to help me in every way and I was always getting phone calls from him, asking if there was anything he could do for me.

Sonnie telephoned. Now that we were divorced, we were almost friends again. Katie was our shared daughter, and it made her happy to have her parents at least talking to each other. 'What's this I hear,' he demanded, 'some bank clerk's supposed to be in love with you.'

'Bank clerk? I don't know any bank clerk,' I said obtusely. 'I wonder if you mean that nice young officer who looks after me when I do troop concerts?'

I felt light-hearted again, and if a young man named Brian Lewis had a lot to do with it, so much the better. My life was full again, one evening I'd appear at the Albert Hall with three enormous bands to back me, and the next day I'd be singing in a tent in Dorset.

Sonnie telephoned again. 'That bank clerk,' he said, sounding quite angry. 'You don't intend to marry him, do you?' Next day he rang again. 'I won't have you going around with cheap little bank clerks.'

'Sonnie dear,' oh, revenge was so sweet, 'he's not little. He's over six feet tall. And he isn't a bank clerk, really, he's an officer. He's in France, fighting for his country.'

Of course I didn't intend to marry again, at least not to a penniless boy of twenty-four. I'd had enough of husbands, they'd never brought me luck.

Brian came home on leave. There was a chance he'd be sent to India, why wouldn't I agree to become engaged? Tony Foreward told me, 'you're ruining Brian's life, he's madly in love with you.' Sonnie telephoned: 'Whatever you do, don't get married.' He had married Beth and they had a son called Robert. Why shouldn't I too have another chance at happiness. Why shouldn't I, too, have a child? On August 9th, 1945, at Chelsea Register Office, I became Mrs Brian Lewis.

Sonnie telephoned. 'So you let him talk you into it. Where's he taking you to live? In a tent on Salisbury plain?'

I could well do without Sonnie's constant telephone calls.

He'd run my life for so long that he couldn't give up the habit. 'Sonnie,' I told him, 'you are no longer my husband. Stop interfering!' As it turned out, it wasn't Sonnie who tried to break the marriage up, it was my ten year old daughter, Katie.

Brian and I found a house outside Farnham. There were high evergreen hedges round a lovely garden, so we called it *'Evergreen'*, and there was a tennis court. We both prepared for the day when Katie would return from her stay with Sonnie and Beth and live with us. Brian bought her a bicycle and hid it in the garage. I was sure she'd be overjoyed for she'd never owned one.

Katie gave Brian a very cool look for a ten year old when he produced his gift. 'A bicycle,' she said disdainfully. 'What a slow way to travel.'

'I didn't do too well, did I?' said Brian ruefully. 'Still, better luck next time.'

He rolled the tennis court, mended the net and bought her a tennis racket. His new ploy was to teach her to play tennis whereby he might gain her confidence. But Katie wasn't having any. I could have shaken her, but I had enough sense to realise that this new relationship was just as hard for her, and it was going to take time and patience.

She still spent the odd weekend with Sonnie and Beth, and she would come back to Farnham with the most hair-raising tales of life in the Hale-Munro household. I felt rather guilty listening to them, but I guessed that Katie's stories to them about Brian and me were just as riveting.

Sonnie would telephone me after her visit. 'Katie's becoming very out of hand. It's the bad influence of that man you've married.' I felt like telling him that Brian had no influence over Katie at all; she never spoke to him. Katie, unconsciously, was learning to play Sonnie and I off against each other, sometimes it was all too much for her. She looked at me under her thick dark lashes. 'Shouldn't I really be called Catharine Lewis?' Did this mean that she was at last learning to like Brian, I wondered. He did try so hard and he was unfailingly kind and patient with her. I knew perfectly well that even if she was sincere, Sonnie would never allow her to take another man's name. 'You're Daddy's little girl, and you must be loyal to him.' Katie promptly burst into tears.

She changed in time and she came to accept Brian, not as an elder brother, and he was too young to be her father, but as someone who lived in the house and was good natured and easy to be with. That had to do. I was happy and suddenly I was in a state bordering on bliss. I was going to have another baby. If she were a girl, we decided, we would call her Victoria.

> Jessie Matthews, the famous stage and screen star has for the second time given birth to a still-born child. Her husband, Mr Brian Lewis, told our *Daily Mirror* reporter that she is heartbroken.

To lose one child is almost beyond endurance, to lose a second is even harder. My strong maternal instincts had made me yearn for a child of my own. All my sisters had children, but I was not to be like other women. Brian comforted me and this time I did not break down. I turned to my work.

At first I did concert tours. Brian came with me as my manager. I didn't need a manager. Even in my palmiest days I had done without one; a secretary had always looked after my correspondence and I'd always known that the best person to pay my bills was myself. But Brian was stage-struck, and there was another reason, Brian was finding it hard to settle down to a job. Like so many young men of his generation the war had unsettled him. After we married he spent three months studying to be an architect. Then, because he had a real flair with machinery, he'd gone into the motor business.

One of my tours was to Scotland and Eddie, my brother, sang duets with me. Eddie was handsome, a good dancer, he had an excellent voice but he lacked a vital ingredient for success on the stage—self-confidence.

'I was bloody awful,' he'd shout in a loud voice as we left the stage. 'Did you hear how I muffed that last note?'

'Keep it quiet,' I'd hiss. 'D'you want the audience to hear you?'

I remember another incident in Dundee. One evening two people came round to see me in my dressing-room. A dark-haired young man who carried a Victorian posy of flowers and his mother, Mrs Currie, a sweet faced little woman. Archie Currie had been my fan ever since he had seen *Evergreen* when he was thirteen years old. That evening he produced an album of press cuttings for me to autograph. I looked at the pictures of the skinny little creature I used to be and asked Mrs Currie if she didn't think I was getting too plump.

'You're a fine figure of a girl,' she answered in her warm Scottish voice, 'but you must concentrate on your acting now and your singing.'

Archie Currie is still my loyal fan. He still makes long journeys to be at all my first nights, and without his collection of press cutting albums to jog my memory, the writing of this book would have been so much harder.

Just as Mrs Currie had advised I was concentrating on my acting. I made a film, I did radio work. I toured in a very happy revue called *Maid to Measure*, which ran in the West End. Brian was still my manager, but it was very obvious that he hadn't the tough personality, the guile and the hard bargaining attributes that were needed. One of the stage-hands said, 'Brian's always happy in a pub with a pint in his hand.' That was the solution, we'd run a country pub.

We bought the Alliance Inn at Farnham. Oak beams on the ceiling, a snug little saloon bar with a bar counter in one corner, horse brasses, cretonne curtains, and Brian in his new role of 'mine host', looking very handsome with a silk scarf knotted at his neck. I sold our house and we moved into the flat over the pub.

'It's a challenge,' declared Brian, master in his own home at last. 'You stay home and run the pub with me.'

We had a lot of customers. At week-ends they poured in, jamming the little saloon bar, overflowing out onto the street. 'Come and have a look at Jessie Matthews pulling a pint.' As landlady of the Alliance Inn I had one failing. I couldn't add up. 'Four gins, a pint of bitter and a shandy.' I'd take the order and sidle over to Brian who was good at sums. 'How much will that be?' I'd whisper. 'Eight and a penny,' he'd say impatiently. I'd ring it up on the till, but I still had trouble with the change.

In the end I was banished to the other side of the bar, and eventually told to go back to the washing up. I turned my talents to decorating and improving the flat upstairs. It was a mess, with uneven floors and wide cracks where the smell of beer wafted through. With the help of a local handyman we straightened it out and brought the furniture and carpets out of store.

One of our first visitors was Brian's mother from Newcastle. She had recently been widowed and needed a change of air.

Wendy, as both Brian and I called her, was a handsome woman who looked very much like Brian. She was just fifteen years older than I was, and at first didn't seem like a mother-in-law at all.

She was a very good cook and Brian's face lit up every time she produced a bread and butter pudding or a jam roly poly. 'Teach me to make them,' I begged, for they pleased Brian so much, and after all slapping pieces of bread and butter together couldn't be all that difficult. Wendy smiled. 'you're an actress, dear, not a cook,' and she kept her culinary secrets to herself.

The change of air lasted much longer than I expected. 'When is she going back?' I asked after six weeks.

'She's not,' said Brian. 'She has to stay for she's sold her house.'

When two women share a kitchen and a man, there are problems, and in the privacy of our bedroom I sometimes used hard names. The walls of our bedroom were paper thin. 'Ssh!' I'd say. 'your mother will hear us.'

'So what?'

'Well I don't want that —— listening in.'

'Brian.' A clarion call from the landing, someone was listening. 'What did your wife call me just now?'

When an offer came to go on tour with a new play I decided to leave my kitchen and my husband to Wendy. I returned six weeks later to find that all the furniture in the living room had been moved.

'Katie,' I called. 'Yes, Mummie.' Katie grinned at me. 'Moving day, darling.' Back would go the furniture. At the end of another tour, the same thing would happen. 'Katie, moving day.'

'Oh dear,' said Wendy sweetly, 'I'd quite forgotten you didn't like it my way.'

I was asked to take over Zöe Gail's part in *Sauce Tartare* and returned to revue on the West End stage. Perhaps forty-two was rather old to play the ingenue, but I'd kept my looks and the reviews were very good. Next I toured in Bernard Shaw's *Pygmalion*.

Our arrangement suited Brian very well. He had a wife with a glamorous career, a mother who looked after him, and a job he enjoyed. I wasn't so sure myself. Every time I kissed him goodbye I felt rather like a sailor going off to sea. I knew that Brian would be delighted to see me when I got back, but sometimes I felt that all I needed was a parrot on my shoulder and I'd be a jolly jack tar.

One evening, just before opening time, I went down the steep steps from the flat to the saloon bar. I wanted to have a word with Brian. He was mixing himself a 'White Lady'. He'd given up drinking beer long ago, the sight of the beer-swillers round the bar had turned him from a five pint a day man to having just an occasional cocktail. He mixed the Cointreau, the gin and the lemon juice together with a long glass spoon.

'Brian,' I said, 'I've had another offer to tour in *Larger Than Life*.'

'Splendid,' said Brian, transferring the mixture to a cocktail shaker.

'Don't you want to know where I'm going?'

Brian began to shake the cocktail energetically. 'Glasgow, Edinburgh, Perth. You name it, I've been there.'

'I shall open at the Princess Theatre.' I watched him closely, 'Melbourne, Australia.'

I saw his hand tighten round the shaker. At last, I thought to myself, now he'll react. 'Are you mad?' he'll say. 'Going to Australia. Leaving me! Out of the question.' He'll take me in his arms, and tell me I must not go, and I shall know he loves me.

Brian poured the cocktail into a small glass, added a cherry, lifted the glass, tasted it, closed his eyes for a moment. Finally, he opened them, smiled at me and said, 'Splendid!' Then he added as an afterthought, 'so you're off. Good luck, old girl.'

Chapter Twenty

We were sailing down the west coast of Australia, nearing Fremantle. Diggers returning to their homeland paced the decks and swore that the breeze carried the scent of eucalyptus. Tomorrow morning we should be in Australia, and my confidence, which in the happy isolation of a long sea voyage, had soared like an eagle, was now plumetting down. Had I been crazy to come, I asked myself? I didn't know a single soul in that vast continent fast approaching. How would the Australians like me? If they expected the young dancing star of *Evergreen*, they might be surprised.

Whatever happened, it was a relief to be away from England. No more telephone calls from Sonnie. He'd given up calling Brian 'that bank clerk you married'; now he was 'that bar tender you married'. Sonnie and his wisecracks could stay in cold storage for a few months. Of course I missed Brian, but perhaps this separation was what our marriage needed, and when I got home again, Wendy, my mother-in-law, might have moved out. There was no problem about Katie, she was on board ship with me. At seventeen Katie was fast becoming a beauty. Already heads turned when she walked by.

Very early in the morning, we steamed into the river and swung in to come alongside the long, wooden jetty at Fremantle. A handful of wharfies stood about to take our ropes. With a final creaking bump we touched the wharf. We had arrived in Australia. Coloured paper streamers hurtled through the air, a band played on the quayside to welcome the migrants on board. Even before I stepped ashore I knew that I was going to like Australia.

Opening night of our play *Larger than Life* reminded me of pre-war London: the audience were enthusiastic, the ladies wore beautiful gowns, and the newspapers gave us rave notices. It was so gratifying to be given the star treatment again.

Throughout the tour we had wonderful audiences. When it was over I felt almost an obligation to give something back to the Australian public, so I did a circuit of their number two towns playing as guest star. Katie, who had ambitions to become an actress, played a part in *Larger Than Life*. She was so anxious when she came on stage that she used to mouth my lines until her next cue.

The months spent in Australia with my daughter were very happy ones. The sun shone, the streets of the cities looked so gay with the summer frocks of the women. I loved the easy friendliness of the Australians, the picnics, the days at the beach, and most of all the fact that they wanted me, and fresh offers of work still came in.

Katie and I sat on our hotel balcony in the morning sunshine while we opened mail from home. The letter from Brian was gloomy. The pub wasn't doing well, the overheads were eating up the profits, he was worn out, he was fed up, and when was I coming home?

'We've been here six months,' I said. 'Don't you think we ought to go home?'

Katie continued to stare down to the panoramic view of Sydney Harbour. 'November, December, January, let's think about it in February,' she said.

I sat in the sunshine and thought of November fogs, January snow and the smell of beer that floated up to the flat over the Alliance Inn. 'Well, just a little longer, perhaps.'

I wrote a letter to Brian before we left Melbourne that spring. I set out all the reasons why I thought our marriage had gone wrong, and what we should do to put it right. In Colombo, I had a telegram from Brian to say he was waiting for the ship in Marseilles. So my letter had done something at least. I was to find out that this letter had done a great deal and the effects would be with me for a long while.

Katie sailed on to England and Brian and I went to Corsica for a short holiday. We booked into a splendid hotel over a beach outside Ajaccio, we dined well on haûte cuisine fran-çaise, and after coffee on the starlit terrace, still holding hands we went up to our room.

'Tell me,' said Brian casually, 'that letter you wrote . . .'

At three in the morning the quarrel that had started so unexpectedly over my letter had swelled to proportions that matched the thunderstorm raging outside. The lightning flashed over the mountains, the thunder crashed and we had to yell to make ourselves heard over the din. Brian, my easy-going husband, had become mad with jealousy. Other men were the reason I had not returned earlier from Australia, he insisted.

'Be reasonable, Brian. If I'd wanted to be unfaithful, I had every chance in England when you couldn't have cared less.'

'No, you wanted the rough stuff, didn't you? The tough way Australians treat their women.'

The accusations went on. I was finding out how jealous the average English male can become over the imagined exotic foreign male. At last I gave back as good as I was getting. 'Yes, I did want a husband I could lean on, someone who wanted me near him, and who'd tell me so.'

Brian, in his new dominant role, declared that from now on I was going to stay home and be Mrs Brian Lewis. Jessie Matthews and her career were finished.

And yet when we got home nothing had changed. Wendy still sat in my favourite armchair, the draymen still rolled the barrels of beer down the cellar steps. I was saved from a boring existence of doing the flowers and taking the dog for a walk by Brian's hair. He became convinced that the cigarette smoke in the saloon bar was making his hair fall out. We must give up the pub before he went bald.

With a stroke everything changed. Wendy caught a train going north, and Brian, Katie and I moved to Hampton. Years before I had bought a house for my sister Jenny in Hampton. She and her husband were transferred to Cheltenham and the house was ours.

Then I had the bit of luck I needed. The BBC made a tele-vision documentary of my life, called *Spice of Life*, and the day after it was televised the telephone rang with offers of work. One of the nicest offers came from South Africa. I was invited to go to Johannesburg and take the lead in a repertory season.

Brian wasn't doing too well with his job as a car salesman, and we decided we'd start a new life in South Africa. Here we go again, I thought. Brian became my manager once more.

Katie decided to stay in London and try for an acting career, I installed her in a little flat and gave her a £30 a month allowance, telling her to come out to South Africa as soon as she could.

Brian thought that Johannesburg was like Main Street, USA. It was rather. A thrusting, booming, dynamo of a city with tall blocks of flats rising above the dust clouds in the high dry altitude. Johannesburg, in the middle of a hot South African summer made me feel short of breath at first, but I settled down and started rehearsals for *Larger Than Life*. I was looking forward to it. The hotel, old-fashioned and plushy, was very comfortable, it wasn't until I saw the terrible black slums not so far away that I wondered if I could accept the comfort and close my eyes.

Brian loved South Africa. He wanted to find a job and stay, but as my season of the play neared its end Brian still hadn't found anything permanent. Living together in the confined quarters of a hotel bedroom made us both edgy, and Brian complained that he was only invited to receptions and parties because he was my husband. This is a fact of life when you're married to a celebrity no matter how minor, but lately Brian refused to understand. He hated people to ask me to sing at parties, and I'd often see him get up and leave the room if someone pulled me to my feet.

Before the tour closed I received an offer to go to Australia for a ten-week season with the possibility of more work to come. I had to pay my own fare and that of my husband. I tried to make Brian as enthusiastic as I was, telling him how good the sea trip would be for both of us. 'South Africa's a beautiful country,' I said, 'but Australia's where my heart is.'

An unfortunate phrase, I must say, and Brian picked it up at once. The famous letter I had written from Melbourne came back, the randy Australian males were dredged up and we quarrelled . . . and we quarrelled. . . . I looked at Brian—he was sweet natured, he was good looking, what was wrong between us? There was an age difference, it was true, but I'd kept my looks and it didn't really show; now I realised that it mattered very much. I wasn't too old for Brian, Brian was too young for me. I didn't want to look after him any longer.

I sailed to Australia alone and our parting was rather cool.

There was a virus flu epidemic in Sydney when I arrived and I caught it. I had a long expensive stay in a private hospital in Randwick. After I'd paid the whacking bill, the doctor who'd looked after me came in to say goodbye. Now that I was leaving he let his professional mask slip and we talked about my career. He'd seen me in *Ever Green* years ago. I told him how panicky I got when I started rehearsals.

'Stomach in knots? things like that?' he asked. He knew my history of nervous breakdowns, He went on to tell me that there were new drugs, psychotropic medication, that work on the nervous system. 'You take a pill,' he said, 'and it will quiet all those panicky feelings.' They were a great step forward in the treatment of nervous illness, he told me, and he would prescribe me some.

When he had gone, my mind went back to a conversation I'd had fourteen or fifteen years before. I could hear myself asking Henry Rowan, 'Why can't you give me a pill to put me right?' and Henry's quiet voice answering, 'It's only a question of time before I can.' Was this the kind of medicine Henry had meant? After all insulin saved people suffering from diabetes, penicillin had saved thousands of lives, tuberculosis had been vanquished. Why couldn't there be a drug that would do the same for depression and nervous illness?

Tranquillisers, mind benders, we hadn't learned to call them that in those days, but Henry Rowan had been right, the teams of scientists had come up with something that was to change the grim face of nervous illness.

I soon became fit again in the Sydney sunshine and now for the first time in my life I knew that if I needed them there were medicines that would stabilise my moods. A ten-week offer for a season of plays had gone down the drain because of my illness, but my name still had drawing power and Sir Frank Tait asked me to do a tour with a play called *Janus*.

Janus, a modern story of the God who looked two ways, to Olympus and earth, wasn't blessed with luck. On the journey from Sydney to Melbourne the train developed a hot box, and it turned out to be the carriage where all our dresses and props were boxed. We spent Saturday morning turning Melbourne upside down for new props and dresses. We still opened in time for the Gala Performance before the Governor and his Lady. In another town the hot dry air made my voice husky. I never lost it, but every night when I went on there was the terrible interval between the time when I opened my mouth and the time when my voice came through. *Janus* was a lovely play but it gave me some difficult moments.

My personal problems were beginning to worry me. Not so much Brian. He had decided to stay permanently in South Africa and we agreed that our marriage was over. But Katie —Katie who had been enrolled in an art school while she tried the precarious career of an actress, had given it all up and was doing the usual filling in jobs that girls do. I wrote to her, asked her to come out to Australia where she could go on with her art studies or try the theatre.

Katie answered my letter. She was going to stay in London she told me briefly. She couldn't write at length because she was off to Cornwall to stay with Beth. Had I heard the news about Daddy? (Sonnie had left Beth and gone off with a girl friend.) That was her last letter.

I wrote to Rosie. I wrote to Henry Rowan. I wrote to everyone who could tell me what was happening to Katie. Rosie wrote back that Katie wouldn't speak to her any more, she wanted to be left alone. Henry wrote that Katie was rather elusive, but not to worry, I could straighten it all out when I got home.

The first boat leaving Sydney was an Italian tourist class liner. Music blared night and day from the loudspeakers, children and their parents slept in the lounges. Every disgruntled migrant was on that boat and it was a pretty unpleasant voyage. When we docked at Genoa I was one of the first down the gangway and onto a plane for London.

Rosie, looking a little older and tireder, was waiting for me at the airport. There was Lena, as chirpy as ever, and Ray, over from America on holiday with her children. And there was Katie, in London if not at the airport. She hadn't been able to meet me as she was working. Rosie, however, knew where to go and so I paid a visit to the tea shop in Sloane Street that she had mentioned.

The high-pitched parrot chatter floated over my head as

I took a table in the corner. I saw Katie immediately and she went pale. But she looked so lovely that my foolish heart turned over. I sat in my corner determined to speak to her. I had to wait until she left. I walked with her down Sloane Street, a thousand questions on my lips, but knowing that I musn't ask any of them.

'I can't understand why you've come rushing back from Australia, Mummy?' She avoided my eyes. 'I'm perfectly capable of taking care of myself.'

I didn't remind her that I had supported her ever since I left for South Africa. 'I'm staying with Rosie at Ruislip,' I said. 'Will you come down this week-end so that we can talk?'

'I cross here,' said Katie, 'I must go.'

I caught her arm. 'Will you come?'

'Very well,' she said touchily, 'but, Mummy, you may as well know, I'm engaged to be married.'

Rosie wasn't surprised when I told her what had happened. 'You gave her everything that money can buy. You wanted your daughter to have everything you missed,' she said in her downright way.

Years later, with hindsight, after witnessing the drop-out generations, where rebellious youth leave home for no apparent reason, I can understand Katie's actions more easily. But it hurts now, just as it did then. Katie came down to see us, bringing a very nice young man. When they left I knew I had lost my daughter for the time being. She was twenty-two, she could look after herself just as she had said.

Sonnie telephoned me. The same old Sonnie, full of talk and chat and great plans for the future. I chided him about going off with a girl half his age, but I didn't chide him about leaving his wife and two children. His second family had always been a sore point with me.

'My private life's my own, dear girl,' he said blithely. 'You make your mistakes and I make mine. By the way, how's the bar tender? Now I've written this comedy. Great story, there's a scene where you sing and dance, absolutely tailormade . . .'

Sonnie had actually written a play for me, just as he'd always promised to. Next morning in the post was the script, *Nest of Robins*. The plot was based on the old wives' tale that young robins eventually liquidate their parents. I smiled ruefully to myself as I read the script. Sonnie had taken a real life drama being played on his own doorstep. An ex-revue queen with two snobbish children who were ashamed of her. A loud-voiced comedian, for ever telling corny gags, who comes back from Australia to find her.

The press took up the story and went into columns of print about two divorced revue stars together again. 'Only on the stage,' said Sonnie firmly. We opened at the Royal Court Theatre, Liverpool, and when we danced and sang together, matronly and rather middle-aged as we were, we brought the house down. But as soon as the show was over we went our own ways.

Sonnie's complicated private life made him rather irritable. He and his new lady had just had a baby, and although his marriage to Beth was over and she was sueing him, the problems of maintenance and support, which always get through a lot of money, bothered him.

The hoped-for West End opening did not materialise so when the tour was over we parted company. A week or so later I was asked to play the part of the mother in the MGM film of *Tom Thumb* with Peter Sellers, Terry Thomas and Russ Tamblyn. In a roundabout way I heard that it was Sonnie who hád suggested me for the part.

Cold February rain was falling steadily when s.s. *Himalaya* inched her way out of Tilbury Docks en route to Australia. The pressmen had taken their pictures of Jessie Matthews waving goodbye to England for ever. 'There's nothing for me here,' I had told them. 'I'm going back to the sunshine of Australia.'

There was nothing to keep me in England any more. Katie didn't want or need me. I wrote to her asking her to come and see me before I left but she sent a wire saying she'd get in touch if she could. She didn't.

Sonnie had telephoned to say goodbye. 'Sorry I was rather beastly to you at the end of the run. I hadn't been feeling too well. Anyway, good journey and good luck, old girl.'

'Goodbye, Sonnie, good luck.' We talked together for a few minutes and there was warmth in our voices. Once we had spent happy years together and there were links between us that no divorce court could ever sever. I was always glad that we talked together before I left. I didn't know it, but Sonnie was soon to be told that his luck was running out.

There was a small pub on the riverside. As s.s. *Himalaya* drew out into the river I could read the name painted in large white letters on the roof, *The World's End*. I watched until the pub and its white painted roof disappeared into the mist. Would I ever come back and read that name again?

Chapter Twenty-one

I turned my key in the lock and walked inside. At least it was warmer in than out. Walking home the icy winds off the Dandenong mountains had blown right through me. Melbourne in August didn't seem very much warmer than Tilbury in February.

All my treasures, brought from England, welcomed me home: the blue lustre vase on the inlaid desk, the porcelain figurines presented to me by the Mayor of Stoke-on-Trent. Bert, swinging on her perch in the cage in the kitchen, made an unfriendly noise. She could give me 'the bird' better than any audience I'd ever known. She didn't like me and she showed it. I'd brought her home from the pet shop thinking she was a boy and called her Bert. That might have offended her, for I swore she often snarled at me, and had a most evil character for a budgie.

'You'll be the first to go, Bert,' I announced as I walked to the sink and filled the kettle. 'Guess what? This afternoon I got the sack, so put that in your bird bath and drink it.'

I made my tea, the eternal remedy, and sat down at the kitchen table. I tried to cheer myself up, 'You've had bigger blows. Remember the time you lost the lead in *The Quaker Girl* in 1944, and that was big stuff, a huge salary, not a piddling little £25 a week as drama instructress.'

I remembered my high-flown talk when I'd left England: 'I'm going to open a drama school in Melbourne.' They'd laugh if they could see me now, given the sack from my first job, and I had about as much hope of opening a drama school as flying through the air. It had seemed such a good idea to join a drama school as an instructress, to learn about the business, but I'd reckoned without the other members of the staff.

'Bloody Poms coming out here, pinching our jobs.' One of them had a real chip on his shoulder and he couldn't stand the English. I'd opened my big mouth and forgotten that he was hiding, as usual, behind the drapes. It was true what I'd said, every word—these kids I taught were so nice, so talented, so hardworking, but it was a crime to take their money and assure them that they'd find a job afterwards. There just weren't enough big towns or theatres in Australia to take them.

'That's it, kids,' I told them, 'I'll teach you, and I think you've got lots of talent, but I can't see you making it here in Australia.' They worked so hard to get the money to pay their drama fees, one of them worked as a brickie, another girl worked nights as a waitress. It wasn't fair to take their money unless I told them the truth.

Old Peeping Tom had emerged from his hiding place and made for the director's office like a shot from a gun. Perhaps I should have resigned then and there, but I'd waited for the summons from above: 'If you feel this way about it, Miss Matthews, then I think we're both wasting our time.'

It was the indignity of getting the sack that hurt. At fifty-two, there isn't always another job just round the corner. 'I've had bigger blows,' I told myself, 'much bigger blows. Why should I cry?' There were plenty of reasons, really. I'd upped sticks, sold up, sailed out to Australia, and now I was out of a job and a long way from home.

The doorbell rang. Outside stood three young people, my erstwhile students from the drama school. 'Miss Matthews,' said John, 'will you teach us drama?'

'We told that no-hoper to drop dead,' said the girl called Fay. The other girl joined in, 'I want to learn to speak like you.' And that was how the Jessie Matthews School of Speech and Drama started in my one-bedroomed flat.

From that day things picked up in a dramatic way. With the help of a small advertisement in a local paper my new drama school soon had ten pupils. I enjoyed teaching stagecraft to these enthusiastic young Australians. I tended to teach from instinct for, after all my experience in the profession, I knew most of the problems. Financially the rewards weren't generous, but later on I was asked to star in a radio play for the Australian Broadcasting Company. This led to a series of radio plays and then a TV panel game, then talk about giving English elocution lessons at a modelling school. This school was run by Bambi Smith, a lovely girl with large brown bambi eyes, and a very sweet person. Now she lives in England and is the Countess of Harewood.

Finally, and best of all, Murray came over from Tasmania to see me.

On my way out to Australia, on board *Himalaya*, I'd sat at the Captain's table. Next to me sat a large, rather silent Tasmanian, a good-looking man with a fine head of wavy grey hair. Someone told me that he was making the round trip for his health after some kind of nervous breakdown. Full of good intentions I tried to get him to talk, but didn't get very far, until one night after coffee in the lounge, he suggested we take a turn round the deck before going to bed.

'Do you sleep well?' I asked him.

'Like a top.' He had an attractive voice with just a trace of the flattened Australian vowels.

'Didn't they put you on sleeping pills?'

'Good Lord, no.'

For the first time I began to wonder. 'You *did* have a nervous breakdown, didn't you?'

He threw back his head and roared with laughter. He'd never been ill in his life and he was returning from a business trip to London.

From that uncertain beginning our friendship began. Day to day living in the enclosed community of a great liner brings people into much closer contact, friendship grows more quickly than on land. Warm nights under the stars, and the music of the sea in one's ears. Murray and I became touched by this strange sea magic, and we wanted our voyage to go on for ever. It was an interlude of complete happiness. I grew to admire the quiet strength of this Tasmanian.

The night before we docked in Melbourne Murray talked to me. 'It seemed disloyal to speak about my marriage,' he said, 'but, honestly, it hasn't worked for years. My wife and I made an agreement some time ago that if either of us should want a divorce, the other would not stand in the way.'

I knew Murray was married, of course, he'd told me a lot about his two teenage daughters. But then I had a husband too.

'Would you wait for me?' he asked. 'I can't leave Hobart until my girls go out into the world, but it won't be long now. Then I'll be free to ask you to marry me.'

Letters, telephone calls, and bouquets of flowers came regularly from Murray to relieve my loneliness. By the time he came over to see me I had started my own drama school, and my only worry was whether our feelings had changed and it would turn out to be just another shipboard romance. When I saw Murray, I knew at once that my fears were unfounded. Nothing had changed.

In October my divorce from Brian came through. He planned to marry again. So the next time Murray paid one of his flying visits to Melbourne we could talk confidently about our future, and Murray said he would ask his wife for a divorce on his return. We planned to find a house in Melbourne and turn part of it into a studio for my drama school. I couldn't remember when I'd felt happier about my future.

Katie became engaged to another young man. In November she married. Rosie sent me newspaper pictures of the lovely bride, Catharine Hale-Munro, who had married Count Donald Grixoni at the Church of Our Most Holy Redeemer in Chelsea. Sonnie stayed away. He told newspaper reporters: 'I love Katie . . . but I don't get on with the rest of my family. They don't agree with my way of life . . .' Sonnie's sister, Binnie Hale, was there, however.

I sent Katie a good luck telegram and prayed she'd be very happy. Some time before this I had wired Henry Rowan to ask about Katie's intended husband. He wired back that Donald was a very suitable young man. I hoped it would be just a matter of time before old wounds were healed and Katie and Donald might even come out to Melbourne and meet my new husband.

Out of the blue I was asked to fly to Tasmania and there adjudicate in a Drama Festival to be held in Hobart. I started to put a telephone call to Murray, then I decided to surprise him. After the adjudication I'd ring his office.

The tall contemporary buildings rose against the soft green

hills and the apple orchards of Hobart. 'Everyone in town's here today,' the Mayor told me proudly when he escorted me to my seat on the platform. I looked out at the rows of faces. In the second row sat a large man with grey wavy hair, next to him sat a pretty blonde woman and two teenage girls. I shall never forget the look on Murray's face when our eyes met. I'd done much more than surprise him, I'd given him a near mortal shock. One look at his ashen face and I didn't need to be told the score.

After the adjudication came the reception. One of the first people I was introduced to was the pretty blonde woman, Murray's wife. She chatted to me, completely unaware that her husband had asked Miss Jessie Matthews to marry him, without a suspicion in her head that her husband had ever talked of leaving her. And it was patently obvious, seeing their close little family group, that he had no such intention.

On the plane flying back to Melbourne, I lay back and tried to relax. I had smiled and talked so much that my jaw ached. My heart hurt too. Why hadn't Murray been honest, why had he carried out such a cruel deception? Was his plan just to have a girlfriend tucked away in Melbourne? I didn't know and I refused to give him a chance to tell me. I tore up his letters and I did not answer his telephone calls.

The bruises on my battered pride took a long time to heal. The days crept by with incredible slowness. Someone told me that Sonnie was opening in a new play in the West End. I was glad that the old boy was back in the big time.

I thought a great deal about Sonnie in the next day or two. I had reminders of him all around my flat. By an odd coincidence I was polishing one of his first gifts to me, a door stop, shaped like Punch and painted gold, when the telephone rang. 'London Calling,' announced the operator. Instinctively I knew this would be bad news.

'Sonnie has just died,' said a voice thousands of miles away. 'I thought you should know.'

I learned that leukemia had been diagnosed when we appeared in *Nest of Robins*, but he'd kept his illness secret, going into hospital for transfusions without any publicity. In a few days time he would have opened in a play he wrote, *The French Mistress*, at the Adelphi. Sonnie was a courageous man. I'd always looked up to him, and I knew he was full of talent. His death saddened me and stayed like a dark cloud over my head for a long time. There had always been a deep affection between us; he was the only man I was ever truly married to. He was fifty-seven years old.

In November a letter came from my sister Ray, who had married an American and gone to live in New Jersey. 'What about a real family Christmas with us?' she wrote. That was one of the things I missed most in Australia, the warmth and love of my sisters. Suddenly I decided that I didn't want to live thousands of miles away from the people I loved most in the world. I'd spend Christmas with Ray in America and then go home to England.

As I came down the steps from the plane at London Airport I saw the photographers and the cameras. Instinctively I grew tense with fright. Some of the publicity about my return hadn't made me very happy. 'Stop worrying,' I told myself. 'They're just ordinary men, they can't harm you.' But inside a warning voice said, 'Make one slip and they'll chop you to pieces.'

The cameras were raised, and then it came, a man's shout that seemed to echo above the noise of the airport.

'Is it true you're broke, Jessie?'

I raised my hand and flashed my diamond rings at them just like Harry, my American brother-in-law, had told me to do. I gave them a great big smile, 'Look, boys? Does it look as if I'm broke?'

'Why did you consider flying home with a football team?'

'It's not a football team, it's the Flashing Harps Gaelic Charter Club. My sister in America belongs to it.'

They crowded round me as I started to walk across the tarmac. 'Charter?' someone shouted. 'You must be broke to think of travelling charter.'

I drew in a deep breath. 'It saves half the fare.'

'What are your plans?'

'To get a job.'

One of the reporters shouted, 'Good luck, Jessie. It's grand to have you home again.'

And then it was all smiles and 'Welcome Home', and finally I passed through immigration to find the people I loved.

I settled down with Rosie and George in the little chalet bungalow I'd bought for my father and mother. In an odd way I, too, was back where I'd started from. Rosie, my elder sister, with her strong character still gave me advice, still insisted that I fight my way to stardom again.

'Rosie, I'm older, I've changed.' God knows every year had etched a new mark on my character, if not on my face. 'I don't want the same things any more. I've been teaching the young to act and sing. I agree I should go back to the stage, I will, but please give me time.'

'Time is what you haven't got.'

I didn't know exactly what had happened to me, but I needed time to sort myself out. Some of the events of the last two years had been tough, a great blow to my self-confidence and pride, and Sonnie's death, in a strange way, still worried me. But of all my problems—although I told no one—the one that hurt most was my estrangement from my daughter. The last time I had spoken to her was by telephone from New Jersey, USA, when I was staying with Ray, my sister. I'd heard that Katie's husband had been hurt in an accident, so I telephoned my daughter. We talked, but then she became hysterical and wept. Since then there had been no contact. Somewhere along this long journey I seemed to have lost my daughter. And every night I questioned myself—where had we failed each other?

The dark clouds of depression which hang over me at such times do blow away but I have learned never to make a decision when I feel low. I remember an invitation asking me to be present at one of my old films at the National Film Theatre. I knew with certainty that I did not want to go. I did not want to watch a film of my youth showing Sonnie and myself when we were young and happy. I didn't want to see myself again as a film star.

Against my better judgement, for no one could know the state of my health as well as I, I went along to the National Theatre. Everyone was very kind, they made a great fuss of me, but every scrap of will power I owned was needed to sit through *It's Love Again*.

I did break down on the underground train coming home, but I controlled myself and decided that nothing on earth would induce me to go back and watch the film *Evergreen*. I even persuaded myself that Rosie would understand and she'd say, 'Of course you can't sit through that misery again.'

But how could she understand? I'd kept my worries to myself. She was impatient. 'Don't be so childish, Jessie. You must go. It's your duty, you'll sail through it.'

Alone in the bathroom I jerked open the door of the medicine cabinet. I fumbled for my bottle of sleeping pills. Sleep would give me release . . . if I was ill, no one could force me to go back and watch the film . . . a long . . . long . . . sleep.

I found myself sitting at my dressing table, a glass of water in front of me, white tablets scattered on the glass top. Downstairs I could hear Rosie calling, 'Jessie . . . supper's ready . . . Jessie . . .' Her voice seemed to float in the air and drift away. A bitter taste filled my mouth. I tried to lift the glass of water and drink. It was too heavy. Suddenly I felt dizzy and sick. My hand clung to the edge of the dressing table. I must hold on. What had I done? My face in the mirror was becoming blurred and misty. I felt so ill . . . Rosie . . . Rosie . . . please come! I was still trying to say her name when the black curtain came down.

Chapter Twenty-two

'Just look at the diamonds on her fingers! What the hell's she doing here on the National Health?'

Another woman's voice answered. 'It's always the people with money who do these things. Too much of it, that's her trouble. Come on, Peggy, get a move on.'

I smelled cigarette smoke, heard the swish of curtains being drawn back, the slam of a locker door and the footsteps receded. I carefully withdrew my hand with the offending diamond ring and slid it under the bedclothes. So this was Worcester Ward. I couldn't say my companions sounded friendly. It was a wide dormitory with four beds on each side, around the top of each bed were rails supporting green serge curtains. They were divan beds, not hospital beds, and as I gave mine a trial bounce, quite comfortable. Then there were lockers, a row of wardrobes and on one wall a large sign, NO SMOKING. On top of each locker was a metal ashtray.

It could be worse, I thought, as I sat up and looked around. Here the institutional look was missing, unlike the ward of the main hospital where I'd been admitted after my overdose of pills. I'd been told to report to Worcester Ward the evening before and found everyone but the nursing staff out on a compulsory social evening. After the noisy main hospital ward, the quiet of Worcester had helped me to fall asleep early. I'd met none of the inmates and even now, although the covers of some of the beds were thrown back, there was no sign of them.

'Jessie!' A tall rangy girl wearing the blue uniform and black cap of the hospital loped through the open door. She tapped her wrist-watch authoritatively. 'It is five minutes past seven and you should be drinking your tea.' All this was said in a marked foreign accent. She then flung open a window and let in the cold air. Turning she took a stance rather like a young Ingrid Bergman about to play St Joan, she certainly had her accent. 'It is necessary,' she insisted.

'Well where's the tea?' I asked, listening for the pleasant rumble of the tea trolley.

St Joan pursed her lips and shook her head sadly. 'It is in the kitchen where the others are already drinking. You have not been reading your treatment programme.' She marched round to my locker, produced a stapled leaflet and thrust it at me. 'You must read the rules and follow them,' she said with Swedish firmness. 'Self-discipline is the first rule. Rise at seven. It is necessary.'

To be lectured on self-discipline at seven in the morning by an unknown young girl, no matter how pretty, did not sweeten my temper. Why had I let myself in for this, I grumbled? I could have gone home yesterday. My two weeks' observation period was over.

'Try a week or two in Worcester,' he'd said, that wily psychiatrist. 'You may discover the reason you are here.'

I pulled on my dressing gown, combed my hair, cleaned my teeth and shuffled off to the dining room down the passage. Unpleasant shock number two awaited me. I'd forgotten that Worcester was a mixed ward. In front of me gathered an assorted group of males and females, some in dressing gowns, some in sweaters and slacks. All drinking tea round formica-topped tables and most of them looking pretty dishevelled and surly. Everyone of them stared straight at me. It was as bad as a first night. I could feel perspiration gathering on the back of my neck as I walked towards the members of the Worcester Ward Group Therapy Unit.

Behind me lay a long history of expensive illness. Following too many sleeping pills, I had been taken to the local General Hospital and became a patient on the National Health. After the routine stomach washout, failed suicides spend two weeks under observation. My first few days were spent in rest and medication and the house physician took a full history. Finally I landed up with the psychiatrist.

Dr Max Primrose, small and bearded with a sharp aquiline nose, stood up and shook hands with me. He was shorter than me, a seemingly frail man, and he reminded me vaguely of the Abyssinian Emperor, Haile Selassie. By now I had met up with so many psychiatrists that I knew most of the tricks of the trade. I knew the old maxim, 'First you love him . . . then you hate him . . . then you are cured.' I knew that his job would be to try and unpack my mental box of tricks right down to the bottom layer.

I wanted to be co-operative. 'It was quite out of character for me to do such a thing,' I told him. 'I didn't try to commit suicide, you know, I had to find a way out, something that would prevent me having to watch the film *Evergreen*. . . . Of course I can see I was completely wrong, it was a stupid thing to do.' I'd worked it all out in my mind. 'What I should have done was go back at the end of the film and just be there for the presentation.' Dr Primrose was watching me with dark un-blinking eyes. 'It was a cry for help,' I said finally.

He smiled faintly. 'You seem to understand your character very well.'

'Of course I do. I've had years of being taken to pieces by doctors like you.'

He smiled again, a wintry smile that didn't quite reach his eyes. 'So you understand your own emotions, do you, you understand despair and unhappiness? Please tell me about them.'

I refused to be side-tracked. I was becoming allergic to noise. Whenever I walked in the hospital ground the noise of traffic from the main road overpowered me. If a car came along the private road I shrank away from the din which assailed my ears. If Dr Primrose wanted to help me, he could start there.

Two sessions followed with Dr Primrose. They were filled with mutual wariness, and I was still having trouble with noise. He suggested that I became a patient in his Group Therapy Unit which was attached to the hospital, although it was a completely separate part where the inmates looked after themselves.

'They are all people with a certain intelligence,' he told me, 'otherwise the therapy would go over their heads. Without intelligent co-operation it would fail.'

I didn't want to go to Worcester at all. My two weeks in the main hospital had been painful enough. In the bed next to mine was a woman who thought she was the Virgin Mary. If you addressed her as 'Holy Mother' she was pleasant enough, but if you forgot she was liable to aim a blow at you.

By now I had almost come to terms with my illness. When it struck me, tranquillising drugs seemed to keep it more or less under control. I hated the idea of Group Therapy. All I wanted to do was get away from the gloomy atmosphere of the hospital.

Dr Primrose was firm. 'It's no good going into the outside world if you can't even stand the sound of a motor car.'

I was not persuaded, and it was in this mood that I walked into the kitchen of Worcester Ward that morning. I am a fairly fastidious person, I resented the idea of meeting my fellow human beings before breakfast and meeting unshaven men in particular. My feelings probably showed on my face.

A middle-aged woman with dark greying hair combed into waves and a neat, clean appearance, separated herself from the others and came forward holding out her hand. 'I'm Dorothy,' she said. 'I believe your name's Jessie. We're all on first name terms, here.'

A young man came up behind her. 'Except the good Dr Primrose. Call him Max and you're for it.' He held out his hand too. 'My name's Mike.' He had a pale, gaunt face, red-rimmed eyes and he wore a yellowing white pullover and faded jeans.

The other women came up, one of them called Jennifer, a tall thin blonde, and the other Peggy. I didn't take to Peggy at all. I recognised her voice and realised she had stood next to my bed earlier that morning. She had an uncared-for look, her hair straggling all over her face and shoulders, a cigarette hanging from her lips.

There were six men whose ages ranged from the late twenties to the fifties. One of them, a man called Reg, with a Welsh accent, told me that he knew me. 'You're an actress, aren't you? I've seen your pictures in the papers.' Then he added unkindly, 'Didn't think I'd meet you in a place like this.'

As I drank my tea I told myself over and over again that I'd made a terrible mistake. How could I live with these people in such close contact. It was awful. I could never last out. Years ago, as a scatty young actress, it might have been just possible, but not now. I made fresh mistakes with every step I took. After breakfast, at nine o'clock, there was a community meeting held to discuss grievances. The nursing staff—Greta, the Swedish nurse and Richard, the male nurse—were present. I, it seemed, was the major object of the Group's grievances.

'She was late for breakfast,' said Reg, the Welshman. He was a small wiry man who wore an open-necked shirt with rolled-up sleeves and around his trousers he wore a broad leather belt. 'And she didn't stay to help us wash up.'

'I need an hour to get dressed,' I protested. 'It's too much of a rush. I'll miss breakfast, if that's how they feel.'

'Hark at her,' said Peggy, lighting yet another cigarrette.

'I am sorry, Jessie,' said Greta, 'it is necessary you obey our rules.' Something was always 'necessary' for Greta. She was a good-natured, earnest girl, but I was too old for the boarding school routine. At eleven, after making our beds, cleaning the ward, and tidying up the dayroom, there came another meeting. Three times a week, the patients, the nursing staff, and the doctors met to discuss our problems.

We sat in the dayroom, a nice bright place with comfortable armchairs and long settees, looking more like a hotel lounge than a hospital ward. Dr Primrose sat in one corner with his pad and pencil. I sat between Dorothy, who was Group Leader this week, and the obnoxious Reg, who always seemed to single me out. With a touch of relief I discovered that I was not the only new patient. There was also John. A well dressed, prosperous looking middle-aged man, rather overweight, who looked so relaxed that he might have come in from a round of golf.

The meeting began fairly quietly with Dorothy acting as chairman. Various problems were discussed then John was invited to tell us what his problem was. John took a deep breath and said impressively, 'Three weeks ago I was locked up in prison.'

Jolly laughter greeted this unusual statement. At once four hands were raised in the air, including that of Reg. 'You're not alone,' said Dorothy quietly. 'They've all been in jail.'

Hesitantly John began his tale. It was horrible. He spoke of the slow degradation that came with dependence on alcohol. A fearful story ending only after he was picked up from a gutter and woke up locked in a cell.

Everyone sat quietly for a moment, then to my amazement, Reg shouted: 'What you belly-aching about? Bloody sorry for yourself, aren't you?' Like a terrier after a rat, he tore into John's story. He spat out the shocking details one after the other.

The wife-beating, the petty thieving, the cruelty, the vomit. 'So your doctor says you've got six months to live if you keep drinking. Well, you're still alive, aren't you? Stop snivelling, for Christ's sake.'

That was only the beginning. He castigated John, he called him every filthy name under the sun. John sat there, white and shaken, knocked apart by the cruel words. He seemed to have crumbled into a wreck. 'Shut up,' I shouted to Reg. I couldn't stand the cruelty any longer. 'Shut up. Stop saying such terrible things.'

Dorothy leant over and put a hand on my arm. I pushed her away. 'This isn't group therapy, it's group murder. I won't stay and listen.'

Reg rounded on me. 'What right have you got to butt in? You've only just come. Film star are you now?' His Welsh voice grew more sing-song. 'Rich woman! "I always take an hour to dress",' he mocked. ' "I always wear my diamonds when I mix with the lower classes".'

Dorothy intervened quickly. 'Jessie has a right to speak.'

'All right, then. Let her speak. Tell us why she's come here. We had to roll in the gutter before they'd take us in. What does that dressed-up cow know about that?' He turned towards me and there was so much hate in his face that I was frightened.

'Tell him, Jessie.' I heard Dorothy's quiet voice.

'Why should I? Have my private life chewed over by scum like him?'

'Don't be like that, Jessie.' Mike was leaning forward, smiling, enjoying it all. 'Come on, tell us. It will do you good.'

'Mind your own business,' I shouted. I searched the faces around me looking for one that showed any sympathy. Dr Primrose was writing his notes intently on his pad; Greta gazed at me with wide blue eyes; Richard stared up at the ceiling. 'Why don't you . . .' My voice broke. I felt alone and quite apart from these frightening people. I began to weep.

'Look at crybaby!' Reg was still taunting me. 'In tears. She solves all her problems with tears, just like a baby. Childish! Why don't you grow up, Jessie Matthews?'

I stumbled out of the dayroom to the only place I could go— the ward. Dorothy came after me. She sat down on my bed while I powdered my face and tried to regain control.

'We're not as cruel as you think, Jessie,' she said. 'We're all at breaking point when we come in here. We've all been in hospital, had the full treatment, and in a very few days, left to ourselves, we should all be back where we started from. Closed up again. We must have a "go" at each other to stop that happening. It's all part of the therapy here to make us look and see ourselves as others see us.'

'I'd rather keep it to myself.'

Dorothy patted the bed. 'Come and sit down. Now look at me! A respectable, surburban housewife you think. Well, I was arrested for soliciting.' She laughed, a harsh and ugly sound. 'At my age and the way I look. I'd have sold my soul, never mind my body for a drink.' The bitterness and despair in her voice was like a blow to my smug self-esteem. Dorothy, the picture of respectability, neat jersey suit, pearl earrings, well polished shoes. 'My husband died and I couldn't bear it. Someone said, "Have a drink, it'll make you feel better." In a month, I, who only drank a sherry at Christmas, was on a bottle a day.'

We sat on the bed together and held hands. Two middle-aged women whose lives had capsized. Now I knew that my problems were very small compared to hers.

Even so, the days that followed weren't easy. Apart from Dorothy and Mike, the others in the group showed they resented me, and Peggy and Reg were openly hostile. Most of the group were alcoholics, like Dorothy and Reg. But there were three failed suicides, and Peggy was one of them.

Mike, who was only twenty-five, had been an alcoholic since he was fifteen. It broke my heart to listen to the terrible stories he told, the cars he had smashed up, the hospital beds he had lain in. 'I was in Warlingham Unit last time,' he told me. 'Didn't do any good. They locked us in.' I looked at his poor thin face, watched him nervously smoke cigarette after cigarette. 'It's got to work some time, Mike, or you'll be dead. Can't it be now?'

He brushed the cigarette ash from his old white sweater. All his movements were jerky as if the dregs of wine bottles still choked up his veins. 'I'll kick it one day, you watch.'

We walked round and round the hospital grounds together. He was mad about cars. He knew the sound of every motor. 'Listen to that one, that's a supercharged Bentley—marvellous sound.' He loved cars but he'd never drive again. He'd been disqualified for life. 'Now there's a smooth engine for you. Listen to that one, Jessie.'

Mike cured the car noise in my ears, or perhaps my compassion for him made me forget the roar of the traffic.

The part of the day I liked best was the afternoon when we went over to the main hospital and helped with the patients. Old ladies whose illness was just to be old. They had to be helped from bed to chair, talked to, listened to. Every afternoon I spent there was a long prayer of thankfulness. There were so many others so much worse off than I. There was a woman with brain damage who lay inert, motionless, scarcely breathing, there was no brain to direct the muscle and bone. There was a coloured girl from Jamaica, called Marigold, who had lost the use of her legs. She had been a nurse once. I used to wheel her round the grounds and we'd sing hymns together. Therapy, said our Dr Primrose, is helping others whereby we help ourselves.

With Peggy, it was different. I could make no contact, give her no help and find none from her. She was a very sad character. Something had gone wrong for her, killed off the joy of living. She just couldn't bother. She said she longed to go home to her husband and her two children, but when her husband came to take her home for her child's birthday, she could hardly rouse herself to brush her hair.

Her husband waited patiently in the dayroom while Dorothy and I tried to get her ready. I found her shoes, tried to force them on her feet. 'Leave me alone,' she cried, 'I can't go. I'm too ill.' With a savage gesture she flung her handbag to the other side of the room, then threw her shoes after it. 'What the hell!'

Dorothy and I looked at her. I thought of the wretched man waiting outside, the ten year old daughter who wanted her mother to be there for her birthday. 'You stink,' I said coldly. 'You stink because you're too lazy to wash. You're disgusting. Every day we have to look at you in your filthy blouse and skirt. Why should we have to put up with a dirty slut like you?'

Peggy turned on me. 'Jealous bitch. Just because you haven't got a husband and real kids, you're jealous.'

A lifetime's frustration boiled up inside me. 'Just as you say, I haven't any real kids. But do you know, Peggy, I'd have given anything on earth to have had them. You've got kids, haven't you, but you're too lazy, too eaten up with self-pity to get off your backside and go home and see them. Your husband's waiting outside for you. Yes, you're right, I haven't got a husband. I've no man who gives a damn about me. But you've got one, and you're too bloody idle to bother.'

Dorothy said briskly, as if nothing had happened. 'Come on, Jessie. Let's get the bitch moving. Shove her shoes on.' We got her moving at last and handed her over to her husband. Dorothy and I watched them go. 'You know what you've done, my girl,' she said to me. 'You attacked Peggy, just like Reg attacked you.'

'But she deserved it,' I said self-righteously.

Dorothy smiled.

I'd been in Worcester Ward for over a week, listening to problems I didn't know existed, problems that seemed often insoluble, and the knowledge that mine were so slight in comparison strengthened me. I accepted now that group therapy was helping me discover my weaknesses but I still dreaded those morning meetings at eleven o'clock. Reg still had a 'go' at me, but I found that if I played it carefully, I could divert his attack to someone else.

Reg was his usual obnoxious self this morning. He hadn't slept well and someone had to suffer for it. He complained that I was still having a sleeping pill at night, when none of the others were allowed drugs. 'Self-discipline for the likes of us,' he jeered, 'but anything goes for Lady Muck here.'

It had been a long time since anyone had called me 'Lady Muck' way back in my early Charlot days, but it still made my blood boil. 'Discipline,' I retorted. 'What do you know about discipline? You ought to have been a ballet dancer like I was.'

'Oh, so she was a ballet dancer, was she? Takes damn good care not to tell us about it. What you trying to hide, eh?'

'Oh, leave me alone. You're just like one of your bloody Welsh sheep dogs—always chasing after me. Lay off.'

'Jessie,' Greta leant forward, earnest as ever, 'but we want to hear. You have had more out of life than any of us here. You danced before great audiences.'

'So what! They didn't clap their hands when I was lying in a hospital bed.'

Richard, the male nurse, who usually sat quiet and listened, entered the argument. 'That's self-pity. Why do you talk like that?'

'You're sorry for yourself.' To my amazement I heard Mike's voice. How could he attack me, after all the hours I'd spent listening to his troubles?

'Too fond of herself, that's her trouble. Doesn't want to mix with us lot. Too common.' That was Jennifer, of course.

They were all shouting at me, tormenting me. I knew I must resist. I knew what they were after, it was just a ploy to break me down . . . and then the blow I never expected came. Dorothy turned on me. Dorothy, my one friend in this alarming mass of humanity. 'Why do you think you're so different from us, Jessie?' she demanded, her voice was hostile. 'Are you better than we are?'

'Leave me alone! Oh, God, leave me alone.' I could hear my voice breaking.

'Crybaby,' yelled Reg, 'solve your problems by blubbing like a baby.'

'She can hand it out,' Peggy's voice screamed. 'But she can't take it. Know what she told me? That I stink. That I'm lazy. What does she know about real work? Stuck-up bitch. She ought to have had my life, slaving my guts out, cooking, washing floors, washing kids . . .'

A torrent of words erupted, I couldn't hold them back: 'Washing,' I shouted back, 'I scrubbed floors when I was seven. I washed in a tin bowl, if I could get one. I grew up in a slum, worse than any of you can imagine.' I was yelling at the top of my voice, bringing out these things from the recesses of my memory that I thought I'd forgotten. 'There was never enough food, never enough money, never, even, enough love. My father drank himself stupid every night. Now you know why the sight of you drunks disgusts me. And you have the bloody nerve to tell me that I don't know. All right, so I'm not like you. You all brag how drink brought you down to the gutter, how many times you've tried to kill yourselves. I can't do that. I've had to keep quiet. Everything that ever went wrong with my life had to be hidden. Do you know what it's like to wake up and find your name smeared across the Sunday papers?'

'I wouldn't mind if I was Jessie Matthews, the film star,' shouted Peggy.

'I *hate* Jessie Matthews,' I cried. 'She's taken everything from me. She's spoiled my life. It's not *me* people see, it's that image. She's split me in two, and now the film star's gone, the half that's left, the half that's really me, no one wants.'

'We've all had our troubles,' said Dorothy sternly.

I turned on her. 'You lost a husband. Well, I lost three, and I didn't turn to drink.' I saw my words wound her as if they were knives. 'The men I loved let me down, I lost my children, I lost my darling Katie.' Words poured out, words that tortured and shamed me. The money I'd made and lost. The houses I'd bought, the people I'd supported. The unhappiness, the defeat, the story of my life. 'You say I've had so much from life. All right, I have. But I've paid for it. I'm still paying for it.' My voice faltered. 'Every mistake I've ever made I've paid for. Sometimes I think I shall never stop paying. . . .'

Now I was quiet. I sat in a pool of silence, waiting for the attack to start again, for their voices to beat me down. I squeezed my eyes shut and tried to stop the tears forcing their way out down my cheeks.

I felt an arm around my shoulder. A rough hand touched my hair. 'Good girl,' said the hated Welsh voice. 'Good girl.'

They came up to me, one by one, my nine companions in misery. They put their arms around me, they hugged me. It was the strangest sensation I have ever had in my life. With their touch I felt a comfort I had never known before. When I looked into the corner of the room Dr Primrose was sitting silent, watching us.

Chapter Twenty-three

I left Worcester Ward not quite sure of my ability to cope with the strains and stresses of life outside. The frail walls of my personality had been broken down and now I must rebuild these walls on new foundations. But as the days went by I did feel new strength coming to me. I had learned that there were others far worse off than I was, and in trying to comfort them I had made myself strong. Now I accepted the fact that my personality would always zoom up to the high notes, then plummet down, but I had the help of modern drugs to give me an even rhythm.

So many times in my life a wonderful opportunity has appeared out of nowhere. As happened when I was asked to appear at the London Palladium in *A Night of One Hundred Stars*, to raise funds for the Actor's Orphanage. It wasn't the first time by any means that I had appeared in this once-a-year midnight revue, but this occasion turned out to be a special one, a memory to treasure.

David Nathan in the *Daily Herald* gave me a lovely notice: 'Jessie Matthews came back from two years in Australia to look for work as a straight actress. She came down the vast Palladium stage . . . her gown was flame-coloured . . . the orchestra began playing her most famous song, *Dancing on the Ceiling*. She sang it straight. . . . They were a tough audience to please. Yet this woman caught them by the throat. Jessie Matthews showed that she could still command an audience.'

I did an Arts Council tour with *Five Finger Exercise*, staying in digs that cost fifteen bob a night, bed and breakfast. I did a pantomime at the Old Vic, Bristol, playing Fairy Snowflake. I toured with Ralph Lynn in *Port in a Storm*, and I was asked by Eamonn Andrews to appear as the mystery guest on his show *What's My Line*.

I had decided to mystify the panel with a Welsh accent. While I waited for the car to pick me up, I tried it out on Rosie. 'How does this sound?' I asked her.

Rosie didn't seem very interested. I couldn't understand what was wrong with Rosie today. She was acting like a cat on hot bricks. First she washed her hair, a thing she never did on Sundays, then she put in pins and curlers. Finally, Rosie, who was always immaculate, was still wearing her overall.

'Don't you feel well, Rosie?' I asked her. She'd even refused to come with me to watch *What's My Line*. Rosie said she felt very well. 'Then why don't you change your mind and come with me?'

'How can I,' snapped Rosie, 'with my hair in pins?'

'I'll do your hair for you. Oh, come on, Rosie.'

'For the last time,' Rosie's black eyes flashed with anger, 'I'm not coming.'

She doesn't care, I thought sadly. And I'd do anything to have her with me, I always feel so nervous in front of those television cameras. Because I was upset I clumsily overturned the bottle of red nail varnish with which I was painting my nails. It crashed to the kitchen floor.

'Don't touch it,' screamed Rosie. 'Don't touch it. I'll get you some more. Next door, I'll be right back.'

Before I could stop her, Rosie in curlers and overall, went flying out of the house. She's odd, I thought, my goodness she's odd. She must be sickening for something.

Eamonn Andrews himself was waiting for me in the foyer of the Shepherd's Bush theatre. I was touched by his thoughtfulness. He gave me one of his lop-sided Irish smiles and then caught my arm in a vice-like grip. 'Jessie,' he said, 'there's been a change in the programme.'

I edged away, trying to move my arm. 'What's happened?'

Eamonn's grip tightened, but with his free hand he ripped the poster advertising *What's My Line* off a bill board. Underneath . . . 'Oh, no,' I gasped, 'not that!'

Eamonn, grinning like a Cheshire cat, cried, 'Jessie Matthews, *This Is Your Life*.'

They say it takes different people in different ways. Mine was to almost faint with shock. Now I knew why Eamonn takes such a stranglehold on his victims, it's to hold them up when they pass out. I was still trembling with shock when so many of my dear friends walked back into my life . . . Anna Neagle . . . Buddy Bradley . . . Danny O'Neill. . . .

'And now,' announced Eamonn, 'here are your army of brothers and sisters.'

'Hallo, Jessie. It's me, Rosie.' Treacherous Rosie, looking wonderful with her hair done and a new dress that must have been concealed under that awful overall.

'Hallo, Jessie. It's me, George.' My brothers and sisters came on right down to the last voice that said, 'Hallo, Jessie. It's me, Ray, all the way from America.'

Afterwards Rosie told me, 'They very nearly messed it up. Your car was late, that's why I rushed outside to find a bottle of varnish from a neighbour, and would you believe it, there was the wrong car waiting for me and Lena.'

Poor Rosie, she'd had the brunt of the arranging forced on her shoulders, and the difficult time of keeping the secret from me. The rest of the family brought from their various homes had been living it up in hotels. 'And what did I get?' said Rosie. 'Just two guineas from the BBC and a shocking headache.'

I've always owed so much to Rosie. She was the one who pushed me into my next career. I was painting the dining room walls a lovely warm grey. Rosie marched in, a newspaper in her hand. 'There's a piece in the paper . . . it says they're looking for an actress to play the doctor's wife in that serial.'

'They wouldn't want me, dear.'

'Jessie, come down off that ladder and ring up.' The years had rolled by but Rosie was still the same.

'But I'd feel so humiliated if they said no.'

Rosie always got her way. I climbed down, wiped my hands on my apron and dialled the BBC. 'May I speak to Harold French, please?' Harold had been in the profession since he was a boy actor, we were old friends, but that didn't make it any easier to approach him in his role of BBC producer.

'Harold,' I began uncertainly, 'I believe you're looking for someone to play Mrs Dale? Of course, I realise that I'm not . . .'

'I'm delighted you phoned,' Harold cut in. 'What a lovely idea! I'll arrange an audition for tomorrow morning at ten.'

Fifteen years before, on January 5th, 1948, to be precise, Mrs Mary Dale, a fictional doctor's wife sat down at her desk and committed her little worries to paper and the BBC microphone. Every weekday afternoon since that date, a few million housewives put their feet up, got on with the ironing or made a cake, as they listened to their favourite programme. Mrs Dale, Jim, her husband, Bob and Gwen, her two children, and Mrs Freeman, her mother, were just as real to many women as the family down the street.

The BBC decided that the bromide of *Mrs Dale's Diary* needed a pep pill. They moved them from their nice old house to a new town called Exton. Dr Dale joined the National Health, and the gentle harp music that introduced the programme was gone forever. Mrs Dale stopped worrying about Jim and put her mind to the more serious problems of life. The series was now called *The Dales* and Mary Dale was to be re-cast.

I discovered that about one hundred actresses had been tested to play Mrs Mary Dale, and the audition I gave was very comprehensive. I was given three scenes to study and no time for rehearsal. The first a cosy chat with Jim, the second a quarrel with him, and the third a family comedy scene.

'I was awful,' I told Rosie, when I got home, 'I fluffed so many lines.'

'What a pity,' said Rosie, 'I like the Dale family. They're so nice.' Rosie was a sucker for soap operas. She'd brought me up in the theatre, she must have known that backstage is tinsel, cardboard and make-believe, but she still lived every moment of the drama. In the days when *Peyton Place* was on our television screens, we used to say in our family, 'Don't worry if you miss an instalment. Rosie knows it all by heart, and she'll act it out for you.'

I went back to painting the dining room, and by the time I'd got round to the window frames I'd forgotten all about Mrs Dale. Rosie came in again. 'Harold French is on the phone.' Instinctively, I felt that this would be the polite brush-off, and I was ready for it. After a few minutes social chit-chat, I thought I'd spare Harold his difficult task. 'Do come and have a cup of tea when you're round this way, Harold.'

Harold said, 'I'd love to, Jessie. By the way we'd like you to play Mrs Dale.'

Rosie saw my look of astonishment. I nodded my head furiously. 'Ask him how much?' she whispered hoarsely.

I mouthed my answer to her. '£25'. Her face fell.

'However,' Harold went on. 'There'll be five episodes and repeats. It should work out about £65 a week.'

Rosie digested the new figures. 'No hotel bills . . . no travelling. . . .' Her face lit up. 'Say, yes.'

Good Lord! How polite these new young reporters were. They called me 'Miss Matthews'. They were almost reverent. Their headlines weren't quite so edifying: 'The Highkick Queen of the Thirties who never gave up!' 'The Saucy Pin-up back among the Teacups!' 'Cheesecake Girl Back!'

It was flattering to be back in the limelight; to tell magazine writers how the new Mrs Dale spent her day at home; to be asked to make records; to appear in cabaret at a top London club. And my work for charity, which I'd done ever since I was a Charlot girl, had a new impetus. Now when I opened a bazaar for charity, the takings were high.

I was constantly amazed at the enormous public *The Dales* had. When I appeared on the Royal Command Performance, the Queen Mother told me the programme was one of her favourites, and she tried never to miss it.

The members of the cast of *The Dales* were lovely people. Shirley Dixon, who played my daughter-in-law, was very glamorous and was always knitting for her two little daughters. Charles Simon, my doctor husband, slept a lot and was often woken up by me just in time to step up to the microphone. I was always amazed how wide awake he was in an instant, reading his script, word perfect.

We had lots of spare time, and we all spent it in different ways. Derek Nimmo was always writing, Leslie Heritage answered his fan mail, Dorothy Lane (Mrs Freeman) wrote industriously into a small notebook, and I sewed headscarves for my friends.

It was through this programme that I made the most important friend of my life, Rae Ball. On Mondays, Tuesdays and Wednesdays, I joined the commuters to travel from Watford Station to London to record the programmes. Every morning, through some strange chance, I found myself in the same com-

234

partment with a pretty dark woman. In time, we smiled at each other and saved each other a seat. We chatted and finally used to meet for lunch in the West End. Rae Ball worked in electronics, and she lived with her husband Charles, an accountant, in a Hertfordshire village. She had a dachshund called Sam that she talked about a great deal. I envied her, for Rosie didn't like animals and wouldn't have one in the house.

I also found myself a manager. Vincent Shaw, who was Charles Simon's agent, asked me if I would be interested in doing a television commmercial. I suppose everyone knows that a TV commercial is as good as a win on the pools. I donned a white overall, held up my snowy pillow cases and confided to the British viewing public that the detergent I used made my washing, 'Fresh air fresh and sunshine white.'

Rosie was now disillusioned with the whole entertainment business. 'You've worked like a dog for forty years, and for that little flash on the television screen you earn as much as if you'd slaved for months in a West End show.'

No matter how unjust show business could be, I found the money very useful. We moved to a much nicer house in Northwood and I still had some money left burning a hole in my pocket. I didn't intend to buy a cottage. I blame a lovely summer afternoon when Rosie and I were driving down to Bournemouth to appear in a show. We saw the 'For Sale' notice, the thatched roof, the bulging whitewashed walls, the black beams and the roses round the door.

'Very nice,' said Rosie, 'but you wouldn't get me living out here.'

Inside, the cottage was very dilapidated. A huge stone fireplace with logs piled at the side, a wide staircase, a long, low-beamed drawing room. 'I bet there's woodworm,' whispered Rosie, 'and you couldn't swing a cat in that kitchen.'

But I was dreaming of myself in front of the fire, a dog snoozing at my feet. I told Vincent about it when I got back to town. He was very good as an agent, but as a property man he would let enthusiasm carry him along. 'You're asking £8,900,' he said to the owner when he drove down with me for a quick look round. 'All right, we'll give you £8,000 cash, now!'

'Vincent, you're out of your mind. I can't buy it.'

'Cash on the nail,' said Vincent.

'Vincent,' I wailed, 'I can't afford it.'

'Done,' said the owner with a happy smile.

As we drove off I told Vincent what I thought of him. 'It hasn't even been surveyed. It's probably riddled with woodworm.'

'But you like it.'

'That's not the point. You don't buy houses this way. It needs money spent on it. All right, the television fees will help pay for it, but what about the rest?'

'Relax,' said Vincent. 'You'll just have to work harder. Now there's a new play called *Share in the Sun*. You're going to play the lead.'

Ten years later I'm still paying bills on my cottage. I've spent at least £10,000 putting it right, and I don't regret a penny. Vincent Shaw has been more than my personal manager, he has been a true friend and done his best to protect my professional interests always.

There are times when I sit in front of the log fire down at the cottage warming my toes after a walk through the fields with Bill, my dachshund dog. But in my thoughts I am often half waiting for the telephone to ring. 'How about auditioning for a new musical to open in the West End?' 'Are you free for a summer season at Ramsgate?' Nothing excites me more than to pick up the phone in answer to a call to work. All my energies are aroused at once and I am ready to go anywhere, any time.

When *The Dales* came to its untimely end in 1969 I did not feel unduly downcast. I had been playing Mary Dale for six years, but I had guarded against becoming stale by fitting in other jobs both on television and on the stage. Yet it was sad to say goodbye to the company, we felt rather like a family breaking up.

And now my own family has broken up, in various ways. Only eight of us remain. Carrie was the first to die, she was young, in her forties, then Georgie and then Billy. Jenny and Ray are both in America, but Lena and Eve live in this country, and of course, so does my darling Rosie.

Rosie and I no longer live together, she and her husband have retired to a little bungalow in Ruislip. As for myself, I live at my cottage, and when I have to work in London I stay with my dear friends Rae and her husband Charles.

Rosie, however, was with me on the proud day I went to

Buckingham Palace where the Queen invested me with the most excellent Order of the British Empire. The ceremony over we walked out into the palace courtyard and stood for a moment in the sunshine. Not so very far away lay the place where it had all begun. King William and Mary Yard in Soho. A short walk across Green Park, along Piccadilly, and then a dive into the narrow and mysterious streets of Soho where the barrow boys still shout, 'Lovely bananas! Juicy Oranges!'

One of my greatest joys on that special day was the presence of my daughter Catharine. For a while it seemed that I had lost her for ever, but now all that is past and she has come back into my life.

Every Christmas time I would scan my mail with unusual anxiety. Would Katie remember me? Would she send me a card?

On Christmas Eve 1967, I opened an envelope, drew out a card and read: 'Happy Christmas, dearest Mummy.' I could hardly read the message underneath because the writing was blurred by my hot tears. Catharine was pregnant, her baby would be born in January. 'Why don't you come and see us both?'

The days that passed before I could go to see her were a mixture of joyful expectation and anxiety. Rae came with me, I don't think I could have got there alone.

We found the nursing home in a quiet street in Bath, the nurse showed me into Catharine's room. A girl, now almost a stranger, said to me, 'Mummy, what have you done to yourself? Your hair!' It was almost ten years since she had seen me and my hair had gone silver.

Catharine my daughter, had changed too. Life had not always treated her kindly. Our new relationship, if it was to become established, would have to be treated gently and with wisdom.

'Look at your grand-daughter,' she said, 'and you've got a grandson waiting to see you.'

I picked up the tiny infant and touched her soft pink cheek gently. She felt very frail and I was filled with tenderness towards her and for her mother, Catharine.

'Mummy,' said Catherine.

I raised my eyes from the sleeping child.

'Her name is Jessica.'

Jessica! Named after the child who had danced her way to

the stars. What could I wish for this new baby? Not a life like mine, no, never. I would wish her love, kind friends, the power to give love in return, and, most of all, the gift of good health. There is so much I would wish for you, little Jessica. . . .

I shall always cherish the memory of the first time I held my daughter Catharine in my arms. I prayed that we would give each other happiness. Well, the joy she has given me has far outweighed the sorrow.

The relationship of mother and daughter can be complex, and the added strains that my work as an actress brought, the long months away from her while she was looked after by other people, did not help. My daughter and I were estranged for many years. If I say I do not know exactly what went wrong between us, I may not be believed. Yet it is true. I regret those years when we were apart with all my heart, and I know that Catharine does too.

But now she has given me enough joy to make up for everything: my two grandchildren, Martin and Jessica. I pray that nothing will ever separate me from them, for the sound of their clear young voices and happy laughter is my strength to look to the future.

Index